Early Language Development

Language is of central importance in children's development and vital for their success at school and in the world beyond. Designed for the many professionals involved in encouraging language development, *Early Language Development* will enable them to come to grips with the practical issues of helping children with language difficulties.

John Harris provides an invaluable summary of recent research on language development and how it relates to the practical concerns of language assessment and language teaching. Readers are given a clear account of the ways in which research has expanded our understanding of just what language is and how this has led to different approaches to language assessment. Various theories of language development are summarised and discussed in terms of their implications for language teaching. Dr Harris also describes different ways of encouraging language development and explains how teachers and therapists can overcome the special problems faced by children with particular difficulties, such as visual impairment, hearing impairment, general learning difficulties, and environmental deprivation.

With its emphasis on the relevance of research-based knowledge to practical concerns, the book provides a useful bridge between the world of research and practice. It will be of particular interest to teachers of young children, speech therapists, and child psychologists, as well as to students taking courses on child development, and to parents of young children.

John Harris has taught and carried out research on the language of young children for over fifteen years, and is at present Director of the British Institute of Mental Handicap, Kidderminster.

Early Language Development

Implications for clinical and educational practice

John Harris

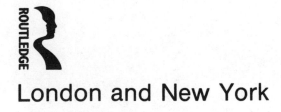

London and New York

First published 1990
by Routledge
11 New Fetter Lane, London EC4P 4EE

Simultaneously published in the USA and Canada by Routledge
a division of Routledge, Chapman and Hall, Inc.
29 West 35th Street, New York, NY 10001

© 1990 John Harris

Typeset by Witwell Ltd, Southport
Printed and bound in Great Britain by
Billings & Sons Limited, Worcester

British Library Cataloguing in Publication Data
Harris, John, *1951–*
 Early language development: implications for clinical and
 educational practice.
 1. Children. Language Skills. Development
 I. Title
 401'.9

Library of Congress Cataloging in Publication Data
Harris, John, 1951 –
 Early language development: implications for clinical and
 educational practice/John Harris.
 p.   cm.
 Includes bibliographical references (p.   ).
 1. Children–Language.   2. Language acquisition.   3. Language
 arts.   I. Title.
 LB1139.L3H277 1990
 372.6–dc20   89-71086
                                                 CIP

ISBN 0-415-01416-6
ISBN 0-415-01417-4 (pbk)

For Daniel, Bethan, and Hannah

Contents

Illustrations

Tables

Preface

For those concerned with children's education and development the area of language has always been of special interest. This is because of the importance of language in all areas of life, including getting along as a member of a family, making friends, fitting in and succeeding at school, and the ability to participate in the wider world of work and leisure. Naturally, teachers and parents are keen to ensure that the children they care for have every opportunity to develop normal language abilities; when they suspect that a child is experiencing problems they often seek the help of professionals, such as teachers with special responsibility for language, speech therapists or psychologists.

Providing help for a child who is suspected of having language difficulties or advising a teacher or parent about how best to proceed is far from straightforward. There are three reasons for this. The first is that the term 'language' does not refer to one specific ability but to a complex set of interrelated abilities. These include translating ideas into words and sentences, employing abstract rules to generate any number of novel grammatical sentences and using language to influence other people in remarkably subtle ways. Second, we are still a long way from having a clear idea about how ordinary children are able to develop all these abilities without any deliberate help from adults and at an age when, in other respects, their capacity to learn from experience still seems very limited. Third, the area of children's language has been the target of a vast amount of research activity during the last 30 years – so much so that it has proved difficult for academic researchers to keep abreast of new developments. It is therefore hardly surprising if professionals in the field of child care and education occasionally feel out of touch with research findings. For all these reasons teachers, speech therapists and psychologists are likely to regard children with language difficulties as representing something of a special kind of challenge.

This book is an attempt to help professionals meet that challenge. It is based on the belief that professionals are most effective when they are able to blend practical experience and their own special personal qualities with research-based knowledge. For this reason there is a sizeable chunk of what might loosely be called 'theory' in the first half of the book. However, even good theories may be of little practical benefit if they are not presented in a readable form and in a way which makes their relevance to practical concerns apparent.

For the practitioner, the two most important practical questions when dealing with children who are experiencing developmental or educational problems are: *How can I find out exactly what the problem is?* And, when I have a clear idea of the nature of the problem, *What can I do about it?* For this reason over half the book is concerned with the practical issues of assessment (Part 3) and language teaching (Part 4). However, before one can assess language, it is necessary to be clear about the range of phenomena which might be examined and precisely what aspects of language should be assessed on this occasion. And in order to answer these questions it is necessary to know something of the various abilities which together constitute language.

The first part of the book addresses these issues by looking at different ways of describing language which have evolved from research concerned with both the mature language of adults and children's language learning. In doing so it provides an account of what we might mean by language and the range and depth of the social and intellectual problems which 'language learning' presents for the child. The insights into language description which come from research provide a set of guidelines which the practitioner can use to determine the range of abilities that need to be taken into consideration when trying to discover how successfully a child is coping with the language learning.

Just as it is important to deal with assessment in the light of recent developments concerning *what* children learn, so issues relating to strategies for intervention can be illuminated by theories which seek to explain *how* children learn language. The chapters on language teaching are therefore closely linked with preceding chapters which deal with processes implicated in children's language development.

At this point it may help to summarise the general layout of the book: Part 1, 'Describing Children's Language'; Part 2, 'Explanations of Children's Language'; Part 3, 'Language Assessment'; Part 4, 'Approaches to Language Teaching'.

Since most of the research on children's language is concerned with ordinary children who are not experiencing difficulties, we might ask how much this can help when we come to deal with children who *are* experiencing problems. The most obvious response to this question is that we need to see all children, including those with severely handicapping disorders, as children first and foremost and not as separate categories of children with special educational or developmental needs. Similarly, when children learn language, it is reasonable to assume that both normal children and those experiencing difficulties share a common challenge and that by studying those who are successful, we may learn how to be more effective in helping those who have problems. If we can discover the strategies and underlying abilities which contribute to normal development, we may be in a better position to understand the implications of specific disabilities for language development and the best way to help such children establish alternative compensatory strategies.

Notwithstanding the importance of research on the language of normally developing children, many developmental difficulties are either directly linked with language or have indirect effects on a child's ability to learn language. A particular concern for developmental psychologists is, therefore, the complex interrelations between motor, sensory, social and intellectual abilities and their role in development. In order to understand why children experience difficulties with language and how they may best be helped, we need to be clear about the developmental implications of, for example, deafness or severe mental retardation. How do these handicapping conditions affect a child's ability to learn language? Should we expect to see widespread difficulties in every area of linguistic functioning or are there reasons to suspect that such children might experience particular difficulty with certain aspects of language? How might these children best be helped?

If remedial intervention is to be effective it must be carefully targeted to provide support where the child most needs help; once again, this depends upon a detailed understanding not only of the normal developmental processes, but also of the relationship between language learning and other areas of functioning. While it is not possible to provide a full account of all developmental disorders which influence linguistic abilities, the penultimate chapter provides a brief overview of the most common handicapping disorders and discusses research findings concerning language development and teaching strategies for these particular groups of children.

The final chapter returns to the question of how those professionals with special responsibility for language can help their colleagues or a child's parents to provide more effective support for language learning. It is now widely recognised that a 'clinic' model, where a psychologist or speech therapist provides short sessions of treatment for individual children, is inefficient and frequently ineffective in helping the child to master skills and abilities which are useful in everyday life. Similarly, when working with pupils in school who are seen as having special difficulties with language, the traditional strategy of withdrawing children from the ordinary classroom for special periods of intensive remedial tuition is now being questioned. While such an approach may succeed in teaching specific skills, it still leaves open the question of how the child will be helped to employ these new skills when she returns to the ordinary classroom. Without close collaboration between the language specialist and the class teacher, these newly acquired skills may be unrecognised and unused.

The alternative to working individually with each child is for the specialist teacher or therapist to work with the child's regular class teacher or the child's parent. Here the goal is to provide an adult who is in frequent close contact with the child with a set of strategies which will enhance the child's opportunities for language learning. Since that learning takes place within ordinary everyday settings, new skills and abilities should be directly relevant to the child's communicative needs and should be effective in helping the child to cope in a variety of situations where language skills are important. If such a strategy is to be effective, then the professional responsible for language must not only be familiar with the processes which contribute to language development, but must also understand how to modify different social environments so that they maximise developmental opportunities for different kinds of children.

Inevitably, in writing a book about children, parents and professionals, there are numerous choices with regard to terminology. Foremost among these is how to incorporate gender-specific pronouns without inadvertently, and possibly subconsciously, exposing a sexist bias. The simple solution taken here is to redress the balance of the past, in which masculine pronouns predominated, and to employ female pronouns whenever the gender of the referent is unspecified or indeterminate. Thus, children, parents and professionals are all referred to in the singular as 'she'.

Second, when talking about the many different kinds of professionals who may work with children I have chosen to use the terms 'teacher' and 'therapist'. This provides specific reference to two of the professional groups for whom this book was written. It also has the added advantage that the terms describe roles which may be filled by any adult who chooses to work in a principled way with children. Since this book is written for all those who are concerned with encouraging children's language development, I leave it to the reader to decide which of these two hats to wear.

Part one

Describing Children's Language

Chapter one

The structure of early language

Introduction

Psycholinguists, studying the rapid and apparently effortless acquisition of language by ordinary children, have addressed two major issues: what are the patterns of growth and change which characterise a child's increasing mastery of language? And, second, how does such change come about? The first question may look relatively straightforward, for it simply involves providing a description of the changes in children's language and communicative skills during that period in which they are learning the language used by those around them. But the complexity of the problem becomes much more apparent when one watches and listens to young children. Here are two girls, aged 4 years and 6 months and 4 years and 10 months.

Siobhan: will you please will you
    give me the scissors and
    then I can have the stool
    and you have this?
    uh?
    yes and I'll be your best
    very friend
Heather: I'm cutting your pictures
    I am not
    that's my picture
Siobhan: this?
Heather: not
    this is my picture this
Siobhan: hope you won't cut this
    wee favourite picture out
    that I cut
    I'm gonna cut these ones
    out so you'd better give
    them to me very fast

> Heather: You've cutted them then
> (Heather hides the scissors).
> (McTear 1985:123)

While the language which these children are using is easily recognisable as English, it is also readily apparent that it is very different from the language of most adults. But exactly how is it different from adult language? And in what ways does it differ from the language of children much younger than Heather and Siobhan? To answer these questions it is necessary to consider the various component skills and the different kinds of social and conceptual knowledge which underlie language. For example, Heather and Siobhan clearly have learned the meaning of a large number of words and they are able to string words together into sentences, although by the yardstick of 'correct grammar' some of the sentences contain glaring errors. They are able to express relatively complex meanings, although these meanings are concerned with their current interests and needs, rather than abstract concepts or events that are distant in terms of time or space. Perhaps most noticeably, they are becoming adept at using language to influence each other through requests, rejections, polite forms ('please') and more direct commands.

One of the main foci of research efforts into children's language acquisition has been the elaboration of descriptive systems. Such systems have resulted in a clearer understanding of just what language is, and perhaps more importantly, they have resulted in a better understanding of the skills and abilities which are implicated in production and comprehension of language at various ages. This concern with descriptions of language is also of central importance for teachers, therapists and clinicians working in the area of language disability. There are two reasons for this. First, a detailed and comprehensive description of the course of normal language acquisition is essential for accurate identification and assessment of children who do not learn language in the normal way or at the same speed as other children. Second, planning and evaluating attempts to remediate language learning with these children will be better organised if teachers and therapists have a clear understanding of the patterns of 'normal' language development.

The question of *how* developmental change comes about has received rather less attention than the issue of *what* changes. Theories of language acquisition have very often gone hand in hand with the emergence of different solutions to the problem of how best to describe language. As views on what a child needs to learn in order to become a language user have changed, so it has become necessary to modify our explanation of the mechanisms involved in the acquisition process. What language *is* determines how language can best be described and the different descriptions have framed our understanding of the sequence of skills and abilities which reflect competence at different stages of language development. The skills and abilities which characterise successive stages of developmental change constitute the data which any theory of acquisition must address. A developmental theory is centrally concerned with the mechanisms which explain *how* a child achieves successive levels of competence.

The major impact of theories of language acquisition has been upon the intervention procedures which have been employed with language-disordered children. As approaches to language description, methods of identification, and the assessment of language-disordered children have changed, so, too, there have been considerable advances regarding the most appropriate ways of helping children with language difficulties. The major contemporary theories of language acquisition are described in Chapters 4 and 5, while Chapters 9 and 10 present different approaches to language intervention.

The first part of the book is concerned with contemporary approaches to describing children's language. It is divided into three chapters which deal with the different descriptive systems; the first considers language as a rule-governed system for expressing meanings in sounds; the second looks more closely at meaning and the semantic representation of meaning in children's early language; and the third chapter examines how the rule system and meanings expressed in language operate within the wider context of interpersonal communication and social understanding.

Structural approaches to language description

From a rather narrow perspective, language might be characterised as a continuous sequence of sounds produced by the expulsion of air through the throat and mouth; as the air passes through the larynx, the vocal cords vibrate at different frequencies and the shape of the mouth and position of the tongue also influence the sounds that emerge. Structures in the ear are sensitive to the airwave vibrations produced in this way and make the detection of speech sounds possible.

Remarkably, the production of soundwaves makes it possible for speakers to encode extremely complex messages and for listeners to decode messages with a high degree of accuracy. The ability to encode and decode the meanings in the sound sequence indicates that both speakers and listeners know the **rules** by which meanings are translated into sounds; this is referred to as 'grammatical knowledge'. Grammar is concerned with the way in which sounds are organised or structured to communicate meaning.

Perhaps the most important and challenging aspect of grammatical knowledge is that it facilitates productivity; that is to say, given the finite number of discrete sounds which occur in any language, a speaker who knows the grammar of the language can produce and understand an infinite range of novel but grammatically correct and meaningful sentences.

Figure 1.1 Examples of grammatical and ungrammatical sentences

Complex grammatical sentence

1 I know that you believe you understand what you think I said, but I'm not sure you realise that what you hear is not what I meant.

(Richard Nixon)

Ambiguous sentence

2 Teenage prostitution problem is mounting.

(*Columbia Journalism Review*)

Semantically anamalous but grammatical sentence

3 Free trade parrot dogs Heath's steps.

(*Guardian*, July 1988)

Ungrammatical sentence: inappropriate word order

4 Problem teenage mounting prostitution is.

Ungrammatical sentence: inappropriate verb agreement

5 This man are driving his car.

Ungrammatical sentence with phonological patterning

6 Inty ninty tibbety fig Deema dama doma nig.

(Grunwell 1982)

Grammatical knowledge makes it possible to discriminate well-formed from ungrammatical sentences, even when such sentences are unnaturally convoluted, and to recognise ambiguous and semantically anomalous sentences (see Figure 1.1).

Grammatical rules can be thought of as comprising three interrelated components or subsystems which operate at different levels. Beginning with a sequence of sounds which is produced when a speaker utters a sentence, it is possible to identify within any given language a restricted number of sounds which carry meaning, and rules which describe permissible sound sequences; these sounds are referred to as 'phonemes' and rules governing the combination of phonemes represent the first level of grammatical description. In Sentence 6 above, although this is not a grammatical sentence, the sounds are derived from English and they are organised according to the phonemic rules of English.

Individual sounds can be organised into strings which constitute recognisable words. There is also an intermediate level of analysis which is more general than the specification of phonemic strings and more detailed than the separation of words from non-words. For example, a word such as 'sportsman' can be broken down into separate elements, only some of which count as words in their own right; sport s man. Alternatively, more elements can be added to make a longer word, as in 'unsportsmanlikc' (un sport s man like). Each of the elements in the word comprises a phoneme or sequence of phonemes which significantly alters the meaning of the word. These elements are referred to as 'morphemes'.

The third subsystem of a grammatical description is concerned with the way in which words can be ordered in sequences to express more complex meanings. Descriptions at this level are concerned with the rules of syntax.

In summary, a description of the grammatical rules which specify the way in which a sentence is structured from discrete sounds includes:

Phonemes – rules for generating strings of sounds to produce morphemes.

Morphemes – rules for combining and modifying individual words.

Syntax – rules for ordering and modifying separate words within sentences.

This chapter will deal with each of these three subsystems separately, beginning with descriptions of children's language in terms of phonological rules.

Phonological rules

A description of the way in which sound variations contribute to meaning is fundamental to an understanding of language as a rule-governed system. There are a number of different ways in which linguists have approached this problem (Grunwell 1982). First, there is the area of traditional **segmental phonology,** which is concerned with the specific sounds that occur in a given language and the ways in which these can be sequenced to produce words. However, words can also be pronounced with different degrees of stress or emphasis, and the way in which intonation varies over words in a sentence can influence meaning. For example, compare 'John hit Bill and then Mary hit him,' with 'John hit Bill and then Mary hit *him*.' The way in which stress is used to influence sentence meaning is referred to as **prosodic phonology** (Grunwell 1982) or **supra-segmental phonology** (Crystal 1981).

A third area is known as **sociophonology** and is concerned with the way in which speakers modify pronunciation in response to the perceived characteristics of different social situations. Fourth, the area of **metaphonology** is concerned with the extent to which children and adults are aware of the significance of the phonological system – for example, in relation to rhyming words, puns and the social significance of variations in accent.

Limitations of space mean that this section will concentrate on segmental phonology as a key area of language description.

Segmental phonology

Segmental phonology is concerned with the rules which can be devised to describe the regularities that occur in a language with respect to the sound sequences that count as words. In any language it is possible to identify phonemic strings which are words – for example, in English, 'cat', 'big', 'bicycle', 'navigate' – and strings which are potential words since they conform to the same rules as real words. In English, such non-words are 'splug', 'clant', 'wilop'. There are also words from other languages which are not permissible in terms of English phonology – for example, 'tsetse' and 'pneumatic'. While such loan words have been incorporated into English in terms of spelling, native English speakers invariably modify the pronunciation of the initial consonant pairs to avoid inadmissible sequences of phonemes. On the basis of observations such as these, it is possible to describe rules which determine the sound sequences which do occur or could occur in a language and those which are not permissible. Such rules are normally specified in terms of phoneme sequences. But what exactly is a phoneme?

Phonemes represent a relatively abstract characterisation of sounds in that they indicate the *sound contrasts* which are employed within a language to distinguish different words. In English, the sounds 'p' and 'b' are recognised as different phonemes because words which are only differentiated by these sounds will, nevertheless, be recognised as different words: 'big/pig'; 'sop/sob'. Alternatively, regional variations in respect of pronunciation of vowels in such words as 'butter', 'plastic' and 'coal' give rise to recognisable accents, but do not lead to word confusion. Such differences are treated as permissible variations in pronunciation of a single phoneme and are referred to as **allophones.** Phonemes do not therefore represent a specific way of articulating a sound, but rather the range of pronunciations which are consistent with the maintenance of contrasts between words. Within any language the extent to which allophonic variation is consistent with listeners 'hearing' a single phoneme will vary from phoneme to phoneme; some will have a very narrow range of variation, while others may allow considerable latitude without creating confusion. Figure 1.2 shows the set of phonemes which are generally recognised as constituting the sounds of English. The symbols are used by linguists and speech clinicians to represent the way in which individual speakers produce word sequences. The **phonemic transcription** of speech using these symbols differs from the more detailed **phonetic transcription** in that the former seeks to identify only those phonemic variations which are associated with changes in word meaning.

Figure 1.2 English phonemes

Vowels

1 Simple

/ɪ/	pit		/ʌ/	putt
/e/	pet		/ɒ/	pot
/æ/	pat		/ə/	potato

2 Long vowels and diphthongs

/i/	beat		/iə/	beer
/eɪ/	bait		/eə/	bear
/aɪ/	bite		/uə/	tour
/ɔɪ/	boy			
/u/	boot		/ɜ/	Bert
/oω/	boat		/ɔ/	bought
/aω/	bout		/ɑ/	bart

Consonants

Plosives	/p/	pin	Fricatives	/f/	fin
	/b/	bin		/v/	vine
	/t/	tin		/θ/	thin
	/d/	din		/ð/	then
	/k/	kin		/s/	sin
	/g/	gain		/z/	zinc
				/ʃ/	shin
				/ʒ/	measure/'meʒə/
Affricates	/ʧ/	chin			
	/ʤ/	gin			
Nasals	/m/	ram	Approximants	/l/	lime
	/n/	ran		/r/	rhyme
	/ŋ/	rang		/j/	yet
				/w/	wet
				/h/	hen

Source: Hawkins (1984)

Phonological sequences

In learning a language children must learn not only to distinguish the range of sounds that 'count' in terms of creating meaningful differences between words, but they must also learn to recognise and pronounce specific *sound sequences*.

As has already been suggested, while there are many different phoneme sequences, the number of permissible combinations is restricted. A **phonotactic** description is concerned with the way in which phonemes are sequenced and the extent to which an individual's speech reflects the

Figure 1.3 Emergence of phonotactic sequences

C = consonant;   V = vowel

9 months–2 years	CV	CVCV		
2 years–3 years	CV	CVCV	CVC	
3 years and beyond	CV	CVCV	CVC	CVCCV
	CVCCVC	CVCVCV	CCV	
	CCVC	CVCC	CCVCC	

Source: Adapted from Grunwell (1981)

phonotactic rules of the language. For example, consider the consonants /s/ /p/ and /r/. Of all the possible pairings of these consonants, in English, only three occur before a vowel:

s p r	spray; spring
s p	spy; spot
p r	pry; private
p r s	—
p s r	—
p s	—
s r	—
r s	—
r p	—

(Grunwell 1981)

Children initially begin to sequence sounds to produce simple syllables (a vowel preceded or followed by a consonant) at between 9 and 18 months of age. Although phonologically constant forms (or PCFs) may be produced consistently in relation to social or physical situations or psychological states (Dore 1973, 1974), they do not necessarily resemble conventional words. The first sequences to appear are consonant-plus-vowel ('ma', 'ba', 'da') and consonant-vowel-consonant-vowel ('mama', 'dada', 'baba'). Even when children begin to produce recognisable words employing a conventional phonotactic structure, there is little evidence that they are developing a system of phonemic contrasts. Instead, they seem to be learning sounds and sound sequences in relation to specific words (Ferguson and Farwell 1975; Ingram 1974, 1976). For example, the word 'yellow' is frequently mispronounced by young children as *lellow,* even when the initial phoneme has been mastered in respect to other words. Similarly, Smith (1973) found that his son mispronounced 'puddle' as *puzzle* and yet pronounced *puddle* when attempting to say 'puzzle'.

Subsequently, there appears to be a relatively orderly development of phonotactic sequences (as is shown in Figure 1.3) and increasing signs that the child is constructing a system of phonemic contrasts even though these may not always reflect the phonemic contrasts in the adult language. For example, a child who makes the following pronunciations for conventional words has clearly learned to produce the sounds /p/ /b/ /k/ and /d/.

Word	Child's pronunciation
top	dop
bed	bet
pin	bin
but	but
time	dime
knob	nop
hide	hite
sleep	lip

(Hawkins 1984)

However, the phonemes here do not serve the same contrastive function as they do in the adult phonological system. The sounds /b/ and /d/ occur only at the beginning of a word and the sounds /t/ and /p/ occur only at the end of a word. This suggests that, for the child, the sound pairs /b/ and /p/, and /d/ and /t/, are not separate phonemes which are necessary to differentiate words, but simply different ways of producing a single allophone depending on whether the sound comes at the beginning or at the end of a word.

The obvious differences between the contrastive use of sounds, in children's language and the ways in which sounds are used to differentiate meaning in the adult language, have created considerable interest in the possibility of describing the phonemic systems which are operative at different stages of development. Such an approach clearly has important implications for the assessment of phonological disabilities and for different approaches to remediation. However, before these issues can be discussed, it is necessary to consider the other levels of structural description, and also the way in which phonemic descriptions can be applied to children's language.

Morphological rules

A sentence comprises a string of words and the words themselves can be divided into smaller units. For example, in the sentence 'The little girls kissed their dolls,' the words 'girls' and 'dolls' can both be represented as nouns with plural markers (/s/) while the word 'kissed' is a verb with a past tense marker (-ed). These units – 'girl', 'doll', 'kiss' – cannot be further subdivided without destroying their meaning. Such minimal meaningful units are referred to as **morphemes** and are usually defined as the smallest phonemic strings which can convey meaning. Whereas 'girl' and 'kiss' can occur in sentences as independent words, /s/ and -ed do not constitute words and thus cannot occur in sentences in isolation. Morphemes which are also words are referred to as **free morphemes,** while those such as /s/ and -ed which can only occur when joined to free morphemes are termed **bound morphemes.** While free morphemes indicate the relationships which exist between the major sentence constituents (in this example, girls kissing dolls), bound morphemes serve different functions. In this example, they indicate that the action (kiss) occurred in the past and that there was more than one girl and more than one doll. The examples of /s/ and -ed illustrate just two of the ways in which bound morphemes may combine with free morphemes within sentences.

Morphemes can also be divided into **derivational morphemes,** which provide information regarding the way in which aspects of meaning are shared by different words ('bomb', 'bombardier', 'bomber', 'bombastic'; 'history', 'historical', 'historian'), and **inflectional morphemes,** which are introduced specifically in relation to grammatical rules for creating sentences. English has a highly complex system of rules governing the use of inflectional morphemes to mark such aspects of meaning as person, gender and number as well as tense. This not only creates problems for linguists who are concerned with describing morphological rules, but it also presents considerable difficulties for children learning language and those who are concerned with helping children who have language disorders.

In a study of three children in the United States, Brown (1973) found that between the ages of 2 and 4 years children gradually included a variety of different morphemes in their spontaneous utterances. Although there was little correspondence between the inclusion of separate morphemes and chronological age, there was considerable similarity regarding the sequence in which the different morphemes appeared. The order of appearance of morphemes seems to be governed partly by the complexity of the semantic distinctions which are expressed (Cromer 1981) and partly by the complexity of the grammatical rule employed (Slobin 1973). Brown studied fourteen morphemes which are obligatory in English. The sequence in which they appeared in the language samples of the three children was as follows (approximate ages are shown in parentheses):

1 The present progressive affix on verbs (-ing), denoting an activity in progress – for example, 'He's drawing.' (19–28 months)
2 The preposition 'on' – for example, 'Put it on the table.' (27–30 months)
3 The preposition 'in' – for example, 'It's in the cupboard.' (27–30 months)
4 The plural /s/ – for example, 'Dogs bark.' (24–33 months)

5 The irregular past tense of verbs – for example, 'It broke'; 'He ran away'; 'I made it.' (25–46 months)
6 The possessive /s/ – for example, 'Tom's book.' (26–40 months)
7 The uncontractable copula 'be' form (that is, where the 'be' form is used with an adjective, preposition or noun phrase and cannot be abbreviated) – for example, 'He is.' (In response to 'Who's there?') (27–39 months)
8 The articles 'a' and 'the' (counted as separate morphemes). (28–46 months)
9 Regular past tense forms – for example, 'Sally picked a flower.' (26–48 months)
10 The third-person singular /s/ for present tense verbs – for example, 'John rides the bike'; 'He likes my dress.' (26–46 months)
11 Irregular, third-person singular present tense; the verbs 'have' and 'do' become 'has' and 'does' for third-person sentence subjects – for example, 'He has two eyes'; 'Mummy does the shopping.' (28–50 months)
12 The uncontractable auxiliary 'be' form (that is, where the 'be' occurs with a main verb and cannot be abbreviated) – for example, 'He is.' (In response to 'Who's coming to the party?') (29–48 months)
13 The contractable copula 'be' form (that is, where 'be' occurs with an adjective, preposition or noun phrase and where abbreviation is possible) – for example, 'They're inside'; 'The boy's dirty.' (29–49 months)
14 The contractable auxiliary 'be' form (that is, where 'be' occurs with a main verb and abbreviation is possible) – for example, 'He's laughing'; 'Mummy's cooking dinner.' (30–50 months)

As we shall see in Chapter 7 this kind of developmental sequence has important implications for the assessment of children with language difficulties.

Syntactical rules

The rules for ordering words in sentences do not operate on specific words, but on classes of words such as nouns, verbs and adjectives. This has the advantage that a relatively small number of syntactical rules can account for the production of a very large number of sentences. For example, the simple rule:

S→article + noun + verb + article + noun

(where → stands for 'can be rewritten as') means that an infinite number of sentences with this structure can be produced – for example:

The man sees the house.
This dog chases that ball.
The president makes a speech.

Application of the rule depends on knowledge of the lexical classes to which different words belong. Thus, the rule assumes that words are categorised according to their status as nouns, verbs, articles, adjectives, etc. However, determining the lexical status of a word – that is to say, exactly where it fits into rules for generating sentences – is not as straightforward as it might at first seem.

Lexical categories

Although it is usual for nouns to be thought of as 'naming words' and verbs to be described as 'doing words' or 'action words', it is doubtful that these lexical categories can be defined so easily. In fact, the identification of a word as a noun or verb is closely linked to the role that the word can play in a sentence (Maratsos 1983; Maratsos and Chalkley 1980). For example, 'red' names a colour, but it cannot appear in the same slots within a sentence as nouns.

Categories of word meanings are related to lexical categories, but they do not correspond to such an extent that one can be predicted from the other: while some verbs clearly describe action relationships between nouns (for example, 'kick', 'throw', 'run'), others are much less directly concerned with action (for example, 'like', 'know', 'hear', 'belong', 'want', 'wish'). Conversely, there are non-verbs which have a strong connotation of activity, such as 'noisy', 'rapid', 'violent', 'turbulent'.

The way in which the rules of grammar permit a word to appear in a sentence – that is, the word's privileges of occurrence – also contributes to the definition of lexical class, although the role taken by a word in one sentence is not sufficient for accurate identification of its lexical status. For example, although a verb stem can be combined with the bound morpheme /s/ within a sentence, this structural feature alone is not sufficient to identify the word as a verb, since nouns can also be combined with the same morpheme. The distinction between the two lexical classes lies in the fact that verbs take an /s/ morpheme to indicate present tense while nouns do so to indicate plurality. Thus, lexical categories can only be adequately defined on the basis of the changes in meaning which occur in sentences when the words appear in different structural contexts (Maratsos 1983; Maratsos and Chalkley 1980).

In order to generate grammatical sentences, a speaker needs to know something about word meanings and something about the way in which structural variations influence meaning; and these two aspects of grammar are not independent but closely interrelated.

Sentence subject and logical subject

So far the sentence

The girls kissed the dolls

has been identified as indicating a past tense relationship between girls and dolls; the two nouns are co-ordinated by a verb which describes that relationship as 'kissing'. However, it is also evident that the verb 'kiss' expresses a *direction,* in that it is the girls who kiss the dolls and not the dolls who kiss the girls. In active sentences, the *direction* of the verb is normally conveyed by the sequence noun-verb-noun. It is this syntactical arrangement of words in sentences which enables the reader/listener to assign the roles of *agent* to the girls, since they are performing the action, and *patient* to the dolls, since they are receiving the action.

In active sentences like this one, the noun which precedes the main verb and indicates the agent, is also the grammatical subject of the sentence. The grammatical subject indicates the sentence topic – that is, what the sentence is about. It is also implicated in the grammatical rules which determine how verbs are modified with inflectional morphemes to agree with the number and aspect of the noun subject. For example, compare the following sentences:

The girls kiss the dolls.
The girl kisses the dolls.

However, in English, it is common for the role of grammatical subject to be taken by a noun which does not refer to an agent. For example, in the sentence

That car belongs to me

'that car' is the sentence topic and the grammatical subject; it therefore determines the presence of the /s/ morpheme suffix on the verb to agree with the singular noun. 'That car' is not, however, the agent which performs the action 'belongs' in the same way 'the girls' is the agent which performs the action of 'kissing'. Furthermore, when a sentence does include a noun in an agent role, that noun is not necessarily the subject of the sentence. In passive sentences, the role of grammatical subject is taken by the direct object of the verb – for instance, 'The dolls were kissed by the girls.'

This ambiguity in the semantic status of nouns which are sentence subjects and sentence objects illustrates the distinction between the way in which meanings are expressed in the **surface structure** of sentences and the underlying semantic relations or **deep structure** of sentences.

Deep structures and surface structures

In the sentence

The boy was helped by the teacher

'the boy' coming immediately before the verb 'was helped' is easily identifiable as the subject of the sentence. However, the person performing the action described by the verb is not the boy but the teacher; in this sentence, the logical subject is separated from the grammatical subject. Carrying this distinction further, Chomsky (1965) proposed that sentences be described in terms of their surface structures and deep structures. The deep structures are seen as being mapped directly on to some set of underlying ideas and relationships which a speaker may wish to communicate. But deep structures are never directly represented in language. Before the deep structures can be realised in sentences, they must first be reorganised to conform to the grammatical rules of a particular language.

In English, this reorganisation permits a number of choices to be made including, for example, whether the logical subject or deep-structure subject, will occupy the role of sentence subject. It is also possible to express the same underlying deep structure as a declarative sentence, an interrogative or a negative. Thus, the following surface structures all express the same set of deep-structure relations:

The teacher helped the boy.
The boy was helped by the teacher.
The teacher did not help the boy.
Did the teacher help the boy?

Chomsky argued that it was possible to specify, through a set of grammatical rules, the relationship between deep structures and surface structures and hence between any set of surface structures which are derived from the same deep-structure relations. Since these rules make it possible to see how deep structures are transformed into surface structures, they are termed **transformational rules.** Transformational rules do not operate directly on the words in the surface structures but on sentence constituents; these sentence constituents are derived from an additional set of rules called **phrase-structure rules.** The relationship between surface structures and deep structures is presented diagrammatically in Figure 1.4.

Phrase-structure rules

The phrase-structure analysis specifies rules which are able to generate novel sentences of a particular kind. For example, simple active declarative

Figure 1.4 Rules for relating deep structures and surface structures

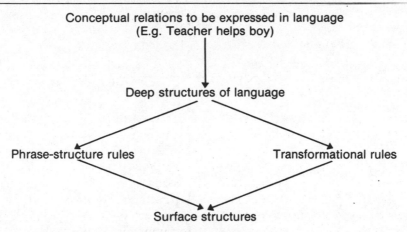

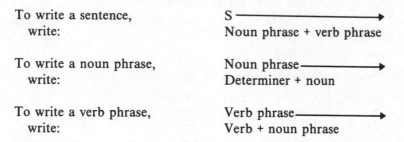

E.g. Active sentence: The teacher helps the boy.
Passive sentence: The boy is helped by the teacher.
Negative sentence: The teacher does not help the boy.

sentences can be assembled from the following rules (note: the right-hand column shows the conventional shorthand expressions for writing grammatical rules, while the left-hand column gives a gloss):

To write a sentence, write:

S ⟶
Noun phrase + verb phrase

To write a noun phrase, write:

Noun phrase ⟶
Determiner + noun

To write a verb phrase, write:

Verb phrase ⟶
Verb + noun phrase

These simple rules indicate that a sentence comprises a noun phrase (a determiner plus a noun), together with a verb phrase (a phrase beginning with a main verb and ending with a noun phrase). Note that one of the rules, the noun phrase specification, is reused to indicate the constituents of the verb phrase. This recursive nature of the phrase-structure grammar is largely responsible for its ability to generate complex sentence structures using comparatively simple rules. A final set of rules is also needed to indicate the relevant words which fit the lexical categories of noun, verb and determiner. For example:

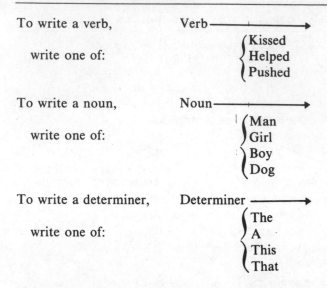

To write a verb,

    write one of:

Verb ⟶

⎧ Kissed
⎨ Helped
⎩ Pushed

To write a noun,

    write one of:

Noun ⟶

⎧ Man
⎨ Girl
⎬ Boy
⎩ Dog

To write a determiner,

    write one of:

Determiner ⟶

⎧ The
⎨ A
⎬ This
⎩ That

Depending on the number of words known and identified as belonging within the lexical categories noun, verb, determiner, this set of rules would generate a large number of simple sentences. However, all of the sentences would be simple active declarative in form.

Transformational rules

A transformational rule indicates how the phrase-structure constituents can be reordered to produce different surface forms with the same underlying relationships preserved. For example, a simple active declarative sentence in the past tense such as

    The man walked the dog

can be expressed in phrase-structure rules as:

    S = noun phrase(1) + verb + noun phrase(2)

The sentence can be transformed into a passive sentence by reordering the constituents according to the rule:

    S (passive) = noun phrase(2) + was + verb + by + noun phrase(1)

Note that the reordering deals with the phrase-structure constituents as single units of analysis, even though they might stand for a number of words in the surface structure. For example, in the sentence 'The teacher helped the boy', the transformational rules work equally well with the sentence 'The kindly old teacher with soft blue eyes helped the naughty little ginger-haired boy,' since 'the kindly old teacher with soft blue eyes' is analysed as the first noun phrase and 'the naughty little ginger-haired boy' is the second noun phrase.

    This example has been used to illustrate the principles of transformational grammar. When the rules are extended to deal with more complex surface forms – such as embedded sentences and different tenses – they become far more complicated. However, Chomsky's claim is that this approach does make it possible to provide a formal description of a set of grammatical rules. As such, it has a number of advantages. First, as we have seen, the transformational rules, together with the phrase-structure rules, specify the relationship between deep-structure meanings and the surface-structure forms. Second, the rules are generative and account for all acceptable sentences in English and no ungrammatical or inadmissible surface strings. Third, the rules suggest the kind of knowledge that adult speakers must have in order to understand and produce completely novel utterances. While Chomsky's transformational grammar is widely accepted as the most successful attempt to describe syntactical rules, and hence the knowledge which underlies sentence production in adults, the relevance of this and other structural approaches to the language of children is more problematical. It is to this issue that we now turn.

Are structural descriptions relevant to children's language?

While the previous sections introduced a variety of structural descriptions of language, the question now arises as to the applicability of these descriptions to the language used by children. This is an important question since it determines the kinds of language assessment procedures which are considered appropriate for children with language disabilities and the areas to be addressed by intervention procedures. Underlying strategies for assessment and intervention, is the assumption that the descriptive framework which is employed is much more than a system imposed upon children's language. Rather, such descriptions are seen as reflecting the processes involved in language development and thus may indicate both the problems which children face in learning language and the ways in which these problems might be overcome.

The relevance of structurally based descriptions can be addressed in two ways. First, do the descriptions fit children's language or, perhaps more accurately, does children's language fit the descriptions provided? Second, are there grounds for believing that the descriptions provide an accurate characterisation of children's knowledge at different stages of development? This latter question is concerned with the psychological validity of descriptions of children's language (Maratsos and Chalkley 1980).

Language is a developmental phenomenon, and all normal children eventually come to possess skills which reflect an enormously sophisticated knowledge of the grammatical system. But how does this knowledge arise? While studies of the language of 10- and 11-year-old children indicate a mastery of most, but not all, of the grammatical rules of English (Chomsky 1969), it is much less clear whether the language of very young or language-disordered children differs from adult language simply in terms of complexity – that is, the number of rules learned – or whether there are more fundamental differences. Is it the case that young children are learning grammatical rules but, because they are young, they have only acquired very simple rules for ordering and modifying linguistic structures? Or is it that the language of young children is not in fact based on the acquisition of structural rules at all?

If structural rules do seem to capture the developing child's linguistic knowledge, it would suggest that language development is in a sense controlled by the child's search for the rules of the adult grammar. This in turn might be regarded as support for assessment procedures which focus on language structures and a reason for trying to teach language-disordered children grammatical rules.

Phonological rules in children's language

It is clear that children do gradually improve and extend their articulatory skills so that the sounds they produce more closely resemble the sounds of the adult language. Since most children do eventually master the adult system of sounds – and for those who do not, the adult system represents the goal of any therapeutic intervention – it seems reasonable to try and describe development in terms of the phonological rules found in the adult language. Thus, if a child produces *pup* instead of 'cup', this might be identified as an error whereby one sound has been substituted for another.

The major problem with this **error-analysis** approach is that, by focusing on the accuracy of individual words, it prevents an analysis of the patterns of error which might provide insight into the child's developing knowledge of sounds as a *system* of phonemic contrasts. It is for this reason that linguists favour a **contrastive analysis,** in which samples of speech are examined to discover regularities in phonemic errors across words and with respect to the position of phonemes within words (Grunwell 1981; Hawkins 1984). Such an analysis, it is argued, can provide insights into the child's own developing system of sound features and indicates the extent to which this differs from the adult system.

It should be emphasised that here the term 'system' has two important characteristics. First, it implies that sounds are learned in terms of the ways in which they contrast with other sounds and therefore contribute to the communication of meaning (see pp. 8–9). Second, it implies that when additional contrasts are acquired – for example, when 't' in 'train' is distinguished from 'ch' in 'chain' – the contrast will be reflected throughout the system and other words with the same phonemic contrast will be differentiated (for example 'trees/cheese'; 'trip/chip'). A failure to extend a contrast in this way would indicate limitations in the organisation of the child's phonemic system.

There are two criticisms which have been directed at this approach. The first is concerned with the validity of any representation of a *system* of phonemic contrasts, since the notion of a system implies some degree of stability over time and in relation to different contexts of use. Grunwell points out that neither of these assumptions is valid and that the pattern of errors in children's language tends to be in 'an almost constant state of change' (Grunwell 1981: 78) and highly sensitive to the speech of others.

The second criticism concerns the status of the phoneme. Single phonemes' range, in terms of the allophones which they embrace and the allophones that count as variants of a single phoneme, will depend upon the position in which a phoneme occurs in a word. Furthermore, the distribution of allophones with respect to phonemes seems to be totally arbitrary. This raises the question of the degree of allophonic variation which should be permitted when a child is credited with having mastered a phonemic contrast. Menyuk and Menn (1979) argue that the phoneme is best viewed as a convenient abstract device for describing sound patterns, but that there is no reason to suppose that it represents the basis for the child's organisation of the sounds within a language. Instead of beginning by attributing to the child a knowledge of phonemic contrasts, they argue that developmental linguistics must determine *how* that knowledge is acquired.

The obvious fact that most children do eventually master the phonological system of the adult language suggests that there must be mechanisms by which these phonemic contrasts are assimilated into an immature yet perfectable system underlying the child's utterances. A description of such a mechanism would both explain and predict phonemic errors in children's speech. Three such approaches will now be considered.

Distinctive features

One approach has been to look 'beneath' the abstract level of phonemic descriptions in an attempt to devise a descriptive framework which is more closely related to the mechanisms of speech production. The 'distinctive features' approach (Chomsky and Halle 1968) suggests that phonemes of all natural languages can be specified by a relatively small number of features concerning the functioning of the articulatory apparatus in sound production. For example, some sounds (such as /b/ and /d/) are 'voiced', while others (such as /p/ and /t/) are not; some sounds are produced with a nasal resonance (/m/ /n/ and /ng/); and, for some, the tongue is raised in the mouth. In each case the articulatory feature can be present or absent. Thus, any phoneme can be uniquely specified by the presence or absence of a set of distinctive features derived from the mechanisms of sound production.

While the mechanisms for producing the features are presumed to be innate, the child's problem is finding out which combination of distinctive features fits with the phonemes of any given language. It is assumed that mastery of the adult system occurs through the gradual accumulation of distinctive features; initially, a phonemic contrast in the adult language might be distinguished by the presence or absence of only one distinctive feature but, gradually, with increasing experience, the child recognises that reproduction of the sounds in the adult language requires specific combinations of a number of distinctive features.

In spite of the claims that this approach is anchored to the mechanisms of speech production and therefore provides a link between speech sounds and word meaning, it has been widely criticised as being inconsistent with the evidence from children's language. Grunwell (1982) argues that the distinctive features are themselves abstract concepts which are remote from the reality of speech production and inappropriate to the description of speech errors, while Carney (1979) suggests that the approach leads to inaccuracies in the specification of phonemes in ordinary speech.

Generative phonology

In contrast to the distinctive-features approach, generative phonology is based on the assumption that, from a very early age, children have an underlying representation of the adult phonological system and that errors arise because of difficulties in the production process. Such a view is given some support by the evidence from experimental studies which indicate that even very young infants have a well-developed ability to detect phonemic contrasts (Morse 1972, 1979). Phonemic description, therefore, focuses upon the errors a child makes in relation to the adult system. Such errors are described in terms of additional rules which account for the difference between the child's underlying (adult-like) representation of the phonological system and the child's own productions.

Once again, there are a number of criticisms which may be directed at this approach. First, the experimental evidence regarding children's responses to speech sounds is ambiguous, since it conflates detection of sound differences with perception and interpretation of the meaning of those differences. Second, since this approach assumes that the child's speech is constrained only by production difficulties, it predicts that a new phonemic contrast, once learned, will be applied appropriately to all words in the child's vocabulary, but without any over-generalisation to other phonemes. Grunwell (1981) points out that, in fact, over-generalisations do occur – for example, Smith (1973) reported a child who produced *led* for 'red' and, on occasion, *let* for 'yet'. When /r/ was mastered in relation to 'red' the child also introduced another variant for 'yet' – *ret*. Finally, the approach is implausible from a developmental point of view; the child is seen as beginning with an immature system which, because of the production rules required to account for phonological errors, actually has more rules than the target system.

Simplification processes

The third approach to be considered here is also based on the view that problems in production are a major source of speech errors among children. According to Stampe (1969), the structure of the articulatory apparatus is such that some sounds are easier to produce than others. Given a phonemic contrast in which one sound is easier to pronounce than the other, the child will inevitably produce the easier sound whenever one member of the contrasting pair is required.

There are a number of putative simplification processes which, it is claimed, account for children's phonemic errors (Grunwell 1981; Ingram 1976). For example, the process of **weak-syllable deletion** results in unstressed syllables being abandoned so that 'banana' becomes *nana* and 'again' becomes *gen*. **Cluster reduction** accounts for errors whereby consonant clusters are reduced to single consonants ('plane' becomes *pein* and 'brown' becomes *bown)*, while **consonant harmony** occurs when different consonants within a word are modified to produce similar consonants either side of a vowel (for example, 'dog' becomes *gog)*.

These simplification processes have the advantage of describing, in a relatively straightforward way, the relationship between the child's errors and adult pronunciations. However, they are subject to a number of important limitations. First, in so far as they focus exclusively on errors, they do not provide an account of the child's emerging understanding of the phonological system – that is, those aspects of phonology which the child gets right. Second, there is some disagreement regarding whether the simplification processes are more closely concerned with production (Stampe 1969) or with perception and representation of speech sounds (Ingram 1976). Third, while the simplification processes are attractive in terms of providing a summary of children's errors and in terms of describing the relationship between the adult system and children's knowledge of that system, they are circular: the processes arise only in so far as it is necessary to account for the observed disparity between adults' and children's speech sounds.

While there is wide agreement that a system of phonemic contrasts is a useful way of linking the sounds in the adult language to a description of words and sentences, there are serious limitations to its adoption as a descriptive framework for describing what children know about the organisation of sounds in the language. The alternative phonemically based descriptive approaches reviewed have also been subject to serious criticisms. As yet, no description of the child's emerging phonological system can claim accurately to represent the child's underlying knowledge of the ways in which sequences of sound contrasts are organised within a language. A contrastive analysis does lead to the identification of regularities and patterns of error in a child's speech and, in spite of its limitations, it remains the most popular approach to the description of phonological errors.

Morphological rules in children's language

Applying morphological descriptions to children's language is dependent upon two relatively simple criteria: first, is it possible to identify separate morphemes within children's utterances? And, second, where segments which would be identified as separate morphemes in adult speech do occur, are they used appropriately to mark semantic distinctions? Where these criteria are met it may be assumed that a morphological description is an accurate reflection of the child's knowledge regarding the relationship between different combinations of morphemes and the expression of meaning (Brown 1973).

The evidence for dividing the utterances produced by children into morphemes derives from a distributional analysis of a speech sample. For example, if a simple utterance such as 'Daddy gone' occurs in a speech sample, it is quite possible that this represents a single morpheme which has been learned by rote in response to comments from adults, such as 'Daddy's gone to work,' being repeated on different occasions. It is only when the two morphemes occur either singly ('gone', 'Daddy') or in combination with other words ('ball gone', 'kiss Daddy') that it is possible to identify them as separate morphemes in the child's developing language system. Similarly, with bound morphemes, the occurrence of a plural marker – for example, /s/ in 'toys' – does not count as a separate morpheme until the noun without the /s/ has been used to identify a single instance of the referent 'toy'. Thus, the identification of morphemes in children's language is closely tied to the semantic distinctions which are made by their appropriate use.

Whereas a speech sample may make it possible to identify separate morphemes positively, the absence of evidence does not lead unequivocally to the conclusion that the child is not able to make specific morphemic distinctions. It is possible that the opportunity for making a specific distinction did not occur within the period during which the child's speech was sampled. Although this problem is ultimately insoluble, the difficulties it presents can be considerably reduced by basing morphemic descriptions on large samples of speech – usually 100 utterances – and, whenever possible, taking account of the relationship between the child's utterances and the context in which they are employed. For example, if the child who uses 'toys' to refer to a group of toys also uses the morpheme /s/ when referring to a single toy, this is evidence against /s/ being regarded as a separate morpheme in the child's language system.

The close relationship between morphemes and the child's expression of complex meanings creates the possibility of a summary measure of sentence complexity or, put another way, a measure of the amount of meaning a child is able to express through conventional sentence structures. As the child becomes able to express major relations within a sentence in words (for example, 'Daddy go work' instead of 'Daddy go' or 'Go work' and, later on, 'My Daddy went to work') so the number of morphemes in a sentence rises. Similarly, as bound morphemes are introduced to indicate tense, plurality, possession, etc., the number of morphemes within an utterance increases.

Brown (1973) reported a high degree of consistency with regard to the sequence in which different inflectional morphemes were learned and this provides additional support for the idea of using the length of utterance, as measured in morphemes, as an index of grammatical complexity. Not only does the number of morphemes in an utterance provide a direct measure of the child's mastery of conventional grammatical markers and the complexity of the ideas being expressed, but Brown's data suggest an underlying pattern to this growth; similar changes in utterance length across children will tend to reflect mastery of the same inflectional morphemes. Brown suggested that the most useful measure of grammatical complexity is the Mean Length of Utterance (MLU), which is the average length of utterances from a continuous sample of spontaneous speech. Procedures for collecting samples of child language and calculating the MLU are described in Chapter 7.

Syntactical rules in children's language

The first overt sign of grammatical structure, and hence a knowledge of primitive syntactical rules, is the emergence of two-word utterances within a single intonational contour. These first combinatorial utterances have received a considerable amount of attention and an increasing understanding of the underlying knowledge upon which they are based has served as a stimulus to the exploration of the more complex utterances that occur later. Less obviously, they also provide a better appreciation of the processes involved in communication at the single-word stage.

What kind of description might be appropriate to the following utterances?

Here milk	This light
Here fix	This one book
Here car	This book
Here hat	This here book
Here music	This one cookie

Want milk	Can-I fix it
Want car	Can-I have ball
Want get	Can-I have bite
Want fix it	Can-I have put in
Want blow	Can-I have break it
More music	Look (at) that
More hat	Look (at) light
More cookie	Look (at) chicken
More put in	
More spoon	

(Adapted from Braine 1976)

Is there any reason to suggest that such utterances are ordered on the basis of syntactical rules or lexical classes? Such simple two-word rules seem to offer little opportunity for attributing to the child a knowledge of complex grammatical rules. The evidence, such as it is, will be derived from (a) the consistency with which a child places a word or group of words in first or second position in an utterance, and (b) the extent to which sequence regularities can be attributed to a child's knowledge of a word's grammatical or lexical status. More specifically, it has been suggested that for a child to be credited with syntactical knowledge, two- and three-word combinations must pass the following tests (Bowerman 1973a; Braine 1976; Brown 1973):

1 For words within a particular grammatical or lexical class, is there evidence for regular orderings, such that words in one category always take the same position in the utterance?
2 Is there evidence of productivity, such that novel sequences which are unlikely to have been produced by imitation, also follow such regular orderings?
3 Is the sequencing rule extended so that a wide range of words within the child's repertoire are incorporated within it? For example, if the rule is concerned with the position of words which fill the role of grammatical object, is a wide range of possible words used to fill that role?
4 Is there evidence of a more general grammatical rule which would explain the sequencing regularities without crediting the child with knowledge of abstract grammatical classes?

Subject and object relations in children's early utterances

When language samples from children who are using two- and three-word utterances are examined using the above criteria, they do not support the view that these primitive sentence structures are organised on the basis of knowledge of either grammatical or lexical categories. For example, Bowerman (1973a) pointed out that many children do seem to have a preference for placing some words in the subject position, at the beginning of an utterance, but typically this involves a narrower range of words than would be predicted on the basis of the words in the child's vocabulary which *could* have been grammatical subjects (Criterion 3). Similarly, for words which occur in the second position in two-word utterances, Braine (1976) pointed out that the range of meanings expressed is often restricted. He argued that a number of utterances which seemed to conform to the verb-plus-object pattern, were more easily interpreted in terms of a simple rule of the kind:

S→word indicating 'request' plus word indicating 'object requested' (Criterion 4)

Thus, there is little justification for crediting children with knowledge of lexical categories such as 'noun' and 'verb' when the words which fill those roles in the adult grammar can be described in terms of more general rules which credit the child with less abstract knowledge. For young children, 'nouns' generally refer to objects and 'verbs' generally describe actions, but this is not invariably so – for example, as with the child who when given a hot drink requested his mother to 'cold it'. Braine (1976) describes a child who placed 'want' with both object words (putative nouns such as 'cup') and with other action words (putative verbs such as 'go'). However, other action words ('hold' and 'roll') were used only in combination with 'it' ('hold it', 'roll it'). Thus, on the basis of Criteria 3 and 4, it would be inappropriate to describe those utterances as indicative of lexical knowledge regarding nouns and verbs. In addition, since phrase-structure rules are dependent upon grammatical categories such as 'noun', 'verb', etc., it follows that this evidence also invalidates the application of phrase-structure rules to children's first word combinations (Bowerman 1973). It is still not clear exactly when children's language warrants the inference that they possess an understanding of lexical classes and hence of phrase-structure rules.

Pivot–open grammar

Even though the abstract concepts which describe adult grammar may not be applicable to the two-and three-word combinations found in the language of young children, this does not remove the possibility that children are putting words together on the basis of some set of structurally based rules. Perhaps rather than learning adult grammatical rules, children construct their own rules for producing ordered sequences of words. This reasoning has led a number of researchers to carry out a detailed distributional analysis of language samples from different children. A distributional analysis involves scanning a corpus of utterances for words which appear in the same positions relative to other words, without trying to impose a priori grammatical or lexical descriptions. Such an analysis might indicate a totally random approach to organising word combinations, any word combining with any other word. On the other hand, such an approach might indicate regularities in terms of selection strategies for words which are combined together and systematic word orders.

The first results from such an approach were reported by three groups of researchers in the early 1960s (Bellugi and Brown 1964; Braine 1963; Miller and Ervin 1964). It was suggested that children's two-word combinations were derived from three simple, structurally based rules. The rules operated on words which were classified as belonging to one of three categories. 'Pivot words' (Braine 1963) formed a relatively small set and could occur only in combination with a word from the larger class of 'open words'. Furthermore, the pivot category was subdivided on the basis of privileges of occurrence – some pivot words could occur only in the first position in a two-word sentence and some could occur only in the second position. Finally, the distributional analysis indicated that open words could combine freely with both categories of pivot words and with one another. Thus, the rules for two-word sentences were:

S→Pivot (1) + Open word
    Open word + Pivot word (2)
    Open word + Open word

Considerable interest surrounded this view of young children apparently carrying out their own distributional analysis of the sentences they heard, and actively creating primitive grammatical rules. The excitement carried over to the field of language disorders and prompted a number of researchers to focus on pivot–open grammar as a basis for assessment (Lee 1966) and intervention (Jeffree *et al.* 1973; Willbrand 1977). However, such enthusiasm was premature and it is now clear that pivot–open categories are no more successful in meeting the criteria for structurally based linguistic knowledge than the descriptions based on grammatical and lexical categories derived from adult language. There are many examples of two-word utterances which do not conform to the pivot–open rules and, at the same time, the rules gloss over important distinctions which children do seem to make with these early utterances. They are thus both too narrow and too general to account for the data on children's language (Bloom 1971). Finally, as we shall see in Chapters 2 and 3, there are alternative frameworks for describing children's first sentences which fit the data more successfully.

Transformational rules in children's language

As children's utterances become longer and, in terms of their surface structures, more complex, it becomes increasingly plausible to consider them in terms of the transformational rules which have been used to describe adult language. Some researchers (Bloom 1970; Bowerman 1973a; Brown 1973) have explored the possibilities of applying a transformational grammar to children's first word combinations, although for a variety of reasons this was not considered successful. It is also tempting to move beyond the point of straightforward language description and ask whether transformational rules are psychologically real. Do transformational rules provide a description of what it is that children learn in order to produce grammatical sentences and is progress in language development determined by the child's knowledge of transformational rules? If such a view were confirmed, it would not only provide a very elegant account of developmental progress towards adult proficiency, but it would also have important ramifications for assessment and intervention with language-disordered children.

The validity of a transformational description of children's linguistic knowledge has been explored using three different lines of investigation. The first approach is based upon the way in which sentences are assumed to be produced by the application of one or more transformational rules. For example, the sentence 'Mummy shouts louder than Daddy' is transformationally more complex than the sentence 'Mummy shouts louder than Daddy shouts,' since it invokes a deletion transformation of 'shouts'. More complex still is the sentence 'Mummy does not shout louder than Daddy,' which incorporates a deletion transformation and a negative transformation.

If children are learning transformational rules as a basis for sentence production, it is suggested that sentences which involve fewer transformations will be in evidence before those which incorporate more transformations. Using this reasoning, Brown and Hanlon made specific predictions regarding the order of appearance of sentences such as simple active affirmative declaratives ('We had a ball'), interrogatives ('Did we have a ball?'), truncated sentences ('We did'), and negatives ('We didn't have a ball'). On the basis of a detailed examination of the data from a longitudinal study of three children, Brown and Hanlon concluded that 'there is a sequence . . . from those sentences that are derivationally simple, in terms of the adult grammar, toward those that are derivationally complex' and 'the adult grammar does, at least roughly, represent what it is that the child is learning' (Brown and Hanlon 1970: 50).

Against this evidence must be set the arguments that there are additional forms of complexity in longer utterances as well as transformational complexity – for example, the negative sentence is not only longer than a simple active declarative sentence, but it is also more complex in terms of meaning (Maratsos 1983). The order of acquisition might be related to constraints on utterance length and semantic constraints, rather than transformational complexity. Furthermore, there is contradictory evidence to show that in some cases the transformationally more complex forms – for example,

'That's John's' (transformational deletion of object) – occur before the full sentence form (Brown 1973).

The second line of investigation concerns the pattern of syntactical errors in children's early language. For example, children sometimes produce incorrect forms of 'wh' questions, such as 'Where we can go?' Here, it has been argued (Bellugi 1971) that in a sentence which requires two transformational rules to be applied, the child has only succeeded in dealing with one. Unfortunately, this kind of error does not seem to be spread evenly across different types of 'wh' questions (Labov and Labov 1978), which raises the additional question of why children should have difficulty with applying transformational rules for some interrogative sentences, but not others.

The third approach to studying the validity of a transformational approach to children's linguistic knowledge is concerned with the errors which can be predicted on the basis of sentence complexity, rather than those which actually occur. Here, the picture is rather different in that children seem not to have difficulty with constructions such as 'He is going' and 'Did he go?', 'What did he see?' and 'Where will he go?' although they are at least as complex in terms of transformational rules as sentences which do create difficulties such as 'Where can we go?' (Maratsos 1983.)

Thus, the evidence for the psychological reality of transformational grammar is ambiguous. A transformational description of children's language provides a set of good predictions for the order in which various sentence types appear in children's language, but such a sequence is open to different interpretations. Some errors that occur in children's language are consistent with the incomplete learning of transformational rules or problems in the application of more than one rule at a time. On the other hand, if transformational rules are acquired slowly over time, it is difficult to see why children do not make more errors than they do with some transformationally complex constructions.

Chapter two

Meaning in children's language

Introduction

The discussion of structural approaches to describing language presented in Chapter 1 indicated that these approaches provide a relatively elegant and powerful description of the rules which seem to underlie adult language production and comprehension. However, when children first begin to talk their language structures are extremely limited and provide little evidence to support the view of underlying knowledge in terms of traditional grammatical concepts such as sentence subject, noun, verb categories or more sophisticated grammatical systems such as phrase structure or transformational grammar. Bearing in mind that most children do eventually progress to adult levels of competence where structural descriptions are appropriate, the problem remains of the kinds of description which are best suited to early speech and how such descriptions might account for the transition to more abstract grammatical knowledge.

The origins of semantic approaches

Semantic approaches to language description are based on the idea that, for young children, language structure is subordinate to the child's efforts to communicate (Bloom 1973). Since very often the child's utterances seem to be prompted by an effort to communicate specific meanings, it has been argued that it makes more sense to describe children's language in terms of the ideas they seem to be expressing, rather than in terms of the inadequate structural devices which they employ.

The beginning of what is sometimes referred to as the 'semantic revolution' in research on children's language can be traced to Bloom's attempt to apply transformational grammar to children's first word combinations (Bloom 1970). In looking at her transcripts of children's utterances recorded in natural settings, she found a number of examples of the same structure being used to communicate different meanings. For example, the phrase 'Mummy sock' was used on one occasion when a mother was putting a sock on the child's foot, and on another occasion when the child appeared holding one of her mother's socks. Bloom argued that by taking into account the physical and social context within which the utterance occurred, it was possible to infer that the same structure was used to convey two different meanings.

The first message might be glossed as 'Mummy [is doing something with the] sock' and the second one as '[This is] Mummy['s] sock.' (Note that the square brackets indicate aspects of meaning which are not expressed in the surface structure.) It is the availability of contextual cues which enables the adult (the child's mother as well as the researcher) to fill in the structural elements which are missing and thus provide an interpretation of the child's intended meaning. Because this kind of description requires the researcher or clinician to infer what the child might have been trying to say, it is often referred to as a **rich interpretation.**

Compared with structural approaches to description, the emphasis in semantic descriptions has shifted from reading meaning from the surface structure of the words and phrases spoken, to using contextual information to infer the child's *intentions* when speaking. Instead of development being seen as an attempt to master a language *system* by acquiring rule-based knowledge, growing structural sophistication is seen as a consequence of the child's struggle to make other people understand what she wants to say.

Subsequently, the idea of using a 'rich interpretation' of the data on children's language (that is, using contextual information to compensate for structural limitations in the child's utterances) became an essential feature of analysis in research and clinical assessments. The following sections deal with semantic descriptions of single words and two- and three-word phrases.

Semantic approaches to single words

A number of writers (Bloom 1973; Braine 1976; Clark 1983; Nelson 1973) have suggested that children's first utterances are attempts to give verbal expression to ideas or concepts which are already understood in some way. The child's understanding of objects, events and relationships is usually referred to as **conceptual knowledge,** while the expression of ideas and concepts in language is a **semantic representation** of that knowledge. Thus, young children may know much more at a conceptual level than they are able to express in words and sentences.

Single-word utterances provide the first evidence of children's attempts to map the way in which meanings can be expressed in language on to their existing conceptual knowledge of the world. Subsequently, during development there are two important trends. First, children gain increasing mastery of the structural features of a language which provides conventional methods of marking important semantic distinctions. For example, the discussion of morphemic rules indicated the way in which children learn the rule/s/ of English for expressing tense, plurality and possession. As a result, children are able to express more meaning in the surface structure of utterances, rather than relying upon the listener to infer meanings from context. Second, with increasing mastery of structural complexities, children become more able to talk about a wider range of underlying concepts (Cromer 1974).

There are two broad approaches to providing semantic descriptions of single-word utterances. On the one hand, it is possible to consider the words children learn, how these relate to conventional lexical and grammatical categories and, from the way in which they are used, the *conceptual categories* which they express. On the other hand, it is possible to ask whether children's single-word utterances reflect specific *semantic categories* which relate to the semantic distinctions expressed by two- and three-word phrases.

Single words and conceptual categories

One study which throws some light on the way in which children first come to terms with conventional means of expressing concepts was undertaken by Nelson (1973). She studied the first 50 words acquired by a group of 18 children between the ages of 15 and 24 months. The identification of word categories was based upon the way in which the words were used. Thus, the word 'door' was counted as an 'action' word if the child said 'door' when he or she wanted to go outside, but 'door' was counted as a 'naming word' (nominal) if the child merely pointed to a door or touched a door when saying the word. Table 2.1 summarises the categories which Nelson identified during the course of her study.

Given Nelson's descriptive framework, one might suppose that the relationship between the child's use of a word and the child's conceptual knowledge is exactly the same as that which exists between the adult's use of a word and adult concepts. When a child utters the word 'dog', this is a semantic realisation of an underlying conceptual category which can be defined by what a dog is (hairy, domesticated animal with four legs and tail; barks), how one relates to dogs (pats them, takes them for walks, lets them sit on settee) and specific exemplars of dogs (spaniels, retrievers, boxers, etc.). However, is it the case that a child who is able to refer to a dog using the term 'dog' has the same underlying conceptual framework as the adult who uses the same word? The available evidence suggests that the answer is no: when children first learn single words, the way in which those words are used reflects only partial correspondence between meanings attached to the word by adult and child.

Clark (1983) identified five possible ways in which children's meanings might be related to adult meanings:

1 **Overextension.** This is a widely documented phenomenon whereby

Table 2.1 The meanings of children's first words

Category	%	Examples
Specific nominals	14*	People: Mummy Animals: Dizzy (name of pet) Objects: car
General nominals	51	Objects: ball, car Substances: milk, snow Animals and people: doggie, girl Letters and numbers: E, two Abstractions: God, birthday Pronouns: he, that
Action words	13	Descriptive: go, bye-bye Demand: up, out Notice: look, hi
Modifiers	9	Attributes: big, red, pretty States: hot, dirty, all gone Locatives: there, outside Possessives: mine
Personal social	8	Assertions: no, yes, want, know Social expressive: please, ouch
Function words	4	Question words: what, where Miscellaneous functions: is, to, for

*Figures in the second column indicate percentage of single words in each major category.

Source: Adapted from Nelson (1973).

a child uses a word not only to refer to exemplars of the conceptual categories which a word refers to in the adult language, but also extends the word to objects or events which lie outside that category. For example, Clark (1983) reports a child using 'fly' to refer to specks of dirt, dust, all small insects, the child's own toes, crumbs of bread and a toad, in addition to a fly. Clearly, this child's understanding of the conventional semantic possibilities for the word 'fly' is very limited.

2 **Underextension.** This occurs when a child uses a word appropriately, but with respect to a restricted range of referents compared to adult usage. For example, Bloom (1973) reported that her daughter initially used 'car' only to refer to a moving car observed from the living-room window.

3 **Overlap.** It is possible for a child both to overextend and underextend the application of a word. Clark refers to this as 'overlap'. While it is logically possible that overlap occurs in children's language, it is difficult to detect and there are few well-documented examples.

4 **Coincidence.** This represents an exact match between a child's range of referents for a word and the referents considered appropriate from an adult point of view.

5 **Mismatch.** This refers to instances where the child seems to be using a word to refer to a totally different conceptual category compared to adult usage. Bowerman (1976) describes how her daughter began to use 'hi' as if it referred to something resting on or covering hands or feet. This idiosyncratic use of 'hi' seems to have arisen from the occasion when Bowerman showed her daughter finger puppets which nodded and said, 'Hi.'

The evidence for a lack of complete correspondence between adults' and children's meanings attached to single words prompted Clark (1983) to suggest that children learn the meanings of words in a gradual way. She argued that words could be defined in terms of a cluster of semantic features. For example, 'cat' might be defined as applicable to animate beings which have fur, four legs, a tail, climb trees and meow. In learning how to use the word 'cat' correctly, the child would need to learn all the perceptual features that define it. If a child has learned the word 'cat' but has not learned all the defining perceptual features – for example, climbs trees and meows – then the word would be incorrectly applied to all animate beings which have fur, four legs and a tail, including dogs and rabbits!

This view came to be known as the **semantic features hypothesis** and bears a close relationship to the distinctive-features approach to phonological development described in Chapter 1. Where the distinctive-features approach assumes that the mechanism for sound production gives rise to a series of innate and universal sound contrasts (features) which in varying combinations specify phonemes, the semantic features hypothesis is concerned with universal and innate perceptual features which can specify word meaning. Recently, Clark has criticised the semantic features approach for a number of reasons. First, there are serious methodological difficulties in working out what the semantic features for different words might be when they are used by children. Second, the approach creates a confusion between semantic features concerned with word meaning and conceptual features concerned with underlying non-linguistic knowledge. Third, Clark acknowledges the criticism that some words (for example, 'table') simply cannot be adequately specified in terms of underlying perceptual features.

Clark suggests that instead of focusing on semantic features, it is more helpful to base a description of single words on the way in which they are used in communication. She suggests that in trying to express ideas in language, the young child is faced with two principles which determine which words will be learned. The first principle is that words are effective in communication because their meanings contrast. The potential for conveying useful information is greater when words which mark major conceptual divisions (such as 'dog' or 'cat') are used, compared to words which mark smaller conceptual distinctions (such as 'spaniel' and 'retriever'). Thus, it is more helpful for a child to learn the names of different kinds of animals than to learn the names of different kinds of dogs. This is referred to as the **contrastive principle** of word meaning.

The second principle is that in every language community, there are conventions regarding what words are most appropriate for referring to objects, events and relationships and, as Brown (1958) remarked, children generally learn those words which are maximally useful, given the conventions of the speech community. Thus, for a child learning English, it is initially more useful to learn the word to refer to specific items of fruit, such as 'apple', 'orange', and 'banana', before the generic term 'fruit', since it is these words which mark the most convenient distinctions for day-to-day communication. This is referred to as the **convenience principle** of word meaning.

To some extent the contrastive principle and the convenience principle operate in opposition to each other. The contrastive principle indicates the value of words which mark major conceptual distinctions, while the convenience principle is an acknowledgement that the social significance of relatively small conceptual distinctions may mean that they need to be marked in speech. For example, it might be argued that liquid vs. solid is a major conceptual distinction, and that drinkable liquids form a relatively minor subcategory of liquids. Within this subcategory are numerous specific drinkable liquids, such as water, juice, milk, tea and coffee. While the contrastive principle indicates the importance of the liquid–solid distinction, social practices ensure that children usually learn the word for 'drink' (which may be overextended to apply to all liquids) first, and then learn more specific names for drinks ('Coca-cola', 'Ribena', 'milkshake') before the major liquid–solid conceptual distinction is represented in words.

This approach suggests that descriptions of the meanings attributed to single words need to take into consideration three interrelated factors. First, how does the child use the word and what conceptual distinctions does the child seem to be recognising? What evidence is there for overextension, underextension and mismatch in terms of the child's word usage?

Second, what alternative words does the child use and what is the 'conceptual' space between the words? For example, if a child knows only one word for an animal such as cat, it is likely that the absence of contrast words will lead to 'cat' being inappropriately applied to other animals; the conceptual category embraced by 'cat' will not match the more restricted adult category. This does not, of course, mean that the child does not recognise the difference between cats and other animals, only that the child has not yet translated such conceptual distinctions into the words found in the language. If the child knows the word 'dog' it is possible to compare the way in which both 'cat' and 'dog' are used to mark conventional conceptual distinctions.

Of course, the opportunity for a child to mark conceptual distinctions in language will be heavily constrained by the words which are available in the language the child hears. This suggests the third factor which needs to be considered in describing word meanings: what kinds of semantic distinctions are expressed in words by the child's parents, teachers and other caregivers? Children who have English as a second language or who come from homes which place little emphasis on expressing ideas in language, may have been exposed to a relatively restricted range of words for expressing conceptual distinctions. This will inevitably reduce the child's opportunities for learning a rich and varied vocabulary for referring to different aspects of experience and for expressing ideas.

Single words and semantic relations

With the demonstrations by Bloom (1970) and Bowerman (1973a) of the limitations of transformational grammars for describing children's first word combinations, and the fresh insights available from a rich interpretation of the data on children's language the stage was set for the application of semantically based descriptions of children's first words.

The linguist Charles Fillmore (1968) proposed that the deep structure of a language could be described in terms of semantic relations rather than abstract grammatical categories. He developed the notion of **case relations**, not in the traditional sense of noun–verb relations in the surface structure of sentences, but as descriptions of underlying deep-structure relationships. These relationships are concerned with the way in which people perceive and understand ordinary events going on around them – for example, who performed an action, who or what was the recipient of the action and what happened as a result. Each 'case', therefore, represents a distinctive semantic relationship organised around verbs indicating actions. This base semantic relationship is then considered as the input to a grammar and may be realised in the surface structure in different ways. For example, active and passive sentences can be derived from the same underlying case relations. The following sample of the major case relations gives a flavour of the kind of description that Fillmore was proposing:

Agentive: the instigator of an action identified by the verb, e.g. *The man* wrote the letter.'

Instrumental: the inanimate force or object causally involved in the action or state identified by the verb, e.g. *'The wind* blew the leaves'; 'The man cut the rope with a *knife.'*

Locative: the location or spatial orientation of the action identified by the verb, e.g. 'The boy wrote on *the wall.'*

Objective: things affected by the action or state identified by the verb, e.g. 'The wind blew *the leaves.'*

Thus, a sentence such as 'On the way home John used his Access card to buy some petrol,' can be described in terms of the following case relations co-ordinated with the verb forms 'used' and 'to buy'.

On the way home	Locative
John	Agentive
Access card	Instrumental
some petrol	Objective
his	Possession

In terms of children's language, the case grammar approach has a number of specific advantages. Since it does not need to invoke grammatical categories, such as sentence subject, it can provide a description which is more directly linked with the utterances children use. Bowerman (1973a) argued that since nearly all the children she studied initially employed agents as sentence subjects ('Rina sit'; 'Rina cut'; 'Rina draw') but failed to use inanimate objects in the same way (they did not use sentences such as 'Stone wall' to describe a stone hitting a wall), it was not reasonable to credit the children with abstract knowledge of the abstract concept 'grammatical subject'. On the other hand, from these examples, the children's utterances did seem to reflect an underlying knowledge of the case relation 'agent'.

For similar reasons, Greenfield and Smith (1976) suggested that if children's single-word utterances were examined in relation to the context in which they occurred (that is, if a rich interpretation were applied), it would be possible to assign them case relations. Of particular importance for Greenfield and Smith was the possibility of a descriptive framework at the stage of single-word utterances which would dovetail with similar semantically based descriptions of the two- and three-word combinations produced by slightly older children.

A semantically based description of single words

Greenfield and Smith studied two children who were observed and recorded between the ages of 18 and 24 months respectively. During this period, a detailed record was made of all single-word utterances and the context within which they occurred. Subsequently, the authors tried to provide a description of the case relations expressed in these early words. Fillmore's system was adopted as a starting-point, but a number of modifications were introduced to the original set of case relations to take account of the special meanings which the children seemed to be expressing with their first words. The 12 semantic relations identified are shown in Figure 2.1

Semantically based descriptions of two- and three-word utterances

Following Bloom's illustration of the way in which linguistic and non-linguistic context could contribute to a description of the meanings ex-

Figure 2.1 Semantic functions of single words

Performatives: occur as part of the child's actions – for example, 'bye bye' while waving goodbye to someone.

Volition: where the child seeks to obtain some desired response from the person addressed – for example, 'Mama' as a request for something; 'no' to indicate rejection of an approach by another person.

Indicative object: where the child calls for attention to the object named – for example, 'car' as a car goes past.

Volitional object: refers to the object of a demand – for example, the child whines and says 'nana' while reaching for a banana.

Agent: the animate perceived instigator of an action – for example, 'Daddy' when Daddy is heard approaching.

Action or state of an agent: where the child refers to action that requires an animate agent – for example, the child says 'eat' while pointing to food.

Action or state of an object: where the child refers to action and there is an inanimate object present which is only optionally part of the action – for example, the child says 'down' when throwing a ball. (Here the *ball* is considered to be involved since it is the *ball* that goes *down*.)

Object: where the object referred to is decisively involved in an action that changed its state or otherwise directly affected it – for example, the child says 'ball' when throwing a ball.

Dative: where the child's word refers to an animate being who experiences rather than instigates an action – for example, the child says 'dog' while patting a dog.

Object associated with similar object or location: when the child names an object which is not present in connection with an object or location which is present – for example, the child puts a nappy on her head and says 'hat'.

Animate being associated with object or location: where the child names an animate being (usually a person) in connection with an indicated object or location – for example, the child says 'Mummy' while touching her mother's clothes in a cupboard.

Modification of an event: where the child's word concerns the modification of an entire event rather than a single element – for example, the child says 'again' to request an adult to wind a mechanical train.

Source: Adapted from Greenfield and Smith (1976).

pressed by two- and three-word phrases, a number of researchers identified sets of semantic relations (Bloom 1970; Schlesinger 1971; Wells 1974), and in 1973 Brown offered a synthesis of the major meanings which seemed to underlie the child's first combinatorial utterances (see Figure 2.2).

Figure 2.2 Major meanings for two-word utterances

Agent plus action	Daddy go; Mummy sit
Action plus object	Eat dessert; hold hand
Agent plus object	Mummy pigtail (Mummy is making a pigtail)
Action plus location	Put down; go inside
Entity plus location	Sweater down; baby there
Possessor, possessed	Mummy book; Daddy cookie
Entity plus attribute	Old stick; wet nose
Demonstrative plus entity	That candy; here comb

Source: Adapted from Brown (1973); examples from Braine (1976).

Although many of the examples in Figure 2.2 reflect conventional word order in English, identification of semantic relations relies upon contextual information and, for this reason, consistent word order is not essential for categorisation within a semantic framework. Furthermore, semantic relations are equally applicable to other languages which either do not rely so heavily upon word order as English to communicate meaning, or to those languages which employ a different word order to indicate subject–verb–object relations.

Just as Greenfield and Smith argued for a high degree of continuity between the case functions at the single-word stage, and the semantic relations underlying two-word combinations, so Brown (1973) suggested that utterances longer than two words could be seen as straightforward extensions of the rules for expressing two-term semantic relations. For example, three-term relations might simply represent the combination of two-term relations so that:

Mummy sit   (Agent plus action)

and

Mummy there   (Entity plus location)

might be combined to give

Mummy sit there   (Agent plus action plus location)

Brown (1973) refers to this as a concatenation of two-term relations. Alternatively, one term might be expanded within a two-term relation. Thus:

Eat cookie   (Action plus object)

might be expanded to a phrase in which the agent is modified by a possessive relation:

Eat Daddy cookie   (Action plus processor plus
                             possessed)

One of the main problems with a semantic description of children's language is that it relies heavily on adult interpretations of the meaning the child intended to express. While creative interpretation by adults of children's attempts at communication is inevitable and probably extremely important in maintaining 'conversations', it remains a serious problem for researchers who claim to infer specific meanings in children's utterances. Given that children are unable to express their intended meanings accurately using conventional grammar, how much intended meaning is it appropriate for the adult to 'build in' on the basis of *the adult's* interpretation of the context? Clearly, given the adult's more sophisticated understanding of all aspects of verbal communication, there is a danger of endowing the child with intentions which were simply not present or with the attempts to communicate over-elaborate semantic relations (Howe 1975). Braine (1976) suggested that there is a danger of child utterances being cited to *illustrate* interpretations rather than to test their validity.

In order to discover the extent to which the data on children's language provides firm evidence of a consistent set of semantic relations, Braine re-examined the data from 11 children and seven separate studies. He concluded that previous studies, and particularly the review by Brown (1973), had overemphasised the uniformity in the content of the semantic relations across children. In contrast to Brown, he went on to argue that the precise semantic relations expressed by a child at the two-word stage are 'a sample from a probably open ended set of possible conceptual relations' (Braine 1976: 57–8). While some relations do occur more than others, the evidence does not support the suggestion of a 'universal' set of meanings being expressed in children's first two-word utterances.

However, Braine did suggest that there were some common patterns with regard to the consistency with which semantic relations were expressed in children's speech. Initially, children's attempts to express relations are restricted because they do not know enough about the rules for the representation of meaning in the surface structure. Early *groping patterns* are therefore characterised by variable word order. A more stable pattern concerns phrases comprising a constant term which is linked in a fixed order with a range of other words. Such *positional associative patterns* derive their relational meaning from the meaning of the constant term – for example, constructions such as 'all broke', 'all done', 'all wet', 'more cake', 'more drink', 'more toys'. Furthermore, because these patterns tend to reflect English adjectival and participle phrases, Braine argues that they are learned directly from the adult speech the child hears. For this reason, such patterns indicate only a limited understanding of word-order rules.

A third group of relations is characterised by fixed word order and productive innovations in terms of the words which are linked together – for example, 'balloon me', 'swing me', 'ball me'. Such combinations, referred to by Braine as *positional productive patterns,* are unlikely to have been learned by imitation and therefore represent genuine productivity in terms of a child's understanding of how word-order rules can be used to express a wide range of meanings.

Later semantic development

With time, there are a number of developmental changes which occur in children's ability to express semantic relations. First, their command of structural forms improves and so less reliance needs to be placed on con-textual cues, although, to some extent, the meaning of any utterance is based

Co-ordination	My paper . . . pencil
	(My paper *and* pencil)
Sequence	Bye-bye, Daddy, Karen, Ginger
Antithesis	No eat . . . play
	(I don't want to eat *but* I want to play)
Causality (logical)	I can't do it. I not big enough
	(I can't do it *because* I'm not big enough)
Reasons (psychological reality)	You're like that, *because* you didn't know me
Temporal relations	Now I go eat . . . *Then* I play again
	When he goes to sleep he reads
Conditionality	I wear this *while* walking
Temporal sequence	Can I make him a tree, *after* I finish this?
	You better move your legs *before* I run over legs

Note: Where a conjoining term occurs in the surface structure this is highlighted in italics; sentences in brackets indicate an adult gloss of the child's utterance).

Source: Adapted from Miller (1981a)

upon the mutual understanding of a shared context. Second, what the child attempts to say is shaped by the language forms available and, as the child becomes adept at using the structures of a language, so the meanings expressed are extended. Third, the grammar of a language creates the possibility for the expression of more elaborate meanings by conjoining. For example, the relations shown on p. 42 are cited by Miller (1981a) as occurring in an approximate developmental sequence between the ages of 2 and 4 years.

A fourth aspect of semantic development concerns the way in which children become adept at using words to mean more than one thing at a time. For example, when a teacher addressing a class of children says 'I want the girls to line up over here,' the term 'the' serves a number of different functions in expressing exactly what the teacher wishes the children to do. In one sense the word 'the' denotes that the teacher is not just referring to any girls but the girls within the current context. A request for 'a line of girls' would be amenable to a quite different interpretation. Second, the word 'the' serves to indicate that *all* the girls should line up, as opposed to *some* of the girls. Work by Karmiloff-Smith (1979) suggests that an ability to exploit multiple word meanings in this way occurs relatively late on (between the ages of 5 and 10 years) and takes a good deal of time.

How appropriate are semantically based descriptions?

Semantically based descriptions of children's early utterances have a number of specific advantages over structural descriptions. First, they do not invoke abstract grammatical concepts such as sentence subject, or a knowledge of lexical categories such as noun/verb. For this reason, they are less likely to overrepresent what a child actually knows about procedures for expressing meaning in words. Second, semantic descriptions seem to give relatively straightforward accounts of why structural elements are often missing in children's speech. Whereas grammatical approaches indicate additional transformational rules to account for missing elements in the surface structure of children's utterances (Bloom 1970), a semantic description suggests that omissions are direct reflections of the child's ignorance of linguistic devices for representing meaning. Third, there is general agreement that a semantic description opens up more interesting and plausible explanations of early language development in that it suggests links, first, between early conceptual development (for example, Piaget's (1973) description of sensori-motor intelligence) and subsequent linguistic development, and, second, between the meanings initially expressed in combinatorial speech and more complex sentences.

On the other hand, semantically based descriptions are not without problems. Case grammar, as proposed by Fillmore (1968), requires substantial modification if it is not to overrepresent the child's ability to express semantic relations. For example, Fillmore's (1968) objective case subsumes nouns which function as objects located ('chick', 'shoe'), objects possessed ('father', 'clock') and objects acted upon ('Nanny drives car'), and yet it seems intuitively implausible that young children categorise all these nouns as belonging to a single case category. Furthermore, Bowerman (1973a) suggests some detailed technical problems in using Fillmore's original set of categories for describing children's speech. These conclusions suggest that case grammar needs to be modified in the light of the empirical evidence from studies of children's language and, indeed, this is exactly what researchers such as Greenfield and Smith (1976) and Braine (1976) have tried to do.

The success of semantically based descriptions relies upon the ability of adults to fill in the gaps in the child's utterance to reveal intended meanings. This raises the problem that such adult expansions may reveal more about the adult's understanding of children's language than they do about children's intended meanings. Taken to its extreme, this criticism suggests that since children's minds are so different from the minds of adults, it is impossible for the adult to know what conceptual distinctions a child is seeking to express with specific single-word and two-word utterances (Howe 1975).

In defence of semantic interpretations, it must be said that children do communicate with adults and, on many occasions, they seem satisfied with the behavioural response or the fuller gloss which those utterances elicit. More importantly, even young children are well able to indicate that an utterance has been incorrectly interpreted and to indicate requests for clarification or to initiate 'repairs' to the original utterance to facilitate comprehension (Keenan 1974; McTear 1985). Clearly, the greater the structural content of the utterance, the more accurate is any putative semantic interpretation likely to be. While for two- and three-word utterances contextual information provides the opportunity to disambiguate competing interpretations prompted by the surface structure, it seems that a single word can mean more or less anything and that the whole burden of the interpretation rests upon the contextual analysis. The alternative to a description of semantic relations at the single-word level is a semi-grammatical classification such as that provided by Nelson (1973), in which words are assigned to referential categories. While this relies much less on contextual information, it assumes that, when they are first used, single words will conform at least roughly to the lexical slots they fill in adult speech. In addition, this approach says little about any more complex meanings that a child may be trying to express with single-word utterances. For this reason, the referential analyses provided by Nelson (1973) and Clark (1983) are less revealing than semantic systems about possible relations between single-word utterances and later linguistic development.

A final note of caution is necessary with regard to semantically based descriptions of children's language. One of the most important claims of the proponents of this approach is that it reflects what children are trying to express in language and not simply the extent to which they have mastered the structural mechanisms of language. To this extent, a semantic description is an attempt to recover ideas which are in the process of being formulated for communication. However, as Braine (1976) has indicated, there is substantial variation between children in terms of the specific relations they do express, and the potential set of semantic relations for young children may be very large indeed. It is therefore necessary to avoid the temptation to fit any or all of a child's utterances to a set of pre-specified relations. Instead, it is probably better to follow Braine and, for each language sample, to identify productive word combinations which preserve word order and then to examine these for common semantic relations.

Chapter three

Using language

Introduction

Consider the following two interactions between adults and children. In the first an exasperated mother is waiting for a train with three heavy bags of shopping and a young child who seems to have far more energy then she has. She tries to persuade the child to sit and wait for the train on one of the platform seats but the child keeps jumping up and running around the platform. Eventually, after telling the child to sit still on three separate occasions, the mother picks the child up, plonks him on the chair and, with her face about three inches from his she says: 'You just move from there; you just move from there once more.'

In the second interaction a teacher is in a playground with two 5-year-old children. The children have just been involved in an altercation in which one child hit the other. Having listened to the story told by the child who was hit, the teacher turns to the aggressor and says, 'You *hit* him,' pointing to the still-tearful victim. Immediately, the child turns and hits the other child again.

These two accounts are interesting (even amusing) because in each case the listener is required to understand a message that goes beyond the literal meaning expressed in the words uttered. In the first scenario, the mother wants the child to understand her words as an implied threat to the effect that if the child moves again then some dire consequences will follow. The message she wants the child to understand is, in fact, just the opposite of the meaning expressed in the sentence 'You just move from there again.' In the second episode, the teacher uses the sentence 'You *hit* him' as a request for clarification or at least an admission of guilt from the child, but this is misinterpreted as an instruction to repeat the misdemeanour. The child clearly has not read into the teacher's utterance the meaning which she intended to convey.

These two episodes illustrate that in order to understand the meanings expressed in language it is necessary to go beyond what is said and to look at how language is used in different social situations. It is even possible for the same sentence to have different meanings, depending on the social context in which it occurs.

Take the sentence 'It's eight o'clock.' This may be a response to a previous request for information – for example, 'What time do you make it?' Alternatively, if the speaker and listener already share information regarding some imminent event such as a train departure at 8.10, the sentence may be used to bring a conversation to a close ('It's eight o'clock and if I don't go now I shall miss my train'). Here the meaning which the speaker wishes to convey is dependent upon a whole range of presuppositions or shared understandings about how language can relate to social activity. This includes the importance of catching that train, the time it takes to get to the station and the fact that reference to the time now is actually a way of drawing the listener's attention to the speaker's commitments and of inviting the listener to end the conversation. A third interpretation of this sentence would be possible if it were said by a parent to a child whose bedtime is eight o'clock. In this case the sentence operates as a reminder to the child or, depending on the tone of voice used, a command to go to bed.

The relationship between language, the social context in which it occurs and the interpretations which are possible as a result, calls for a descriptive approach which goes beyond the structural or semantic frameworks already discussed. Charles Morris (1938) introduced the term **pragmatics** to describe this level of analysis. Alternatively, since it concerns the way in which language functions with respect to broader aspects of social interaction, it is often referred to as a **functional approach** to language. This chapter considers various functional approaches, beginning with that put forward by the behavioural psychologist B.F. Skinner.

Skinner's functional analysis

The behavioural school of psychology is based upon the belief that the most productive way of studying people is to focus exclusively on their observable behaviour to the exclusion of internal mental events such as thoughts, feelings, beliefs and attitudes. Behaviourists take the view that there are lawful relationships between human behaviour and the events which precede and follow that behaviour. Furthermore, a proper analysis of these relationships will enable psychologists to explain all behaviour, including verbal behaviour. For example, a child who burns her hand on a hot radiator will learn to avoid touching radiators, while a thirsty child will learn to go to a refrigerator to find a drink. The radiator and the fridge can be described as stimuli which indicate which behaviours (approach or avoidance) are appropriate. Avoiding hot radiators prevents the child from being burned, while approaching the fridge enables the child to quench her thirst. These behaviours are learned and strengthened because they have adaptive significance. In particular, when the thirsty child obtains a cold drink from the refrigerator to relieve her thirst, the approach response is reinforced by reduction of a physiological drive (thirst), while avoidance of radiators is reinforced by avoidance of discomfort and pain.

In his classic book *Verbal Behaviour,* Skinner (1957) set out to demonstrate that language can be adequately described as verbal behaviour and that there is no justification for attributing to speakers or listeners mentalistic characteristics such as 'understanding', 'concepts' 'intentions' or 'knowledge of rules'. This implies that a description at the level of the words spoken is sufficient to account for the way in which language is structured, and the way in which it functions with respect to social interactions. (Skinner also argued that this approach provides the basis for a complete account of how children acquire language; this is considered in more detail in Chapter 4.) For Skinner, the 'meaning' of an utterance can be described in terms of the effects it has on the environment and the consequences which follow for the speaker; there is thus no need to consider meanings as existing in people's heads. Verbal responses are adaptive in some way – for example, those that result in avoidance of pain or the reduction of a need state will be reinforced and will occur more frequently, while those which have little or no adaptive value will tend to die out.

Skinner identified five ways in which utterances are related to environmental events and these constitute the five main functional categories.

1 **Mands.** The mand (derived from the words 'demand' and 'command') is an utterance which is reinforced by the effect it has on the environment. It is usually associated with the satisfaction of need states or the termination or avoidance of aversive conditions. Skinner argues that indirect requests such as 'Please pass the salt' and 'Could you please turn the radio down' occur because in the past these or similar utterances have been more beneficial than less diplomatic requests. The mand category includes a range of more specific subtypes, such as requests, commands, entreaties, questions, advice, warning, permission and offers.

2 **Echoic responses.** Whereas mands occur primarily because of their effect on the environment, echoic responses are under the control of similar verbal stimuli. Thus repetition, for example, when children in school take messages from one teacher to another, and requests for clarification both count as echoic responses since they are preceded by verbal stimuli of a corresponding form.

3 **Intraverbal responses.** These responses do not show a point-to-point correspondence with the stimulus as do echoic responses; instead, they represent predictable consequences of one or more different utterances. For example, the response 'Four' to the question 'What's two plus two?'

and 'Margaret Thatcher' to the question 'Who is the Prime Minister of Great Britain' are examples of intraverbal responses.

4 **Tacts.** The tact is a product of the speaker 'making contact with the physical world' (Skinner 1957:81) and is any response which is evoked by a particular object or event or a property of an object or event. The tact is maintained as a response because of reinforcing events which may follow, but while mands are followed by similar responses on each occasion ('Two pints of bitter, please') tacts tend to be followed by a variety of different reinforcing contingencies or by generalised reinforcers such as social approval.

5 **Autoclitics.** The autoclitic is a response which tends to be associated with other categories of verbal behaviour. It operates to qualify or expand the meanings associated with other responses. Skinner gives as examples autoclitics which describe the accompanying response ('I see', 'I recall', 'I guess', 'I believe'), those which qualify ('all', 'some', 'the', 'a') and those which include relations within an utterance (for example, the possessive /s/ in 'the boy's football').

Only two years after the publication of *Verbal Behaviour* the linguist Noam Chomsky published a highly critical review of the behavioural approach to language (Chomsky 1959) and from that point on behavioural research on language and language disorders was conducted independently of the more cognitively based work on children's language acquisition which was stimulated by Chomsky's own work (Chomsky 1965). However, both areas of research contributed extensively to the fields of education and clinical practice. Skinner's approach to language began with the belief that language could be understood within a behavioural framework. Importantly, the most powerful feature of the behavioural paradigm was that it provided an empirically testable account of the relationship between behaviour and environmental events. It was, therefore, ideally suited to educational and clinical endeavours concerned with behavioural change. On the other hand, Chomsky approached the problem as a linguist concerned with the structure of language and the overriding concern of how to provide a description of language as a rule-governed system. For Skinner, a functional analysis of language was necessary so that it could be explained with respect to the same environmental contingencies which had been shown to control other aspects of behaviour. In contrast, for Chomsky the questions surrounding why language occurred and what caused people to speak were of secondary importance to the major issue of linguistic description.

While it was possible for Chomsky to provide a closely argued and compelling criticism of Skinner's functional analysis and the claim that language was a product solely of environmental events, it was more difficult to provide an alternative account of why language occurred and, by implication, how children with language disorders could be helped. While the behaviourists seemed to have developed a powerful technology for behavioural change, Chomsky was arguing that language could not be described simply in terms of behaviour and therefore the impressive array of behavioural techniques were of little use to language therapists. But Chomsky's explanation of language acquisition was also of little help, since it relegated developmental processes to the mysterious and inaccessible workings within the child's head (see Chapter 4). Thus, while stressing that a functional analysis was incorrect, the alternative provided by Chomsky seemed to offer little in terms of strategies for intervention.

As a result of this division, work in the area of language disorders entered a 'schizophrenic' period. Researchers and therapists concerned with assessment tended to recognise the greater descriptive power of Chomsky's transformational grammar and to look to this as a starting-point for clinical practice and the design of assessment instruments. On the other hand, those more concerned with intervention were impressed by the efficacy of behavioural approaches and tended to look towards behavioural technology as a source of inspiration for remedial intervention. Inevitably, this suggested the categorisation of language into Skinner's functional categories. Perhaps not surprisingly, there have been numerous attempts to combine the best of the two approaches by employing behavioural strategies to teach objectives derived from psycholinguistic assessments. A discussion of the problems which such an eclectic approach creates for the language therapist is postponed until Part 4, in which strategies for language intervention are discussed in more detail.

Speech acts

In the two examples presented at the beginning of this chapter, it is clear that the adults are trying to achieve more than a literal understanding of the words they utter. In the first example, the adult is issuing a warning or a threat of the consequences which will follow if the child moves from the seat. In the second example, the adult is seeking confirmation from the child that her account is accurate. While we do not know how much of this additional meaning the child in the first episode understood, it is clear that the child in the second episode understood a completely different message.

Figure 3.1 The component parts of a speech act

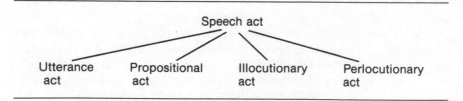

How can we describe this additional level of meaning and how might it be related to the meanings which are expressed through linguistic structure?

To begin with, it is helpful to consider those utterances where the social actions or consequences of the utterance are made explicit (Austin 1962). Sentences such as

> I command you to stop talking
> I promise to tell your mother
> I apologise for losing my temper

are unusual because, unlike other sentences which refer to actions ('I told him the truth'; 'He bought the car'), these sentences actually *perform* actions as they are uttered. For this reason, the verbs 'command', 'promise' and 'apologise', together with a few others, are called **performative verbs** or **explicit performatives.** Performative verbs cannot be uttered meaningfully by just anyone: to be effective and appropriate, they must be uttered by individuals who have certain roles or a particular relationship with those being addressed. Apologising is appropriate only if I have offended someone, and commanding is likely to be effective only with those who have higher rank or status than those to whom they are speaking.

However, as we have already seen, it is also possible to perform actions such as threatening or requesting without using explicit performatives. For example, a teacher might turn to a noisy group of children and ask: 'Did I ask anyone to speak?' Or a child who leaves a door open might be confronted with the question: 'Were you born in a barn?' The implicit performatives here are 'Be quiet' and 'Close the door' respectively; both can be distinguished from the literal meanings of the questions. The performative aspect of an utterance is thus concerned with the effects which the speaker hopes to bring about. These may be very straightforward, as when a teacher tries to explain and make children understand, or they may be more complicated, as illustrated in the example above. It is possible for a listener to understand the literal meaning of the sentence, but to fail to interpret the performative aspect of the utterance. For example, in neither of the above examples is 'no' an adequate response.

Since virtually all utterances express some implied performative function Searle (1969) has suggested that they be analysed as 'speech acts'. A speech act has a number of component parts (see Figure 3.1). 'Utterance acts' relate to the physical production of speech sounds and correspond to structural descriptions outlined in Chapter 1. 'Propositional acts' are concerned with the meanings expressed in the words themselves (see the discussion of semantically based descriptions in Chapter 2). 'Illocutionary acts' are the effects which the speaker hopes to achieve by speaking. 'Perlocutionary acts' are the actual effects which the speaker produces by speaking.

Searle (1975) distinguishes two types of speech act. 'Direct speech acts' are those where the intended effect is consistent with the propositional meaning expressed in the utterance act. Thus, 'Please stop playing football and come in for your bath,' is a direct speech act. In contrast, with indirect speech acts 'one illocutionary act is performed indirectly by way of performing another' (Searle 1975:60). For example, the sentence 'Do you happen to know the way to the nearest supermarket?' is only indirectly a request for directions; superficially it might be construed as an enquiry regarding an individual's grasp of local geography. To understand the question as a request for information requires relatively sophisticated knowledge of the conventions which govern conversational exchanges.

Speech act theory indicates that there is much more to speech production and comprehension than understanding the rules by which language structures are organised to express meaning. It also involves knowing who can say what and to whom; when and where different utterances are appropriate and how the social effects of utterances change as a result of the social context. In order to emphasise the distinction between an individual's command of language structure, often termed 'grammatical competence', the ability to use language effectively in different social situations, and to achieve a variety of interpersonal ends, is referred to as **communicative competence** (Hymes 1971). The importance of communicative competence is most vividly demonstrated by individuals who lack effective control of the functional aspects of language. For example, Blank *et al.* (1979) studied a child who had learned a number of relatively sophisticated grammatical rules and yet could not effectively participate in a conversation with other people:

> John presents us with the picture of a child whose language from a structural and semantic point of view generally represents an adequate description of the physical world (i.e. he describes objects and events accurately), but from a socio-interpersonal perspective it appears to be inappropriate, detached and quite far removed from anything that we intuitively recognise as normal human communication . . . . If his parents were playing shopping with him, a set of sentences concerning stores developed in this setting. Some typical ones were:
>
> Let's go shopping. Where's the money? OK here's the change. Open the door (of the cash register). Pretend it's a shopping centre (talking about a group of blocks). OK, get the elevator: push button.
>
> Thus John appeared to possess a set of highly specialised language-based routines which were tied to specific situations.
>
> (Blank *et al.* 1979: 346–8)

Children's speech acts

The application of speech act theory to children's language raises the question of how children use language and what do they achieve by speaking. This chapter is concerned with how speech act theory can contribute to a more complete descriptive account of children's language, and it is not directly concerned with the separate issue of the process underlying language development. However, it is important to recognise at this stage that learning to use language effectively is not something which children do *after first having mastered the structural and semantic complexities of the language system.* On the contrary, communication is well established *before* children begin to use words, and it seems that children's first word meanings are created by the very fact that the words they use are embedded in social acts which already have communicative significance. Thus, children do not set about learning the relationship between certain words and categories of experience in the world out there; they learn word meanings by dint of their efforts to influence other people, both verbally and non-verbally.

The 'acts' performed by children's first words

Bates (1976) identified two 'acts' performed by children just prior to the emergence of their first recognisable words. In the first, the child attempts to reach for or grasps an object. If the object is out of reach the child may use a combination of gestures, such as looking and pointing together with vocalisation to attract an adult's attention and indicate the desired object. Eventually, the child is able to perform a smooth sequence of gestures which attracts the adult's attention and redirects it towards the object. Bates refers to this as a **proto-imperative** sequence, since the child is beginning to use language to tell other people what to do.

In the second kind of communicative act the child's focus is interaction with an adult and the child seeks to share some aspect of her experience with the adult. The shared experience may simply be mutual eye-to-eye contact and smiling, or it may involve drawing the adult's attention to some third entity through looking or pointing. These non-verbal procedures, designed to share some aspect of experience, are termed by Bates **proto-declaratives** and they form the communicative structure with which the child is able to use words to show or refer to objects and events.

The ability to relate language to those aspects of experience which are shared by speaker and listener is crucial to successful communication. Initially, the child achieves this co-ordination via a well established repertoire of non-verbal communication strategies. However, as the child becomes more linguistically sophisticated, so it becomes possible to establish just what words refer to without such a heavy reliance on gesture. Dore (1977)

Figure 3.2 Children's first speech acts

Labelling. The child uses a word while attending to some object or event but does not address an adult or necessarily wait for a reply. For example, the child says 'eyes' while touching a doll's eyes.

Repeating. The child repeats all or part of a preceding adult utterance. For example, the child overhears her mother say 'doctor' and says 'doctor'.

Answering. The child answers an adult's question – for example, when the adult points to a picture and the child names it.

Requesting action. The child addresses the adult and waits for a response – for example, unable to push a peg through a hole she says 'uh uh uh' while looking at her mother.

Requesting. The child asks a question with a word and waits for a response – for example, the child picks up a book and while looking at her mother says 'Book?' with a rising intonation. Mother replies, 'Yes, it's a book.'

Calling. The child calls the adult's name loudly and awaits a response.

Greeting. The child greets a person or objects by saying, for example, 'Hi.'

Protesting. The child resists the adult's actions with words or cries.

Practising. The child uses a word or phonologically constant form in the absence of any specific object or event and without addressing an adult.

Source: Dore (1977).

suggested the list of speech acts, shown in Figure 3.2, characterised the single-word utterances of children who were just beginning to talk.

In another study of 3-year-old children Dore (1977) identified a slightly different set of speech acts which illustrate how children become increasingly able to use language to facilitate a variety of social interactions. Although 3-year-old children are clearly competent at using language to achieve different interpersonal objectives, Dore's classification suggests that they rely principally on direct speech acts and that they still have some way to go before they are proficient in the tactful deviousness which characterises the indirect speech acts of adults.

While the descriptive categories provided by Dore have considerable advantages in terms of the ease with which they can be applied to language samples obtained from children with language difficulties, they also have some important shortcomings. First, they represent an arbitrary classificatory system which seems to owe much to the functions of language in adult speech. Second, they suggest that even for 3-year-olds each utterance serves only one function. Third, they contribute little to our understanding of the relationship between speech acts of children at the single-word stage

54

Figure 3.3 Speech acts employed by 3-year-old children

Requests. Utterances which solicit information, actions or acknowledgements – for example, 'What's that?' 'Where is the bear going?' 'What did you say?'

Responses. Utterances which directly complement the preceding utterance – for example, 'No, he's not playing with it'; 'But I wasn't the one who did it.'

Descriptions. Utterances which represent observable, verifiable aspects of the surroundings – for example, 'I'm drawing a house'; 'That's a bear with a wheel'; 'It happened yesterday.'

Statements. Utterances which express analytic and institutional facts, beliefs, attitudes, emotions and reasons – for example, 'That's right, good'; 'He wants to go.'

Acknowledgements. Utterances which recognise and evaluate responses which are not requests – for example, 'Right, yes'; 'No, wrong: I disagree.'

Conversational devices. Utterances which regulate social interaction and conversations – for example, 'Okay'; 'Thanks'; 'Here you are.'

Performatives. Utterances which accomplish actions by being said – for example, 'Stop'; 'That's mine'; 'I'm first.'

Source: Dore (1977).

and those expressed by much more able 3-year-olds. The descriptive system developed by Halliday (1975) offers an alternative view of the way in which young children use language and, in doing so, it overcomes some of these shortcomings.

Halliday's functional analysis

Halliday regards language as much more than a rule-governed system for communicating meanings and sees its functional significance as extending beyond speech acts. For Halliday, language is the principal vehicle available to the child for interpreting experience and, in offering the child an interpretative framework for making sense of experience, language facilitates an understanding of the social world and is ultimately a way of learning about broader cultural experiences: 'The child's construction of a semantic system and his construction of a social system take place side by side, two aspects of a single process. A child learns the culture and simultaneously the means of learning it' (Halliday 1975:139).

The functional categories suggested by Halliday emerged from his longitudinal study of his son, Nigel. While the detailed level of analysis made possible by this approach has given rise to some exciting insights, the focus on a single child inevitably raises questions about the extent to which the categories are applicable to other children. However, Halliday's attempt to provide a description of language learning which integrates structural, semantic and functional approaches has had a considerable impact on both research workers and practitioners.

Halliday describes the linguistic system with which the child is confronted as having a 'meaning potential', 'Learning one's mother tongue is learning the uses of language and the meanings associated with them . . . . The structures, the words and the sounds are the realisation of this meaning potential. Learning language is learning how to mean' (Halliday 1973:24). Initially, the child is able to explore that potential only in a faltering and hesitant manner. Without a command of the structures by which meanings are expressed, the child is unable to produce or understand meanings, and this in turn restricts the child's ability to participate in social interactions. Thus, to begin with, the child's opportunities for 'learning how to mean' are restricted by her own limited linguistic abilities.

Whereas the adult is able to use language in different ways and for different purposes, the child is initially restricted to a small number of language functions (see Figure 3.5). Furthermore, while for an adult a single utterance can serve a number of different functions, the child begins by learning how to express single functions. A third characteristic of a child's first utterances is that structure, content and use are inextricably combined so that the content of an utterance is the meaning that it has with respect to a given function. For this reason, it is not possible to focus on meanings in terms of the adult language; instead, it is necessary to ask the question: 'What is it that he [the child] is making the speech sound do for him?' When Nigel was between 9 and 18 months of age (that is, from the time he first began to use Phonologically Constant Forms (PCFs) to indicate meanings until the emergence of two-word utterances), Halliday identified seven goals or purposes achieved through speech (see Figure 3.4).

During Phase 2, which lasted from the time Nigel was 16 to 35 months of age, he began to explore ways of using similar language structures to achieve different effects and of achieving similar outcomes with different language forms. At this point it becomes possible to distinguish between function in terms of social outcomes and function in terms of the way in which structural elements are related within an utterance or grammatical function. Whereas, in Phase 1, each structure could express only a single function, during Phase 2 Nigel was able to use words with the same grammatical functions to achieve different practical outcomes. For example, a word might be used on one occasion to indicate desire or request – 'drink' ('Give me a drink') – and on another occasion to pass a comment ('That's a drink she's got there'). At the same time, the original diversity of language functions is reduced as the child becomes increasingly adept at expressing more than one function at a time. At this stage, the personal and heuristic functions give way to the **mathetic function,** which is concerned with language being used to organise experi-

Figure 3.4 The functions of language: Nigel at Phase 1: 9–18 months

Instrumental. The 'I want' function. Language used to express desire for objects and actions – for example, 'more' ('I want some more'); 'cake' (I want some cake'); 'ball' ('I want my ball').

Regulatory. The 'do as I tell you' function. Language used to influence the behaviour of other individuals – for example, 'book' ('Let's look at a book'); 'lunch' ('Come for lunch'); 'stick–hole' ('Can I put my stick in that hole?').

Interactional. The 'me and you' function. Language used for interaction – for example, 'lalouha' ('hello'); 'Anna?' ('Where are you?'); 'Devil' ('You say, 'Ooh, you are a devil').

Personal. The 'here I come' function. Language used to express the child's own uniqueness – for example, 'star' ('Three's a star'); 'no more' ('The star has gone'); /o/ ('That's funny').

Heuristic. The 'tell me why' function. Language used to explore the environment and measure understanding – for example, /ah-dah/ (What's that called?'); imitation of a name ('Its called a —').

Imaginative. The 'let's pretend' function. Language used to create the child's own environment for make believe – for example, child 'roars like a lion' ('Let's pretend to be a lion').

Informative. The 'I've got something to tell you' function. Language used to communicate information to someone who does not already possess it. This function did not appear until later, when Nigel was 22 months of age.

Source: Adapted from Halliday (1975).

ence. Mathetic utterances are observations or comments, such as 'Ball go under car' and 'That toothpick broken', and do not require a response from the listener. In contrast, the **pragmatic function** which arises from the instrumental, regulatory and interpersonal functions, expresses a desire for action, assistance, materials or information. It is reflected in utterances such as 'Mend train', 'Take it off' and 'Put Bemax on table.'

Subsequently, with his increasing mastery of grammar, Nigel combined the pragmatic and mathetic functions into a flexible language system which enabled him to be both an 'observer and intruder' at the same time. At this point, any utterance can be described in terms of three related functional components.

1 **The ideational function** is concerned with the content of what is said and, developmentally, can be traced back to earlier mathetic, personal heuristic and imaginative functions.
2 **The interpersonal function**, which relates to the illocutionary force of an utterance, derives from the pragmatic function and its antecedents, the instrumental, regulatory and interactional functions.

Figure 3.5 The development of language functions

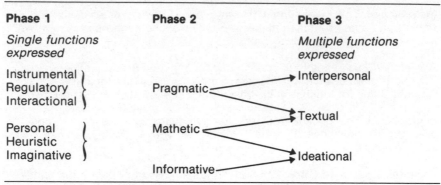

Source: Adapted from Halliday (1975).

3 **The textual function** is concerned with the creation of coherent and meaningful sequences of utterances (or written sentences) within a conversational sequence and within a particular setting (Halliday 1973). In this book the textual function of language is discussed more fully in relation to describing conversational skills.

For Halliday, functional diversity is a characteristic of language throughout development. Young children with restricted knowledge of structure are forced to express single functions separately. With increasing command of the grammatical system, it becomes possible for the child to express a variety of functions with a single utterance. In Phase 1, each utterance expresses a single function. In Phase 2, single utterances express more than one function. In Phase 3, each utterance expresses all three functions (ideational, interpersonal and textual). These relationships are shown in Figure 3.5.

At this point it is possible to see a close correspondence between the functions which Halliday describes at Phase 3 and the main components of speech acts described by Searle (1969); Halliday's ideational component is concerned with meanings expressed in surface structures and corresponds approximately to Searle's propositional acts; Halliday's interpersonal function describes the social effects of language which Searle characterises as illocutionary acts. However, whereas Halliday has little to say about the distinction between intended effects and actual effects of utterances (illocutionary compared to perlocutionary acts), Searle gives little attention to the way in which language is used to organise and influence the structure and content of conversations (Halliday's textual function). It is this last important area of linguistic description to which we now turn.

Conversational skills

Looking at language as a process which occurs within social situations immediately introduces the notion of co-operation and the ability to engage in conversations with other people. In order to be able to 'use language' effectively, a child must come to terms with the rules by which conversations are established, maintained and regulated. In order to speak, not only must a child be familiar with a linguistic code, but she must also understand and be able to organise her behaviour according to a *code of conduct* (Ochs 1983). For example, conversations involve all the participants in adhering to a set of conventions regarding such things as whose turn it is to talk, how turns in conversations are allocated, how to change the topic, how participants indicate misunderstandings and how such misunderstandings can be corrected or 'repaired'.

Conversations are also based on a set of mutual understandings or assumptions regarding the form and content of speakers' contributions. These implicit assumptions were originally spelled out by Grice (1975) and have become known as 'Gricean maxims'. They include the following:

Quantity: a speaker should be as informative as the situation requires but should not provide more information than is necessary. Clearly, this involves making sophisticated decisions about what the listener already knows and how much information is necessary to fill in the gaps.

Quality: a speaker should try to say what he or she believes to be true and should avoid saying things which are known to be false, or for which he or she lacks evidence.

Relations: a speaker should try to make a contribution to the conversation that is relevant to what has gone before.

Manner: a speaker should seek to organise his or her contribution so that it is easily understandable. This involves avoiding unnecessary obscurity or ambiguity, being brief and saying what needs to be said in a sensible order.

When conducting ordinary conversations it is clear that we normally adhere to these conventions and assume that those to whom we are talking will also organise their contributions according to Gricean maxims. Furthermore, these expectations are so well established that they are used to create connections between superficially unconnected conversational contributions. Grice gives the example of a person (A) standing by a stationary car when another person (B) comes along.

A: I am out of petrol
B: There is a garage round the corner.

B's contribution makes little sense and would infringe the maxim 'be relevant' *unless* A assumes that B believes the garage is open and has petrol to sell.

Thus, dialogue involves at least three kinds of ability which go above and beyond those reflected in structural semantic and functional descriptions of language considered so far.

1 The ability to collaborate with another individual so that utterances can be sequenced and structured in an orderly manner.
2 An understanding of how structure and content can be adjusted to fit changing conversational themes or topics.
3 The ability to recognise the communicative needs of the listener and organise conversational contributions accordingly.

Describing children's conversational skills

Even in the case of very young children, their early utterances are embedded within a conversational framework. Thus, while it may be helpful for the researcher or language therapist to consider various components of language performance in isolation, it is important to recognise that, during development, structural, semantic and functional aspects of language are being mastered within a variety of conversational settings. The following is a short extract from a conversation between two boys, aged 2 years and 9 months, with their nanny (Jill).

Jill:	And we're going to cook sausages.
Toby:	Cook sausages.
Jill:	And bacon.
Toby and David:	Bacon.
Jill:	And eggs.

(Ochs 1983)

This sample of conversation shows how the two children are able to participate in a conversation using language which is relatively immature in terms of structure and content. They take turns appropriately, and maintain topic relevance by the relatively simple expedient of repeating key elements in the preceding utterance. The extract at the beginning of Chapter 1 (see p. 3) provides another example of conversational exchange between two slightly older children who have mastered not only a greater variety of structural forms and related meanings, but far more sophisticated conversational devices which enable them to exercise different kinds of social pressure within a well-maintained conversational structure. There follows an overview of the descriptive categories employed by McTear (1985) in his study of children's conversation (summarised in Figure 3.6, p. 62).

Turn taking: this includes the duration of intervals between successive turns, the extent to which turns overlap and how conversational partners organise repairs and overlaps.
Responses: these are classified on the basis of the kinds of initiation to which the child responds (questions, requests for action or statements) and a description of the quality of the child's response (for example, no response; inappropriate or irrelevant response; minimal acceptable response;

response with additional content; other appropriate response). Blank (Blank and Franklin 1980; Blank *et al.* 1978) has developed and implemented a similar approach to the description of children's conversational responses. However, unlike McTear (1985), she has also attempted to categorise responses in terms of their cognitive level (see Chapter 7).

Initiations: these are categorised by McTear into verbal and non-verbal strategies for getting attention, strategies for directing attention, ways of identifying referents which are not physically present, different types of initiation (questions, requests for action or statements) and strategies adopted by the child when initiations are not successful.

Linguistic devices for establishing and linking conversational topics: these include, first, the use of conjunctives such as 'and', 'but', 'because'. A second group concerns the use of ellipsis – that is, a short-form answer to a question: for example, when in response to a question such as 'What did you have for lunch?' the child replies, 'Sausages' rather than 'I had sausages for lunch.' The elliptical response is more natural and, to some extent, more sophisticated than the long form and the language therapist should be wary of intervention strategies which emphasise the importance of children always providing long-form responses when undertaking therapy. The third topic-linking device considered by McTear is anaphora, in which a pronoun is used to refer back to a topic named in a preceding utterance – for example, 'We had sausages. *They* were burnt.'

Repairs: these are concerned with the child's attempts to maintain shared understanding of conversational topics by requesting the speaker to clarify what he or she said, by responding to requests for clarification and by introducing self-corrections.

This section has provided a relatively brief discussion of an area which is rapidly growing in importance, both for researchers of children's language acquisition and for those concerned with assessment and intervention. As we gain a better understanding of the way in which normally developing young children learn language within conversational settings and, in doing so, also become sophisticated conversational partners, so it seems likely that there will be a growing emphasis on understanding the language-disordered child as a social being who needs to be helped towards functionally useful language which can be used to participate in a variety of conversational exchanges.

How appropriate are functional descriptions of children's language?

Skinner's attempt to provide a descriptive framework which makes explicit the relationship between language and the surrounding context was the subject of fierce criticism soon after it was published. Chomsky (1959)

Figure 3.6 A framework for describing conversational processes

How often does the child demonstrate these conversational processes?
Regularly   Occasionally   Rarely   Never

Turn taking
Takes turns
Gaps between turns:
  + 5 secs
  1-5 secs
  less than 1 sec
Overlaps
Repairs to
  overlaps

Responses
Initiation type
  Question/request for action/statement
Response
  No response
  Inappropriate or
    irrelevant response
  Minimal appropriate
    response
  Response plus additional
    content
  Other appropriate response

Initiations
Attention-getting
Non-verbal devices
Attention-directing
Non-present referents
Responses to different
  types of initiation
Reinitiations

Establishing and linking topics
Discourse connectors
Ellipsis
Anaphoric reference

Repairs
Requests for clarification:
  Responses to requests
    for repairs
  Production of requests
    for repairs
Other types of correction
Self-repairs

Source: Adapted from McTear (1985).

rejected Skinner's view that any consideration of internal mental states was unnecessary and beyond the scope of empirical investigation. He argued that Skinner's declaration that language was the product of previous linguistic experience did no more than define the problem; for Chomsky, the central issue was to explain how the child was able to acquire the rules necessary for the generation of complex sentences in the light of those experiences. Interestingly, the success of Chomsky's criticism of *Verbal Behaviour* and the popularity of transformational grammar resulted in researchers and language therapists focusing on the acquisition of language structure and largely ignoring not only the functional categories presented in *Verbal Behaviour,* but also the more general questions concerning language in context for over a decade.

The relevance of Skinner's functionally based categories cannot be separated from the behavioural account of how children learn language; if one accepts the view that external reinforcements play a major role in establishing verbal behaviour, then the categories generated by Skinner are likely to be appealing. On the other hand, if the behavioural explanation of language development is rejected, it is difficult to see how these categories can be useful. A discussion of the strengths and weaknesses of Skinner's account of language development is presented in Chapter 4. While researchers interested in the development of language by ordinary children have tended to reject Skinnerian theory and his functional categories, behavioural psychologists concerned with language intervention have been more sympathetic to both the theory and the descriptive framework. One reason for this is the considerable impact of behavioural technology in changing behaviour and, where necessary, verbal behaviour. The major unresolved issue is whether language behaviour established through behavioural teaching methods is in fact functionally relevant to the child's personal needs and interests, or whether it is merely *language-like* behaviour which is stilted and unresponsive to social situations. (This issue is taken up again in Part 4.)

The more recent approaches to functional descriptions have been regarded much more favourably by researchers in the field of children's language and by clinicians and therapists. There is wide acceptance of the view that the child's ability to use language must be reconciled with more traditional concerns regarding the mastery of grammatical rules and word meanings. At the present time, speech act analysis seems to provide the best integrative framework.

From a descriptive point of view, however, functional approaches share many of the same problems as semantically based approaches: they involve the adult observer in making inferences regarding the child's intention in speaking in the face of limited linguistic and non-linguistic evidence. Awareness of this difficulty has led researchers to concentrate on detailed, fine-grained analyses of speech samples from small numbers of children (for example, Bates 1976; McTear 1985; Ochs and Schieffelin 1979, 1983). The extent to which it is possible to generalise from these descriptive studies to other children remains a matter for present conjecture and future research.

On a more theoretical level, it may be that the subjective nature of adult interpretations of children's utterances in terms of referential meaning and illocutionary force is not simply the product of methodological shortcomings among psychologists and linguistics, but is a fundamental characteristic of linguistic interaction and of language development. Meaning may be better understood not as a child's intention which is more or less successfully translated into words and sentences, but as a social construction which is determined as much by the listener's resources for interpretation as by the speaker's ability to express meaning. It may be helpful, therefore, to think of the ability of a child to participate in conversations and to express language functions as being determined, at least in part, by the kinds of social understanding which speaker and listener are able to construct jointly. From this viewpoint, meanings and intentions are continually created and re-negotiated in dialogue and children may only become aware of what they mean through continued exposure to the interpretations which adults accord to their actions and utterances. This theme will emerge again in Part 2, 'Explanations of Language Development'.

On the basis of this dynamic interpretation of the emergence of meaning and intentionality, it may make more sense to try and describe the *processes* by which children demonstrate their proficiency in linguistic interactions than to try and document the precise social meanings or intentions which lie behind specific utterances. Superficially, it seems likely that descriptions of conversational interactions of the kind provided by McTear are likely to be more robust and to bear a closer correspondence to the phenomena they seek to represent than less clearly defined notions, such as specific intentions and language functions.

Finally, in comparison with the enormous amount of basic research which has been devoted to the development of structural and semantic features of language, functional descriptions are relatively new and it seems likely that much more work will be carried out in this area in the near future. It is probably necessary to await further research developments before attempting a final evaluation of the relevance of specific descriptive systems or the long-term implications of functional approaches for children with language difficulties.

Part two

Explanations of Language Development

Chapter four

Is language learned?

Introduction

At the beginning of Chapter 1 it was suggested that linguists and psycholinguists interested in children's language have addressed two major questions. First, what are the changing patterns of language abilities which characterise development? And, second, what are the processes by which developmental change occurs? The next two chapters are concerned with this second question and present a brief overview of different explanations of how language development occurs.

As we have seen in the preceding chapters, language development gives rise to a complex set of interrelated abilities. Motor abilities, perceptual skills and increasingly sophisticated forms of cognitive representation are all implicated in the mastery of spoken language. Furthermore, an adequate characterisation of spoken language requires the integration of descriptive frameworks from different branches of linguistics and psychology. In view of the complexity of the psycholinguistic abilities which contribute to normal language functioning, it is perhaps not surprising that attempts to explain how these abilities emerge in the first place and are orchestrated into the unified process which we recognise as language have met with only limited success. This chapter and Chapter 5 consider the three most popular theories of language development to emerge in recent years, beginning with the publication of Skinner's book *Verbal Behaviour* in 1957.

At this point it is also worth considering the relevance of theories of normal developmental progress to a book concerned with the assessment and treatment of children with language difficulties. It might be argued that children experience difficulties in the area of language development precisely because the normal developmental processes have broken down. In order to help such children, it is necessary to introduce novel and artificial procedures to assist learning and it is therefore unlikely that an understanding of normal processes will be of any help. The alternative view is that an understanding of how normally developing children learn language is essential, first, in order to understand why a child is experiencing difficulty and, second, to provide insights into the best and most effective strategies for remedial intervention. It is this second view which is reflected in this chapter and the next, and in Chapter 11 on intervention strategies.

Learning, acquisition and development

The terms 'learning', 'acquisition' and 'development' are often used interchangeably and, so far in this book, there has been no attempt to define distinctive meanings. However, a consideration of the processes involved in developmental change invites a more critical view of the way in which these terms are used. It will be suggested here that, because each one of these terms carries with it connotations regarding what these processes are, 'learning', 'acquisition' and 'development' are associated with different accounts of developmental change.

For psychologists *learning* implies the occurrence of new responses or the modification of old responses in the light of specific experiences. Thus, when a child who calls a stool 'chair' is corrected and introduced to its more accurate name and subsequently uses the term 'stool', it would be reasonable to say that the child had *learned* a new word.

The term *acquisition* is more frequently associated with the child's mastery of higher-order understanding which cannot easily be reduced to the additive effect of different learning experiences. Thus, a child may be said to *acquire* the rules of grammar, although it is difficult to see how such rules can be established as a result of numerous discrete learning experiences. 'Acquisition' is often used in the context of innate, non-specific forms of understanding – for example, knowledge of linguistic universals, being realised in respect of specific linguistic categories or rules.

Finally, the term *development* is amenable to a number of different interpretations (Francis 1980), with the most general being 'changes which occur over time'. When *development* is used in the literature on children's language it usually implies acknowledgement of processes over and above learning (for example, Piaget 1970) and an underlying continuity with respect to earlier-occurring relatively simple abilities and later, more complex abilities. The rest of this chapter and the following chapter provide a more detailed account of the processes which are involved in a child's mastery of language from the perspective of learning theory, the acquisition of abstract rules and developmental change.

Language learning: behavioural explanations

Chapter 3 described how Skinner attempted to circumvent the thorny problem of mentalistic descriptions of language by insisting that descriptions of language focus on observable *language behaviour*. This in turn made it possible to consider changes in language behaviour which occurred during childhood as products of the same mechanisms which had been documented in respect of other kinds of behaviour; verbal behaviour was to be understood in terms of the same learning principles which had been derived from studies of the behaviour of rats, pigeons and monkeys.

Skinner argued that behaviour occurs as a function of previous experiences and that, given a clear understanding of the contingent relations between the environment and a specific behaviour in the past, it is possible to predict, with a very high degree of accuracy, the conditions under which that behaviour will occur in the future. Where a behavioural response has, in the past, been followed by environmental events which are pleasurable or which reduce the degree of discomfort experienced, then the same behaviour will be likely to occur in the future. But behaviours are only consistently followed by predictable outcomes under certain conditions – for example, the child's request for a drink is followed by a drink only if an adult hears the child's request. Individuals therefore learn to discriminate the conditions which are associated with behaviours being followed by contingent events which are desirable, from those which are associated with no environmental change or those which are followed by unpleasant events.

A behavioural response is strengthened when it has an increased probability of occurring (frequency) or when it is likely to be performed for a longer period of time (duration). Environmental events which are pleasurable will, if they consistently occur immediately after a behavioural response, have the effect of increasing the strength of the response. When such a relationship is established between a response category and an environmental event, the event is said to **reinforce** the behaviour. For example, Skinner argues that, to the extent that the thirsty person receives a drink after going into a pub and requesting 'a pint of beer', that behaviour, requesting a pint of beer, is reinforced.

Alternatively, if the behaviour is followed by an undesirable or noxious event on a regular basis, the response is likely to occur less frequently under similar conditions in the future. Under these conditions, the environmental event is said to exert a **punishing** influence on the behaviour. An example of a punishing event would be a child at school who is reprimanded for talking during lessons. Where a behaviour has been established under conditions of reinforcement, if the contingent relationship between the behaviour and the reinforcing event is broken so that the one does not consistently follow the other, then the strength of the response will gradually diminish. This is referred to as **extinction.** Extinction might be expected to occur if your local pub stopped selling your favourite drink. Under such circumstances the frequency with which you visited the pub would be likely to decrease gradually over time.

There are two other contingent relations which should be mentioned at this stage. The first concerns behaviours which are followed by the termination or cessation of unpleasant environmental events – for example, when shutting a window reduces the volume of traffic noise or turning on the heating reduces the discomfort from cold. In this situation the contingent relation results in the strengthening of the behavioural response and is therefore described as reinforcing. However, because reinforcement is derived from the *termination* of noxious events, it is referred to as **negative reinforcement.** The second contingent relation is concerned with the parallel relationship for pleasant or desirable events. When a behaviour is consistently followed by the termination of desirable events, the effect is to reduce the strength of that behaviour. For example, a child might be told that certain behaviours will result in the loss of free time; if the child misbehaves, the penalty creates a contingent relationship in which the child has less time to play. Since this relationship is established through the *reduction* of pleasant environmental events, it is referred to as **negative punishment.**

While these four contingent relations between specific response categories and environmental consequences provide an account of how behaviours can be increased or decreased in frequency, they are not sufficient to explain how behaviours might change in form and character over time. Qualitative changes in behaviour depend upon the concepts of **behavioural variability** and **selective reinforcement.** While it is possible to identify responses which are, at first sight, repetitions of the same behaviour, it is evident that each performance of a behaviour introduces slight and, in some respects, insignificant changes. Thus, even routine behaviours which occur many times – such as tying shoelaces, brushing teeth or washing a cup – will never be performed in exactly the same way on two occasions. This gives rise to **behavioural variability.**

If the contingent environmental events are then altered so that certain ways of performing the skill are preferred to others, then some ways of performing the behaviour will be selectively reinforced at the expense of others. For example, if by trial and error I discover that one particular way of ironing a shirt results in the job being completed more quickly, the reinforcement arising from removing a noxious event (I hate ironing) will very likely result in that technique becoming well established. Similarly, behavioural variability means that I sometimes iron with the television on and if this reduces the discomfort I experience from ironing (even though I take longer to finish), **selective reinforcement** from TV viewing while ironing may mean that this also becomes part of my behavioural repertoire. These changes are not so much concerned with the frequency or duration of ironing behaviour as with the precise form of the behaviours which make up 'ironing'. The gradual change in the form or quality of behaviours as a result of selective reinforcement of variable response characteristics is referred to as **shaping.**

Having described the principles of operant conditioning in respect of non-verbal behaviours, it is now time to explore how they relate to speech and language.

Do children learn language?

Once language is described as a category of *behaviour,* it is possible to explain its occurrence with reference to the contingent relationships which have been shown to influence other kinds of behaviour. Skinner (1957) also argued that these contingent relationships between behaviour and subsequent environmental events control language changes during childhood. Thus, a child is said by Skinner to vocalise because this kind of response is strongly reinforced through adult attention and the gratification of physiologically based needs. Because of the way in which adults respond to infants, these early vocalisations occur with increasing frequency. Since adults are also highly motivated to respond selectively to vocalisations which are similar to real words, phonemes and phonemic sequences are gradually 'shaped' until they resemble words in the adult language.

When a child is able to produce phonemic strings which sound like real words, reinforcing adult responses become contingent upon the child's use of words to create meaningful word–referent relations. Once the child has mastered 'Dada', this response will be more consistently reinforced when the referent 'Daddy' is present compared to when he is out of sight. Similarly, the child's mastery of syntax is seen as a product of the adult's ability to respond selectively to those aspects of a child's language which are developmentally progressive.

While shaping describes a mechanism which could theoretically account for numerous changes in a child's language, Skinner acknowledges that it is a somewhat laborious and inefficient way of learning. It is for this reason that the category of echoic verbal behaviour, described in Chapter 3, is particularly important, since it offers a way of 'short circuiting the process of progressive approximations'. For example, a child might be told to say 'She sells sea shells on the seashore' and be reinforced if her response matches the model utterance. Similarly, a child might be taught the names of objects or colours when a generalised reinforcement – for example, 'That's right!' – consistently follows an utterance which names an object or the colour of an object.

The principles of learning theory provide a prima-facie explanation of the linguistic changes which occur during childhood. In spite of the power and continuing influence of Skinner's ideas, it is important that *Verbal Behaviour* is seen more in terms of a set of claims or predictions, which are illustrated with anecdotal evidence and hypothetical examples, rather than a theory which has been tested against research evidence. In fact, most researchers now believe that, on their own, the principles of learning theory are insufficient to account for the child's mastery of language; the bulk of the research on children's language which has been carried out since the publication of *Verbal Behaviour* has been concerned with illuminating other processes which may be involved. However, the learning theory approach to language has continued to receive considerable support from teachers and clinicians concerned with helping children with language difficulties.

Therapeutic implications of the learning approach to children's language

The major advantage of considering children's language as a complex set of learned behaviours is that it gives rise to direct implications for language intervention. If Skinner is right, and children's language is strongly influenced by the way in which those around them respond, how much more effective might the same processes be if they were applied deliberately and systematically. This is the starting-point for behavioural approaches to language teaching. Furthermore, once language is recognised as simply a type of behaviour, it seems to make sense to treat it like any other subject which adults deliberately teach to children.

For the teacher or therapist, behavioural intervention can be considered in terms of a structured sequence of activities. First, it is necessary to determine one or more behavioural teaching objectives. Here, the aim of the therapeutic intervention is specified in terms of the verbal responses which are considered desirable for a particular child but are as yet not part of the child's verbal repertoire. Second, the contingent environmental events which may strengthen or weaken verbal responses are specified and an attempt should be made to identify those contingencies which will operate to maintain the target behaviours in the natural environment once they have been established through systematic teaching. For example, if a child is taught to answer certain kinds of question appropriately, it is important that, after teaching, she will experience lots of opportunities to respond to similar questions and that appropriate responses will be systematically reinforced.

The third step is to describe the child's current level of functioning in terms of verbal behaviour, and to identify the environmental contingencies which serve to maintain that behaviour. Fourth, using this information, it should be possible to establish a sequence of intermediate teaching objectives. These will define the behaviours which a child must learn in order to move from her existing pattern of responses to those described in the teaching objectives. Finally, the programme should describe a set of teaching procedures which will create the necessary contingent relations between the child's language and environmental events to ensure that the child progresses along the sequence of teaching objectives. Inevitably, these procedures will involve the use of reinforcement, but they may also involve more elaborate techniques such as shaping and modelling. A more detailed discussion of behavioural intervention strategies is included in Chapter 9.

Criticisms of the behavioural approach to children's language

The major theoretical problems which arise from explanations of language development as a process of learning verbal behaviours were first presented by Chomsky (1959) and, in many respects, this still represents the best critique of Skinner's position. Only a brief summary of some of Chomsky's detailed arguments are presented here.

Chomsky points out that the principles of operant conditioning were originally derived from experimental studies of animals, in which the experimenter could achieve a very high degree of control over variables which were presumed to influence behaviour. Thus, the contingency relations between environmental events and specific responses could be easily manipulated and measured. Once experimental control achieved in laboratory conditions made it possible to demonstrate that the strength of specific behaviours was indeed a function of environmental events, it seemed reasonable to describe such events as reinforcers. The use of such terminology is, however, appropriate only when a relationship between behaviour and contingent events has been empirically demonstrated. It is not legitimate to extend the use of such terminology prospectively, to naturally occurring behaviour where there is no possibility of testing the contingent relations through experimental investigation. Chomsky is therefore highly critical of the way in which Skinner uses operant terminology to account for language. For example,

> The phrase X is reinforced by Y . . . is being used as a cover term for 'X wants Y', 'X likes Y', 'X wishes that Y were the case', etc. . . . Invoking the term 'reinforcement' has no explanatory force, and any idea that this paraphrase introduces any new clarity of objectivity into the description of wishing, liking, etc., is a serious delusion.
>
> (Chomsky 1959:38)

Since the terms which describe the process of behavioural change cannot be tested against examples of natural language, Chomsky concludes that Skinner's whole account of language is fatally flawed:

> As far as acquisition of language is concerned, it seems clear that reinforcement, casual observation, and natural inquisitiveness (coupled with a strong tendency to imitate) are important factors, as is the remarkable capacity of the child to generalise, hypothesise and 'process information' in a variety of very special and apparently highly complex ways which we cannot yet describe or begin to understand, and which may be largely innate, or may develop through some sort of learning or through maturation of the nervous system. The manner in which such factors operate and interact in language acquisition is completely unknown. It is clear that what is necessary in such a case is research, not dogmatic and perfectly arbitrary claims, based on analogies to that small

part of the experimental literature in which one happens to be interested.
(Chomsky 1959:43)

The questions to which Skinner has addressed his speculations are hopelessly premature. It is futile to inquire into the causation of verbal behaviour until much more is known about the specific character of this behaviour; and there is little point in speculating about processes of acquisition without much better understanding of what is acquired.
(Ibid.:55)

Additional criticisms of Skinner's position have arisen from empirical studies of children's language. It has been pointed out that, far from reinforcing grammatically correct speech, adults typically respond to children's utterances in terms of their perceived communicative value and the intentions which they seem to express. In doing so, adults will often 'reinforce' ungrammatical word combinations (Brown and Hanlon 1970). While this evidence makes it unlikely that children learn grammar through reinforcement of 'correct' utterances, it leaves open the question of the role of reinforcement in the development of different language functions.

Research has also raised doubts about the role of imitation in children's learning of language. It was suggested in Chapter 1 that children's utterances are frequently characterised by novel combinations of morphemes and words which are not found in normal adult speech. It is, therefore, highly unlikely that imitation of adult models can explain their occurrence. The fact that such grammatically incorrect combinations are frequently systematic (Berko 1958; Ivimey 1975) suggests that children are organising their utterances on the basis of a knowledge of rules, rather than simply in response to environmental contingencies, and that such rules are, at least to some extent, generated spontaneously. For example, the application of the regular past-tense morpheme -ed to irregular verbs ('go-ed'; 'run-ed') or the use of the irregular plural /s/ with irregular nouns ('sheeps'; 'mouses') suggests that children overgeneralise simple rules to non-appropriate target words. Such 'incorrect' utterances seem to reflect the child's search for underlying order in language, rather than reinforcement by adults. While simple imitation fails to explain the occurrence of such novel utterances, a number of researchers have presented evidence indicating that imitation may nevertheless play a significant role in the child's mastery of vocabulary, syntax and pragmatic functions (Bloom *et al.* 1974; Clark 1977; Folger and Chapman 1977).

One of the ways in which the seemingly enormous differences between the ideas of Skinner and Chomsky may be reconciled is to recognise that, to a great extent, they were interested in quite different aspects of language. For Chomsky, language is an abstract system of rules which is used by human minds for transmitting and receiving ideas; the natural focus for research is a description of the rules by which that system is organised. In contrast, Skinner regards language as part of the process by which human beings interact with their environment and this points to the relations between utterances and their environmental effects as the natural focus for research activity. In other words, the differences between the two may come down to the fact that one is a linguist interested in grammar, while the other is a psychologist interested in the functional relations between language and the immediate context.

Even though it is generally recognised that, at best, the principles of operant conditioning described in *Verbal Behaviour* contribute but a small part to our understanding of the processes of language development, this does not immediately rule out the possibility of employing techniques based upon operant conditioning to help those children who are not developing language in the normal way. Perhaps where 'natural' processes have failed, it is sensible to apply 'non-natural' teaching techniques. In fact, it might be argued that because teaching techniques based on operant conditioning are derived from a scientific analysis of behaviour change, they offer, potentially, an approach which will be more effective than natural processes (Kiernan 1981).

A considerable body of literature now exists to demonstrate the efficacy of operant conditioning for producing changes in the language behaviour of language-impaired children (Garcia and DeHaven 1974; Mowrer 1984; Ruder 1978; Snyder *et al.* 1975). However, there remains considerable controversy concerning how far changes in language behaviour resulting from these procedures are similar to naturally occurring changes observed in normally developing children (Harris 1984a; Rees 1978). In particular, it is widely recognised that behavioural methods often result in relatively rigid language patterns, and that subsequent generalisation beyond training sessions and the spontaneous combination of taught elements into novel combinations continue to be problematic. Finally, the recent emphasis on the pragmatic aspects of language during development have raised further questions regarding the suitability of learning theory approaches for language intervention (Rees 1978).

Are linguistic abilities innate? The case for language acquisition

For Chomsky (1965) and McNeill (1970) the problem posed by children's mastery of language was how such inexperienced and, in other respects, immature human beings could learn to speak in accordance with the rules of grammar. Grammatical rules are seen as existing independently of the child, and changes in the child's language in the direction of conventional syntax and morphology are seen as indicative of the child *acquiring* the rules which make up the grammatical system. An outline of the phrase-structure and transformational rules identified by Chomsky is provided in Chapter 1.

Chomsky's view of the problem of language acquisition can be simply illustrated. On the one hand, the child hears people speaking; like the linguist studying children's language, children have access to a corpus or sample of language in the utterances they hear. This appears to be the only source of information available to the child regarding how phonemes, morphemes and words are organised into meaningful sentences. On the other hand, after a period of some four to five years' (and after only two to three years of first speaking words) exposure to the language of those around them, children seem to have mastered the underlying rule system which enables them to produce an infinite variety of relatively well-formed, complex sentences.

An additional problem for the child language learner is created by the imperfect relationship between a speaker's knowledge of grammatical rules (usually referred to as 'competence') and the language which is actually spoken (usually referred to as 'language performance'). Under ideal conditions, ordinary speakers of a language are quite capable of demonstrating their grammatical competence by producing fully grammatical utterances and by distinguishing grammatical from ungrammatical utterances (see Chapter 1). However, in every day settings, limited attention, distractions and interruptions interfere with the process by which competence is translated into performance. Ordinary speech is therefore usually a very imperfect representation of the underlying rules of grammar and appears not to provide a sound database for the derivation of these rules.

There is thus a gap between rapid acquisition of complex and highly abstract knowledge by individuals with very limited cognitive resources and the degenerate information, in the form of spoken language, which seems to provide the only source of information the child has to work on. Chomsky filled this gap by suggesting that infants are born with innate knowledge of the properties of language. This can be seen as a kind of intermediate position halfway between the child as a *tabula rasa* with no innate knowledge of the world and the child being able to speak at birth. Clearly, children cannot speak at birth, but Chomsky wishes to credit them with two distinct kinds of knowledge. First, he argues that infants possess an understanding of the basic features which are common to all human languages. This might include a set of rules for relating the surface form of an utterance to its underlying meaning, and certain grammatical categories such as sentence subject and object of the verb. Clearly, to be useful, these features must be common to all languages, since children seem to be able to learn any language with equal facility. For this reason, they are referred to as **linguistic universals.**

Second, Chomsky suggests that children are born with a knowledge of appropriate processing strategies for analysing the language they hear and determining the patterns which are indicative of the underlying rule system. Together, the knowledge of linguistic universals and the innate processing strategies are referred to as the 'Language Acquisition Device' or LAD.

Thus, the LAD needs to contribute enough (but no more than enough) innate knowledge for the child to learn the grammar of a language from the utterances which she hears in the first four or five years of life.

Implications of the acquisition approach for language teaching

Although Chomsky's description of language in terms of transformational grammar has had a considerable impact in respect of work on language intervention, the influence of his theory of language *acquisition* has been much more limited. This is mainly because this account of the mechanisms of language development attributes the major role to hidden processes in the LAD. Not only does this make it difficult to test the theory empirically, but it also creates problems regarding recommendations for intervention. For a child with long-term language difficulties, an appropriate interpretation might be that the LAD is damaged in some way but, without a more detailed analysis of the processes at work and how they contribute to language performance, implications for intervention which stem directly from this theoretical position remain elusive. Even were descriptions of the relationship between LAD operations and specific aspects of language functioning to emerge, it seems likely that they would be highly abstract and therefore of very little value in planning therapy.

Criticisms of the language acquisition approach

The acquisition theory of language development is an attempt to explain how children acquire the rules of grammar. To the extent that transformational rules have been challenged as accurate accounts of children's emerging knowledge of the rules for organising language structures (see Chapter 1), the LAD is suspect. Furthermore, it is now recognised that in learning language, children are doing far more than acquiring the rules of grammar and it may be that the key to the mastery of abstract grammatical rules lies in the socially mediated learning of functional language skills (Bruner 1983; Halliday 1975; Wells 1981).

Chomsky's invocation of the LAD was at least partly attributable to the apparent speed with which acquisition occurred. However, studies of children's communicative abilities prior to the onset of spoken language have indicated that the origins of communication may be traced back to the earliest days after birth, and that full mastery of the morpho-syntactic devices for expressing complex meanings may not be fully understood until early adolescence. The period of language acquisition may therefore be much longer than Chomsky originally thought.

A third point of criticism concerns Chomsky's declaration that the child was exposed to 'degenerate' examples of language which did not accurately reflect the underlying rules of grammar. Abundant research over the past two decades has indicated that the language employed by most adults when addressing babies and infants is, in fact, highly simplified and largely correct in terms of grammar. While this indicates that the language young children hear may provide useful input for learning the rules of grammar, it does not, of itself, rule out the need for an innate ability to process speech sounds (Gleitman and Wanner 1982). Finally, while Chomsky assumed that without a priori knowledge, a distributional analysis of a naturally occurring language sample would inevitably fail to identify correspondences between words and their respective lexical roles, more recent studies have suggested that this view may have been unduly pessimistic (Maratsos 1983).

In conclusion, the nativistic position presented by McNeill and Chomsky may have overestimated the contribution to language learning which must be ascribed to innate knowledge and underrepresented the part played by child–environment interactions. While the criticisms outlined above do not obviate the necessity of some nativistic assumptions, they do suggest a different way of addressing the problem. Chomsky started by defining the nature of the learning objective – that is, adult grammatical proficiency – and then worked backwards to determine how much of the workload in language learning had to be borne by innate knowledge. An alternative approach is to seek a better understanding of the *developmental processes* which seem to be at work by studying young children as they involve themselves in getting to know the language. As more and more is understood of the way in which interactions between the child and the environment create privileged opportunities for language learning, so it may be possible to reduce the burden of explanation which has fallen on innate factors.

Chapter five

Developmental approaches to children's language

Introduction

Perhaps the most distinguishing features of psychological approaches to the study of human development are the assumption of underlying continuities between behaviours at different points in the lifespan, and the attempt to understand how interactions between the individual and the environment at one point in time make possible more elaborate interactions at some later point in time. A simple example concerns the question of continuities between early motor abilities, such as crawling and reaching, and later, more sophisticated abilities, such as walking and pointing. Needless to say, when developmental psychologists are studying language, the 'environment' includes not only the physical environment provided by objects and materials, but also the social environment provided by other people.

In general terms, developmentalists take the view that it should be possible to examine the ways in which infants and young children interact with the physical world and with other people and to determine how they change as a result. The behaviour of even very young children is often highly complex, as for example, in the case of language. As we have already seen, attempts to explain the rapid changes in complex behaviour simply in terms of contingent relations between behaviour and the environment have not been particularly successful. For this reason, developmental psychologists frequently introduce descriptions of mental models, cognitive representations or conceptual understanding to provide a link between the kinds of learning which may have occurred at one point in time and the relatively sophisticated behaviours which are subsequently observed.

While such mentalistic constructions may sound implausible at first sight, they are justified in three ways. First, it is argued that mental events are a fact of life and, therefore, a legitimate object of psychological enquiry. Second, it seems that any adequate account of language must include descriptions of abstract knowledge which makes production and comprehension possible (see Chapter 1). Third, from a methodological perspective,

Figure 5.1 Behaviour–environment interactions and developmental continuity

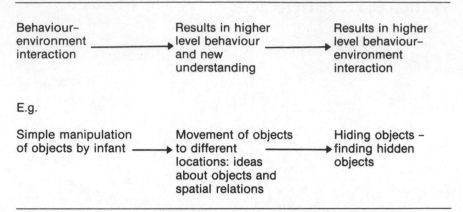

Behaviour– environment interaction ——▶ Results in higher level behaviour and new understanding ——▶ Results in higher level behaviour– environment interaction

E.g.

Simple manipulation of objects by infant ——▶ Movement of objects to different locations: ideas about objects and spatial relations ——▶ Hiding objects – finding hidden objects

perspective, mentalistic accounts are seen as valid so long as they are closely tied to observations, so that any proposed link between behaviour and underlying knowledge is subject to rigorous scrutiny and ultimately to falsification through additional empirical enquiry (see Figure 5.1).

The account provided here of the developmental approach to the child's mastery of language will be dealt with in two parts. The first part considers those pre-linguistic experiences by which the child establishes patterns of behaviour and levels of cognitive representation which permit the learning of spoken language. These will be referred to as developmental foundations for the mastery of language. The second part considers how interactions between the child and her linguistically more competent caretakers may create privileged opportunities for language learning, and thereby constitute a form of environmental support for the child's mastery of language.

Cognitive foundations for language development

One of the motivations for children to speak is that they have ideas which they wish to communicate to other people (Bloom 1973). A *sine qua non* for language development might therefore be the emergence of ways of understanding the world which are amenable to expression in language. At this point it may be worth reiterating a distinction made in Chapter 1 concerning *conceptual* levels of understanding and the *expression* of related ideas in language. Here, the argument is presented that conceptual levels of understanding are necessary precursors to the emergence of spoken language, since language is, in effect, the linguistic realisation of those conceptual distinctions already established at a non-verbal level. When conceptual distinctions are expressed in language they are referred to as *semantic relations.* While emphasising the interdependence between semantic expressions and underlying cognitive concepts, this approach also implies that not all of a child's understanding of a particular experience may be expressed in language, and that a child may *intend* to express more than she is actually able to encode formally in language structures. For example, Chapter 1 discussed the ways in which researchers have introduced the notion of a 'rich interpretation' of utterances such as 'sweater chair', 'Daddy car' in order to disambiguate alternative meanings.

Is it possible to determine the ways in which children think prior to the emergence of spoken language and, if so, what kinds of description can be offered for the conceptual understanding which precedes the expression of ideas in language? These two questions represent the focus of a considerable amount of research by developmental psychologists over the last 30 years. While this is not the place to explore that research in any detail, it will be helpful to describe briefly the kinds of understanding which are believed to be present in young children by the time they begin to use language. This summary is based on the work of Jean Piaget (Piaget 1970; Piaget and Inhelder 1969).

Piaget's work is important because it provided one of the first developmental accounts of the emergence of logical thought. For Piaget, the adult's ability to think logically, to manipulate symbols in meaningful ways and to solve complex problems can be traced directly back to the infant's first attempts to make sense of her surroundings. And, by the same token, the emergence of language is made possible by the developmental achievements of the first two years.

Piaget viewed the emergence of intelligent thought as a process of *construction,* in which the infant actively seeks to make sense of her surroundings and, more particularly, the relationship between her own actions and the contingent events in the environment. However, unlike Skinner, Piaget believed that development is best explained by describing the ways in which children understand such relations. One useful analogy for understanding Piaget's theory is to view the child as a scientist who is seeking a 'theory' to explain complex phenomena; like the scientist, the child at play carries out practical 'experiments' by acting on the environment and observing the outcomes. In the light of these observations, the child constructs 'theories' which are then used as a basis for further experimentation and observation. An important aspect of Piaget's approach is his claim that, since children the world over are very similar physiologically and neurologically, and since the world they explore is regulated by the same laws of nature, progress, in terms of their ability to make sense of the world, will be broadly consistent across all children. Extensive research in a number of quite different cultures has largely corroborated this assumption and vindicated Piaget's decision to base his theory on the detailed investigation of a relatively small number of children.

Here, we are concerned with the way in which Piaget described children's 'knowledge of the world' at different stages of development. Once again, constraints on space make it necessary to address only the first stage of development, which occurs between the ages of 0 and about 18 months.

Piaget's name for this important first stage in the child's long struggle to make sense of her environment was the **sensori-motor stage**, since at this time the child is seen as only being able to make sense of what is happening around her in terms of establishing relatively simple relations between her motor actions and the associated sensations. For example, as a 3-month-old baby waves her hand in front of her face, she gradually becomes aware of the relationship between the act of waving her hand in this way and the visual changes which accompany waving.

At birth, Piaget sees the infant as having no a priori knowledge of her environment or of the way in which she can act upon it. Babies are profoundly egocentric in that they are unable to view themselves as having an identity which is separate and distinct from the world which they are aware of through their senses. Only after a considerable period of experience do infants give clear signs that they are aware of the extent of their own bodies and the division between themselves and the wider world. But by the age of 18 months children seem to have a relatively clear understanding of the actions over which they have direct control and the events in the material world which they can influence only indirectly via their actions or the actions of other people.

During the first year of life children seem to become aware of objects and to realise that objects behave in quite different ways to themselves and to other people. Experience of objects is mediated by the senses, and it takes some time before the child appreciates that objects are best understood not as functions of action and sensation, but as entities which have an existence that is independent of the child's own actions and experiences. For example, infants of 8 months of age will continue to search for an object, such as a toy, which is repeatedly hidden behind the same cover. If the toy is subsequently hidden under a different cover or in a different place, infants of this age will almost invariably search under the cover where the toy was *last found,* and *not* where it was last seen to disappear. For Piaget, this indicates that the infant still thinks in terms of 'making' or 'materialising' objects through action, rather than 'discovering' objects which have simply been hidden from view.

Emerging concepts about objects are closely linked to the child's growing understanding of space, spatial relations and the notion of objects and people being located in a common space. By exploring the world in terms of the actions and their effects, young children come to realise that objects can be acted upon in different ways and that actions often result in objects changing their location; they may be moved to a new place, positioned with respect to other objects or located *on* surfaces and *in* containers.

The child's actions on the material world also provide a stimulus for conceptual development. Piaget suggested that, in performing actions, the child has first-hand experiences of the relations implicit in physical causality. The relationship between 'cause' and 'effect' is illustrated when a child's action 'causes' a particular event or 'effect' to happen. By the age of 18 months or so, the child is able to understand the extent of her own ability to make things happen and the reciprocal powers of other animate beings. She will also be able to establish mental goals and to organise a linked sequence of actions designed to achieve a particular objective.

Perhaps the most significant achievement of the sensori-motor stage is the child's ability to let one aspect of experience stand for, or represent, another. For example, a child may use an action previously performed as part of a game to signify that she wishes the game to continue. Here, the action *refers to* a game which has ceased. Similarly, a child at play may use a stick as an aeroplane or a settee as a car. Here, the child is using one object to *represent* another. This kind of representational ability is thought to be a particularly important developmental achievement since the essence of early language is the child's ability to use speech sounds to *represent* or *refer to* objects, actions and locations. This ability to use gestures and to engage in symbolic play is considered a necessary *precursor* to the child's understanding of the way in which meanings are represented in words and sentences.

How might the conceptual abilities described by Piaget as part of sensori-motor development be related to the emergence of spoken language? A number of researchers have suggested that the semantic relations which seem to characterise children's two- and three-word utterances bear a striking resemblance to sensori-motor concepts and this in itself presents a case for an underlying developmental continuity (Brown 1973). More specifically, it has been suggested that the language which children hear from adults contains frequent examples of those two- and three-term semantic relations which also occur in the language of young children (Snow 1977). The child's problem is to figure out the precise way in which the conceptual categories established during the sensori-motor stage map on to the semantic categories which are expressed in adult speech (Edwards 1973).

Unfortunately, we still have relatively little idea of how the child is able to move from a practical understanding of how, for example, objects change location as a result of actions performed by people, to the more abstract and general understanding of *semantic categories* such as agent, action and object, which provide the basis for early syntax (Bowerman 1976). One possibility is that conversational interactions are structured in such a way that they provide additional support for the induction of grammatical generalisations. This suggestion is discussed in more detail below. A second possibility is that the child is able to employ a set of relatively sophisticated strategies for analysing adult speech. For example, Slobin (1973) has put forward a number of 'operating principles' as a way of accounting for the appearance of language forms which suggest this kind of abstract grammatical knowledge. Only four examples are given here to illustrate this approach.

1 **Pay attention to the ends of words.** This strategy is particularly important for learning inflectional suffixes.
2 **The phonological forms of words can be systematically modified.** This is a basic assumption for the child to recognise that a single word might be realised in different forms, depending on its grammatical function.
3 **Pay attention to the order of words and morphemes.** This is a basic requirement for understanding the way in which word order is related to the expression of word meaning.
4 **The use of grammatical markers should make semantic sense.** This is important since phonological variation in words is not arbitrary but bears a direct correspondence to expressed meaning.

If, indeed, such principles are a feature of children's attempts to understand adult language, it remains to be seen whether they can be seen as the outcome of earlier developmental processes or, as seems more likely, innate abilities and therefore features of Chomsky's LAD.

Social foundations for language development

While it may be true that, in speaking, children frequently express in words underlying conceptual distinctions, a number of researchers have suggested that the ability to use language to communicate needs, interests and desires to other people presupposes another, rather different, set of developmental abilities. For these researchers, language is, first and foremost, a social process and its utilisation implies social understanding and a variety of social skills. This section provides a brief overview of those social abilities which are thought to be development precursors to the emergence of spoken language.

From birth, the environment in which babies find themselves is an intensely social one and almost inevitably they become enmeshed in a network of social interactions (Richards 1974; Schaffer 1977). Thus, while Piaget emphasised the importance of the child's actions upon the world, other researchers have focused upon the child's reactions to other people and the interactions which occur when adult and infant act and react towards each other over a period of time. But what evidence is there that babies acquire social knowledge and that their behaviour to other people is qualitatively different from their behaviour to inanimate objects?

First, a number of studies have shown that babies respond in quite distinct ways to stimuli which have social significance (see Bremner 1988 for a review). For example, they show an early preference for face-like configurations compared with other equally complex geometrical designs, and this soon develops into an interest in real faces. Similarly, infants as young as 6 weeks of age consistently show preferences for familiar as compared to unfamiliar faces. In the same way, infants seem able to discriminate voices and, under optimal conditions, they will respond preferentially to their mother's voice compared to the voice of a stranger. Experimental studies have also demonstrated that young babies can separate a continuous stream of speech sounds into discrete phonetic units and that they are sensitive to phonemic changes – for example, the difference between /p/ and /d/ – only a few weeks after birth (Eimas *et al.* 1971; Gleitman and Wanner 1982; Morse 1972, 1974).

Second, some responses are specifically social in nature and create opportunities for adult caretakers to interpret the infant's behaviours as indications of social responsiveness. For example, most infants smile to visual stimuli at about 5 weeks of age. Although smiling may be illicited by a range of social and non-social stimuli, it is used by adults as a cue to the child's emotional state. Mothers are able to discriminate different kinds of crying pattern and they typically interpret crying in terms of needs and emotional state. Further evidence comes from detailed observational studies of adult child interactions which have suggested that infants are able to synchronise gross motor activity with the intonational contours of adult conversation (Condon and Sander 1974) and that imitation of an adult's facial expression can occur as early as three days after birth (Meltzoff and Moore 1977, 1983).

Third, it seems that most adults are predisposed to respond to infants as social beings, and they are prepared to spend a considerable amount of time and energy in establishing a degree of social rapport. Initially, this may simply involve the elicitation of a sequence of sounds or actions which can be endowed with social meaning. For example, an adult may focus on a non-social action, such as tongue-poking or arm-waving, and interpret this as if it were, in fact, performed as an expression of some kind of social intention. It is as though the adult needs to see the infant as intentional and her actions as purposeful in order to respond appropriately. The significance of the adult's capacity to *attribute* meaning to actions which are not performed with communicative intent lies in the learning opportunities which are created by the adult response. When the adult responds to a particular behaviour *as if* it were socially significant, the infant is provided with a demonstration of the communicative potential of her own actions. She is placed in an ideal position to appreciate that actions and gestures can in fact be used *deliberately* to express social meanings (Newson 1979).

The first obvious signs that infants are able to participate in social interactions comes from repetitive sequences in which adult and child take turns. For example, a mother and infant might establish a simple play routine which involves each partner taking a turn to 'blow a raspberry'. Over time, more complex social routines may be established as adult and infant begin to build up a set of expectancies or joint understandings regarding the meanings of particular behaviours. For example, Bruner (Bruner and Sherwood 1976; Ratner and Bruner 1978) described a game of 'peekaboo' in which the adult covered the infant's face with a soft cloth and then used vocalisations to build up dramatic tension before the infant pulled the cloth away. The climax to this game suddenly dispels the tension and is followed by mother and infant laughing.

Bruner argues that social routines such as this form a framework within which young children learn a variety of social skills which are important developmental precursors to spoken language. For example, although, initially, children separate actions on objects from interactions with people, at between 8 and 16 months of age infants become able to organise their activity to include both objects and people. This development places extra demands upon the infant's powers of attention and requires that she co-ordinate her behaviour with respect to both the object and the other person. The demands of this kind of social experience are perhaps most acute when the infant wishes to communicate to the adult *about* the object – for example, if the child wishes to draw the adult's attention to an object or request an object from the adult. In each case, the child must not only find a way of getting the adult to notice the object, but she must do this in such a way that the adult is aware of what she is doing and why she is doing it. It is only if all these conditions are met that the adult is likely to respond appropriately (see acts performed by children's first words, Chapter 3).

These relatively complex communicative demands establish the conditions in which simple gestures, such as pointing, are particularly useful. However, in order to be used successfully, pointing must be carefully co-ordinated with the child's vocalisations and her direction of gaze and be performed at a time when the adult is attending to the child (Lock 1980a). In using a symbolic device, such as a pointing gesture, to communicate with another person about something – for example, an object – it is clear that the child has learned many of the social skills necessary for linguistic communication. Some researchers (for example, Bates 1976; Lock 1980a) have gone a step further and proposed that the non-verbal communicative skills which are displayed in 'showing' and 'requesting' objects are direct precursors to the linguistic functions of 'telling' or 'giving information' and 'asking questions'.

The following section will describe how patterns of non-verbal communication established in well-rehearsed games and social routines help in another way by providing an important source of environmental support for the development of spoken language.

Environmental support for language development

The developmental view of children's language suggests that, in addition to establishing prerequisite cognitive and social skills, the child must have access to a number of environmental support systems (see Bruner 1983). These support systems arise principally from the maintenance and elaboration of the social routines described in the preceding section, and the special characteristics of adult speech addressed to infants and young children.

Social routines as environmental support for language

It has already been noted that interactions between infant and adult lead to the development of pre-verbal communicative exchanges in which adult and child are able to refer to objects and events; successful joint reference makes it possible for these external objects and events to become 'topics' for further exchanges. In this way, the infant is not only learning to communicate with another person, but also to communicate about *something*. This form of pre-verbal communication may then provide a highly supportive context for the child to interpret adult speech and actively to test her own hypotheses about how words can be used to assist communication. Bruner has made some specific suggestions about the nature of the 'scaffolding' which occurs during adult–child interactions.

First, and perhaps most importantly, the existence of communicative understanding at a pre-verbal level means that the precise meaning of the words spoken by the adult are likely to be redundant. Or, to look at it from the child's point of view, the words the adult uses will be interpreted in the light of the forms of social understanding which have already been forged non-verbally. For example, if the adult holds an object, such as a doll, in the child's line of gaze, the child is likely to look at the object and then immediately glance at the adult's face to check that they are looking at the same thing. Establishment of joint reference in this way serves as a basis for agreement on communicative 'topics' (Bruner 1975). If at the same time the adult says, 'Look' or, 'What's this?' it seems plausible that the words will be interpreted by the child in terms of the communicative acts they accompany – that is, as 'attention-getters' and devices for locating conversational topics. On the basis of past experience the child is likely to try and interpret the adult's next act as some form of 'comment' on this topic. If, instead of acting physically, the adult names the object – 'dolly' – the child is likely to interpret the vocalisation not only as referring to the object, but as a description of the 'doll' as an entity (Ninio and Bruner 1978).

Second, the action sequences which constitute social routines may provide the child with the basis for making some initial hypotheses about the relationship between syntax and meaning (McNamara 1972). For example, consider a child who already understands that joint visual reference to an object she is holding, followed by the adult extending a hand with upturned palm, means: 'I want you to give me what you are holding.' Suppose this child is also familiar with the names of some common objects. Repeated exposure to the 'give and take' routine and the associated words – 'Give me the doll', 'Give me the ball', 'Give me your spoon' – provides the child with opportunities for interpreting the basic grammatical elements for requesting specific objects: 'give me' plus name of object requested. It should be emphasised that these opportunities do not constitute 'language development' nor do they ensure that development will take place. Rather, they help us to specify more precisely the nature of the problem with which the language-learning child is faced.

Third, pre-verbal procedures for joint understanding enable the adult to maintain a constant check on the child's verbalisations. Even if the child's articulation is poor, the adult is likely to be able to make a good guess as to a likely meaning. Similarly, contextual support and existing levels of shared understanding about routines mean that the adult is well placed to endow a child's utterance with meanings which extend or elaborate on those expressed. For example, an utterance such as 'juice' might be glossed as 'That's juice', 'I want some juice' or 'The juice is all gone', depending upon the situation and the child's behaviour. The guess as to the most plausible interpretation of the child's utterance will guide the adult's own actions which, in turn, provide the child with feedback regarding how successful she has been in making her needs and intentions explicit. The child's behaviour may then cue the adult as to how successful was the initial interpretation.

Fourth, the adult's ongoing assessment of the child's ability to understand what is being said and to make herself understood, may determine what the adult talks about and the way in which adult language is related to the context. Bruner (1983) refers to this as a 'communicative ratchet' which enables adults gradually to increase the demands which are placed upon linguistic communication, while at the same time minimising the consequences of misunderstandings. It seems that adults who provide optimal conversational support for language learning are those who are sensitive to the child's conversational needs and are able constantly to adjust their own contributions to match those of the child (Wells 1981; Wood 1988). When the child is communicating fluently and clearly, the most appropriate adult response may be to listen and encourage. Here, adult contributions might be reasonably elaborate, in that they might add new information or extend what the child has said. In contrast, when the child is having difficulty, the adult may need to make more frequent contributions of a different kind in order to help the child express her ideas in words.

The final way in which social routines may provide support for language is that they create the conditions whereby the child is motivated to speak. It is not clear whether this motivation arises from a pragmatic desire to influence other people in order to achieve common objectives, or whether social interctions act as a catalyst for the child's intrinsic curiosity about language as a system for communicating with other people. However, it is clear that social interaction and play routines create the conditions within which children become enthusiastic conversational partners and, in doing so, actively promote their own language development.

Adult speech as environmental support for language acquisition

Chomsky's claim that the young child is exposed to degenerate samples of language which distort the relationship between surface forms and meanings has been challenged by a considerable amount of recent research. This has shown that the language which adults address to young children is different in many ways from the language of adults talking to one another. The remarkable consistency with which adults and, particularly, mothers modify their language when talking to young children has encouraged researchers to term this form of address 'Motherese' or 'Babytalk'. Some of the key differences observed in the speech of adults addressing younger children compared to adults talking to each other or to older children are summarised below (for more detailed reviews see DePaulo et al. 1978; Snow 1977).

In terms of structural characteristics, mothers talking to young children employ shorter sentences, a lower mean length of utterance, more single words, fewer complex sentences and a more restricted vocabulary. Grammatical errors are very infrequent. Motherese tends to be produced at a slower rate, with more pronounced pauses and exaggerated intonational contours.

The semantic characteristics of adults talking to children are that adults talk about objects and events in their immediate surroundings and they frequently focus on topics identified in the child's talk. The semantic relations encoded in 'Motherese' are generally limited to the restricted set of relations which the children themselves use.

In terms of discourse characteristics, 'Motherese' contains a high frequency of self-repetitions and imitations of the child's language. Often imitations are extended to provide a more accurate rendition of the child's intended meaning or elaborated so that new but related information is added.

This kind of evidence led many researchers to suggest that simplified input of the type found in 'Motherese' might be implicated in language learning. However, 'Motherese' is composed of many different characteristics and it seems reasonable to suppose that there is considerable variation among adults in respect of how far these features are reflected in their speech to young children. Is it therefore possible to separate out those aspects of 'Motherese' which make a positive contribution to language learning from those which are merely incidental and possibly those which are actually detrimental?

A number of studies have attempted to do this both by comparing the rates of progress of children whose caretakers employ different styles of 'Motherese' and by deliberately seeking to modify adult input. Similar studies have also been conducted with children attending pre-school play-groups and nursery schools, where the caretakers have been either voluntary helpers or professionally trained nurses and teachers (Wells 1981; Wood *et al.* 1980). However, the results from such studies are far from consistent and there is considerable disagreement about precisely which features of 'Motherese' actually contribute either positively or negatively to language learning.

Some researchers noted a consistent relationship between the mean length of utterance of the adult's speech and that of the child so that, during development, the adult is invariably using slightly longer utterances than the child. This gave rise to the 'fine-tuning hypothesis' which suggested that learning opportunities are maximised if the adult is able to 'fine tune' her speech so that its structural complexity is always slightly in advance of that of the child. More recent research has not only failed to support this view, but has also laid open the possibility that simplified input may not be particularly useful. Instead, it has been argued that exposure to complex sentences is necessary so that the child can adequately test inferences about the relationship between grammatical form and meaning (Gleitman *et al.* 1984).

In terms of the semantic features of 'Motherese', there is considerable evidence to support the view that talking about objects and events in the immediate surroundings is helpful. It has also been shown that children benefit when adult contributions are semantically related to their own utterance. Examples included direct imitation, expansion of the child's utterance into a phrase or sentence which captures the child's intended meaning, extensions which include a novel contribution, and recastings in which the child's meaning is reflected back in a different syntactical form (see Chapter 10).

Adult speech which contains a relatively high proportion of statements or declaratives has been associated with accelerated language development in young children, while studies of pre-schoolers have indicated that conversations are more likely to be maintained over a number of turns if adults make positive contributions by adding new information (Wood *et al.* 1980). Similarly, there is agreement from research with very young children and with pre-schoolers that 'acceptances' ('yes', 'good', 'that's right') and 'phatic' responses ('oh, I see', 'really') are positively associated with progress. However, there is some disagreement about the role of questions. With young children, a high proportion of questions seems to be beneficial (Nelson 1973), but in slightly older children at pre-school, questions were found to be detrimental to the maintenance of conversational exchanges (Wood *et al.* 1980).

One danger with this emphasis on the language of adults is that it easily leads to the conclusion that adults actually cause developmental progress by the way in which they speak to young children. In contrast, the actual role of modified linguistic input may be to provide the child with a restricted set of choices, any number or combination of which may ultimately lead to developmental progress. The range of choices which are made available to the child may not be determined by the adult so much as by the nature of the interactions which are jointly established between adult and child. Hence, the child may actively influence the kinds of learning opportunities which are represented in the language she hears. Furthermore, children may be born with, or acquire at a relatively early stage, processing biases which will constrain the forms of adult input to which they will be most sensitive. Under such circumstances characteristics of adult language input would be reflected in differential rates of progress only to the extent that they coincided with the child's existing 'style' of learning language (Gleitman *et al.* 1984).

Language as process

The emphasis placed on pre-verbal social interaction as a precursor to spoken language, and the pre-eminent position of dialogue, in this developmental account of language acquisition, is indicative of a particular view of *what language is*. In contrast to the grammarian's concern to represent language as a rule-governed system for expressing meanings, recent psychological studies of children's language have increasingly addressed language as part of a larger social process broadly concerned with the regulation of joint activity. Here, it is suggested that symbols such as words and gestures are introduced and initially learned as devices to mediate interaction. The meanings expressed by specific words are only apprehended as a result of the effects which are achieved when they are used. The use of words and symbols to influence other people in predictable ways requires that the child must be able to represent mentally the relationship between the symbol (word or gesture), the meaning for which it stands and the intended effect on the other person. In learning to communicate, therefore, the child is also learning to *represent experience* and, most importantly, *learning to think*.

This view was most effectively expressed by writers such as G.H. Mead (1934) and L.S. Vygotsky (trans. 1962, 1978) over 50 years ago. Both Mead and Vygotsky proposed that communication between the child and older children or adults provides the essential conditions for emergence of 'mediation', whereby a word or gesture can stand for an aspect of experience. For Vygotsky, all higher mental processes are established at the level of interpersonal interaction and are, therefore, social in nature. It is only subsequently that 'inter-mental' processes are understood to the point where the child can dispense with the adult and manipulate symbols 'intra-mentally'. Language is first learned as a means of relating to other people where those others provide social and psychological supports which enable the child to be an effective communicator. In this sense, the child's conversational partner creates the conditions which make meaningful communication possible.

Through participation in the process of communication the child gradually becomes aware of the significance which can be attributed to her own actions and vocalisations. At this stage, the child is able to achieve, in consort with a sympathetic adult, far more than she could possibly achieve alone. Vygotsky called this range of 'adult-supported' activity the **zone of proximal development**:

It is the distance between the actual developmental level as determined by independent problem solving and the level of potential development as determined through problem solving under adult guidance or in collaboration with more capable peers.

(Vygotsky 1978:86)

It is of particular importance because it offers a way of anticipating developmental achievements: 'What a child can do with assistance today, she will be able to do by herself tomorrow.'

The extent to which the 'potential' revealed by the child's adult-supported activity is realised depends to a great extent on the way in which the adult interacts with the child. The process of scaffolding the communicative abilities of young children is not straightforward and depends on how the adult interprets the child's verbal and non-verbal communication. Optimal scaffolding is that which promotes the highest level of functioning with the minimal level of support; a child who is having difficulty in making herself understood may require a great deal of support; a few minutes later that same child dealing with a different topic may become relatively fluent and require a much lower level of adult participation. Too little support when the child is having difficulty, or too much intrusion when the child is succeeding, will have the same effect of reducing the child's opportunities for developmental change.

Implications of the developmental approach

One of the attractions of this developmental explanation of children's language is that it is a very rich source of ideas for remedial strategies. This section provides only a brief indication of the way in which therapists and clinicians have adopted and adapted this approach in working with children who have language difficulties.

The importance of developmental prerequisites

If ordinary children build their linguistic abilities on antecedent social and cognitive abilities, these may, in fact, be necessary prerequisites for the emergence of language. This view has led a number of researchers to question whether some groups of children are slow to develop language because their pre-verbal social and cognitive abilities have not developed to the point where the child is ready to begin using spoken or sign language. Studies with Down's Syndrome children in particular have indicated that if these children are provided with enriched opportunities for developing pre-linguistic abilities, their understanding and production of language is enhanced compared to children who do not have such opportunities (Bricker and Bricker 1973; McClean and Snyder 1978).

The importance of social routines

One of the problems with many children who experience difficulties with language and communication is that they also experience limited opportunities for engaging in social routines. This may be because their communicative impairments limit their scope for participation and places a heavy burden on any adult who seeks to engage them in routine activities. Alternatively, it may be because particular educational placements have very limited opportunities and few resources for this kind of activity. A third possibility is that teachers and care staff may not recognise the importance of such activities.

Recently, a number of researchers have drawn attention to the importance of providing language-impaired children with opportunities for learning language in contexts where language is both natural and appropriate (Harris 1984b; McClean and Snyder 1978; Nelson *et al.* 1986). Rather than treating language as a 'learning topic' which can be compartmentalised and taught in a formal setting such as a classroom or a clinic, an increasing number of therapists and teachers are beginning to explore ways of dealing with language as an integral part of the communicative process which surrounds any social activity. Any naturally occurring activity, such as dressing, feeding, shopping, cooking, or playing games, which provides a context within which communication is necessary, is a potential context for language learning.

Adult speech as environmental support for language learning

The important role attributed to 'Motherese' in language development among normally developing children, has, in turn, fuelled speculation that some forms of language impairment may arise from the child having insufficient exposure to adult language or, alternatively, being among adults who adopt inappropriate styles of talking to young children. The quality and quantity of language a child hears from adults may result in variations in speed of acquisition (Clarke-Stewart 1973) and knowledge of the ways in which language can be used (Heath 1983). These problems may then lead on to additional difficulties at school, especially if the teaching staff mistake linguistic delay as indicative of limited intelligence, or interpret differences in a child's ability to *use* language as a sign of impaired ability to *learn* language (Heath 1983). However, young children's ability to develop language is extremely robust, and unless there are additional cognitive or emotional problems, children learn the language *of their community* even under conditions where exposure to adult input seems to be remarkably impoverished. It is therefore extremely important when assessing any child for language impairment to ask what kind of language is appropriate for the child's home and immediate environment, and whether or not the child's ability is consistent with her experience and the expectations of those around her. This will help teachers and therapists to distinguish between problems of language development, on the one hand, and social and educational problems on the other.

A separate issue concerns whether adults who care for or teach children who have impaired language adopt appropriate forms of speech and styles of interaction in the light of a child's specific difficulties. Here, the question of what constitutes useful linguistic support for the child is much less easy to answer. Speaking as you would to an ordinary child, of a similar level of linguistic ability, may be the most natural response and in most cases this is likely to be a safe strategy. However, the fact that the child has language difficulties is probably a good indication that exposure to the kinds of language which enable most children to learn will not be sufficient to enable this child to make progress; she may require adult input which is specially tailored to help compensate for particular areas of weakness. In support of this view, a number of studies have indicated that language-impaired children make significant improvements if the adults around them are induced to make systematic changes in certain aspects of their language (Howlin 1984; McLean and Snyder 1978). Unfortunately, at the present time, little is known about the kinds of adult language which may be most helpful for children who experience different forms of language impairment.

A second, more serious, problem is that, very often, the nature of the child's language problem makes it impossible to speak to the child 'naturally'; the adult is forced to employ 'unnatural' language and to adopt *ad hoc* conversational strategies. Once again, it remains problematical as to whether this kind of input is appropriate and to what extent a child who has serious language difficulties actually restricts adults' ability to provide appropriate linguistic support.

Language as process

The notion that language development is best thought of as part of a process for regulating joint activities, rather than as a subject, has profound implications for helping children with language difficulties. Most obviously, it shifts the focus from what children *know* about language and their command of language structure, to how they *use* language and the extent to which they are able to utilise conventional language forms in order to satisfy interpersonal needs. This might include exploiting various language functions in different social contexts, as well as being able to participate in conversations. This approach also suggests that the most important language is that which represents the child's attempts to express her own needs and intentions rather than language which arises as the child tries to express ideas supplied by the teacher.

Finally, Vygotsky's description of the 'zone of proximal development' provides a clear indication of the way in which environmental support is likely to be effective. It is not so much a matter of deciding in advance which activities and what kinds of adult input match the child's level of development, either in terms of language or cognitive abilities; rather, it is a matter of the adult being sensitive to the child's changing communicative needs and adjusting her speech and actions from one moment to the next. In this way the child's performance is continually sustained by the adult who, almost paradoxically, is always seeking to withdraw so that the child is able to participate in interactions as an independent and autonomous individual.

Criticisms of the developmental approach

In the light of the available evidence the ideas presented in this chapter must be regarded as the 'front runners' in terms of a satisfactory explanation of how children master the language system. However, this should not be taken to imply that this approach does not have its critics or that all researchers working within the developmental paradigm are in agreement regarding the more detailed aspects of language development. It should also be recognised that while this chapter has stressed the view of language as a process, it is nevertheless the case that, at some point, children do reach a level of mastery where it makes sense to describe them as having acquired knowledge of an abstract set of rules which can be used to express meanings. What is at issue is whether young children begin by addressing the problem in this way or whether they approach grammatical competence via a circuitous route which begins with pre-verbal social interaction.

Perhaps the most important criticism of this approach is that much of it is essentially speculation about how language development *might* occur and that there is relatively little conclusive evidence that this is indeed how young children do, in fact, master language. In addition, close scrutiny of any one part of the process quickly reveals additional questions about how such developmental changes take place in the light of what still appear to be impoverished and often infrequent learning opportunities (Shatz 1983). As a result, research in this area is not only clarifying the possible role of pre-requisite abilities and environmental support, but it is also resulting in some very strong indications that infants are, to a remarkable degree, pre-adapted to the kinds of learning necessary for language acquisition (for example, see Gleitman and Wanner 1982). Inevitably, this is likely to be perceived as gloomy news for those concerned with therapy and teaching. However, this is still a new and exciting field of research which no doubt has many surprises to spring before the mysteries of early language are solved. Furthermore, it is likely to take many years of research and practical work on intervention before we will be clear about the implications of this approach for children with language impairments.

Part three

Language Assessment

Chapter six

Practical and theoretical issues in language assessment

Why assess language?

There are many reasons why it may be regarded as helpful to gather information about a child's language, and the uses to which any formal assessment results may be put will influence decisions about how assessments can best be carried out. This chapter will begin by considering the reasons for carrying out language assessments and the ways in which information from language assessments is used.

Identification of children with language difficulties

On many occasions assessments will be carried out because it is suspected that a child is experiencing some difficulty with linguistic communication, or because there are other areas of functioning in which the child is having difficulty which may have implications for language development. Here, the aim of assessment is simply to identify whether or not the child's language is unusual or atypical compared with that of other children of a similar age or in respect of other aspects of development. For example, a child with language which is less advanced than the language of other children of that age would be regarded as having **delayed language;** in contrast, children whose language stands out because it is deficient when compared with the way in which they perform on other social and intellectual tasks may be regarded as having a **language deficit.** On the basis of this analysis, a child with severe learning difficulties might have both delayed language, in that she would be functioning at a level below that normally expected for children of her age, *and* a deficit if her language skills were more severely affected than other areas.

Screening assessments are normally carried out using tests which enable teachers or therapists to obtain a broad-spectrum view of the child's language abilities. While such tests should ideally sample structural, semantic and pragmatic aspects of language, this is seldom feasible and frequently language screening occurs as part of a more general screening assessment which considers other aspects of a child's social and psychological functioning. While many language tests are relatively quick and easy to use, they do not generate the quality of information desirable for diagnostic statements or the formulation of remedial intervention strategies (see Chapter 9).

Placement

A child who has problems in any area of development may be regarded as being likely to benefit from some form of special educational placement, either full time or part time. Similarly, a description of a child's linguistic abilities may be influential in determining what kinds of educational provision are most likely to meet that child's special needs. Recommendations regarding placement will need to bear in mind not only a child's existing abilities, but also the progress a child is likely to make in different educational settings.

The extent to which a child is able to take advantage of the learning opportunities, which are made available within a particular setting on a day-to-day basis, will be a major factor in influencing how much progress occurs. For this reason, assessments intended to provide a basis for making decisions about placement should consider not only the child's performance under 'test' conditions, but also the child's capacity for engaging in linguistic interactions in 'naturalistic' settings. For example, a child who is sociable, and is likely to benefit from social and linguistic interactions with other children, may be best placed in an ordinary classroom but with special periods devoted to those areas of language which are giving cause for concern. On the other hand, a child who has difficulty in establishing social contact with others may find the unpredictability of an ordinary classroom overpowering and be better placed in a special class or unit.

Special classes usually have the advantage of lower teacher–pupil ratios and it is therefore easier for teachers to organise activities in which the child's level of participation in social and communicative activities can be carefully monitored and adapted to suit existing abilities. Similarly, the gradual introduction of more challenging activities intended to facilitate language development is likely to be more easily accomplished in a small class with specialist teachers.

Diagnosis and prognosis

In the field of medicine, disorders are recognised according to their pattern of symptoms, since it is usually the case that similar symptom patterns are indicative of illnesses that have similar underlying causes. An understanding of the aetiology of disease makes it appropriate to target treatment on the underlying cause or causes of an illness rather than the symptoms. For this reason, accurate diagnosis of underlying causes on the basis of visible symptoms plays a major part in the treatment of physical illnesses and will often enable doctors to provide accurate predictions about the future course of the illness.

The success of the 'symptomatic' approach to physical illness has led to its adoption by other, paramedical, professions concerned with helping people with other kinds of disability. In the field of clinical linguistics, there are many conditions which, it is often assumed, have similar causes and which can be treated in similar ways. For example, Cantwell and Baker (1987) devote a chapter to 'Differential diagnosis of syndromes involving speech and language'. However, they acknowledge the difficulties in applying this kind of taxonomy to language disorders:

> We wish to preface our discussion of syndromes involving abnormal language development with the disclaimer that, while these categories may delineate separate *psychiatric* categories, it is not yet clear that each of these categories represents a unique type of linguistic disorder.
>
> (Cantwell and Baker 1987:70; emphasis added)

Here, the only justification for the introduction of these syndromes is that they reflect a psychiatric (i.e. medically based) taxonomy.

Crystal (1984) points out that attempts to classify linguistic disabilities have led to considerable confusion and that terminology is seldom used systematically. The most obvious reason for this is that neuro-science has not yet reached the point where it is possible to describe language as a direct manifestation of underlying physiological of neurological states. Instead, the best accounts of the 'causes' of language are social and psychological, where language is seen as occurring as a result of interactions between people and their environments. It is therefore seldom appropriate to treat disorders of language and communication by trying to influence presumed underlying causes.

Even when it is possible to tackle the perceived origins of language difficulty, this will not immediately result in the affected individual being cured. For example, a child who is experiencing language difficulties brought about by severe environmental deprivation will be saved from further harm if removed to another, more stimulating, environment. However, this does not in itself overcome the language problems which have arisen during the period of isolation. This can only be achieved by working prospectively on the child's future environment and by deciding which new experiences may be introduced to compensate for those which, in the past, have proved to be inadequate for language development.

Similarly, a child who has language problems because of hearing loss caused by a temporary blockage (otitis media) may have her hearing corrected by surgical intervention, but this will not automatically remedy the child's problems with language; this will require additional treatment to create the possibility of appropriate learning (Downs and Blager 1982; Quick and Mandell 1983; Godowski *et al.* 1986).

This analysis suggests that the identification and diagnosis of language disorder is unlikely to provide the basis for more than relatively crude speculations regarding the child's prognosis. While it may be possible to say, on the basis of a diagnosis, that a child will continue to experience considerable difficulties with various aspects of language, it remains true that the course and speed of language development will depend, to a great extent, upon the kinds of experience to which the child is subsequently exposed.

Over and above these difficulties, there are considerable variations in the way in which different authors use the term 'diagnosis' (Crystal 1984). For example, while Cantwell and Baker (1987) imply that diagnosis is in some senses indicative of *aetiology,* Ingram (1976) restricts his use of the term to the *description* of speech and language difficulties using a particular theoretical framework. In this book, **diagnosis** will be used in the traditional medical sense: to designate a process of classification on the basis of presumed causes. The description of speech and language difficulties which draws on recent psycholinguistic research will be referred to as the process of **assessment.** Assessment may provide the foundations for an intervention programme because it describes an individual's strengths and weaknesses, irrespective of the presumed underlying causes of those difficulties.

The rationale for using assessment procedures to diagnose different kinds of language disorder rests principally on the assumption that different treatments can be evaluated with respect to different conditions (Cantwell and Baker 1987). If it is found that a particular form of therapy is effective for a group of individuals with a particular pattern of language difficulties, or for those who share a common aetiology (that is, they have the same diagnosis), it may be that others with similar difficulties may be helped by the same form of therapy. For example, hearing impairments provide a common aetiology for linguistic difficulties among deaf children and for this reason it is usually assumed that deaf children will respond to therapy in similar ways. Likewise, children with 'acquired childhood language disorder' may be recognised as having similar kinds of communication difficulties (irrespective of specific causes) and, on the basis of this diagnosis, they may be recommended for certain kinds of therapy (Cantwell and Baker 1987).

It is important to note that the reasoning here is as follows: assessment→diagnosis→treatment. Thus the crucial determiner of the therapeutic experiences to which the child will be exposed is whether or not the child is categorised as 'having' a particular condition. There is, therefore, a danger that the assessment is carried out solely to determine the diagnosis and that treatment is designed for the diagnosis rather than for the child. Given the present state of understanding regarding the causes and appropriate forms of intervention for children with language difficulties, this kind of short-cut is likely to lead to inadequate assessment and ineffective treatment. Diagnosis may facilitate communication among professionals in obtaining an appropriate placement for a child. However, it should be stressed that diagnosis is only one of the aims of assessment and diagnosis on its own may be of limited value in developing strategies for intervention (Crystal 1984).

Communicating with other professionals

Very often assessment of a child's language is required in order that it can be presented to other professionals who are seeking to help that child. The information from the assessment may be presented orally at a case conference or it may be presented in the form of a written report. It may also be reported informally in the context of more general discussions or 'chat'. In whichever way the results of an assessment are communicated, it is reasonable to assume that they may have important implications for the way in which the child is dealt with in the future. This information may also influence the way in which other people perceive the child and, consequently, the way in which they interact with the child on an individual basis.

The information which may be derived from an assessment can be roughly divided into two types: first, there is the information which is obtained from the assessment procedures and, second, there is the interpretation which is placed on this information. For example, in terms of the discussion in the preceding section, a diagnosis is an interpretation of the evidence obtained from the assessment. In the interests of maintaining objectivity it is always helpful to keep these two kinds of information distinct and to indicate clearly how an interpretation is derived from the evidence presented.

Communicating with parents

One of the most important roles for any person who conducts a formal language assessment on a child is to communicate the results of the assessment to the child's parents or guardians. This raises rather different issues compared to communication with other professionals, since the child's parents are likely to be much more involved, both personally and emotionally. For this reason, it is necessary to consider not only what information to provide for parents, but *how* this information can be most usefully presented.

Parents will frequently already be aware that the child is experiencing difficulties with various aspects of language, although they may not have considered the implications of these problems in any great detail. However, they are likely to appreciate a straightforward summary of the results of the assessment which places equal weight on the child's abilities as well as on her disabilities. Once again, it may be helpful to distinguish between objective evidence obtained from an assessment and the conclusions which are drawn from this. It will also be necessary to consider the extent to which the evidence involves technical data and the extent to which any particular parent is likely to find this kind of information helpful. In many cases, parents will be more interested in the way in which the professional uses information from the assessment to answer practical questions, such as 'Will she need to have speech therapy?', 'Will he be able to go to the same school as his brothers and sisters?' or 'Will she be able to speak like other boys and girls when she is older?'

Many parents will have experienced considerable anxiety prior to the assessment because of the uncertainty of suspecting that there is something wrong with their child but not knowing what. They may therefore approach the post-assessment consultation in the expectation of being given some definite information regarding the child's difficulties and the likely prog-nosis. However, as has already been mentioned, providing clear predictions about the course of any child's linguistic and communicative abilities is extremely difficult. It may not, therefore, be possible to give direct answers to many of the questions which parents may ask. It is then up to the teacher or therapist to help the parents accept that an assessment may be useful as a way of helping the child without necessarily providing a diagnostic label or a clear statement regarding the child's future.

Very often, parents can be helped by a clear description of the child's abilities and the areas of relative weakness, especially if this is written down so that they can take it away and read it at their leisure. This may also help parents to be more aware of language and communication in ordinary, everyday settings and to notice when and on what occasions a child's lang-uage seems to be improving. This may not only be encouraging for the parents, but it may also provide the teacher or therapist with valuable in-formation about the child's functioning which would not otherwise be avail-able.

In addition, some parents may find that it is easier to cope with a child who has a serious language problem if they are able to participate in the process of assessment and intervention. This may require the parents being given some special activities to be carried out each day, or it may involve more general and less highly structured activities, such as looking at books or playing with toys. In these cases, it is important that the parents are given regular feedback regarding progress and that activities are frequently modified to reflect even modest progress. It may also be necessary to ensure that parents do not become over-zealous in their commitment to a particular kind of therapeutic activity to the extent that it limits, rather than expands, the child's experiences, or dominates the lives of other members of the family.

Measuring changes over time

An important function of assessment is that it can help determine the extent to which a child's language is subject to changes over time. This involves carrying out two separate assessments and comparing the results. Clearly, the longer the time interval between the two assessments the greater the chances that there will be differences. Such differences may be indicative of more elaborate language and progress in the direction predicted by normal developmental trends, or the child's language may be deteriorating. It is also quite likely that there will be a mixture of positive and negative changes which need to be carefully interpreted.

One particular difficulty in assessing change over time is that any differences between the two assessments will be influenced by a host of extraneous factors which may either conceal or exaggerate the real changes in the child's language. Some published language tests provide data regarding the variability to be expected in test scores if the test were to be repeated on the same child at relatively close intervals. Under such conditions, it is assumed that there would have been no 'real' changes in the child's language and that any differences in the two test scores would be due to error arising from the limitations of the test itself (see Chapter 7). It is only changes in test scores which exceed these reliability estimates that can be regarded as reflecting real changes in the child's ability.

Unfortunately, other forms of assessment do not lend themselves to precise measures of test–retest reliability and the clinician may need to judge how far situational factors might have influenced the two assessments. For example, a sample of naturalistic speech, on a tape recorded in the child's home, is probably not directly comparable with a sample taken while the child is in a school or clinic. Even in the case of language tests, it is possible that situational factors will influence a child's performance and hence make comparisons between two sets of scores difficult to interpret. For example, a child who is assessed while slightly under the weather or simply in a bad mood will be likely to perform below par, and a comparison of this assessment with a prior or subsequent assessment will provide a distorted impression of any real changes which have occurred.

Evidence of change may be useful in deciding whether or not a child requires special placement, and it is likely to be particularly helpful when discussing the child with other professionals or parents. However, in addition to providing information about the child, an indication of change over time may also be helpful in evaluating the success of previous attempts at remedial intervention. It might reasonably be expected that a child placed in a special class would make more progress after the placement than during a comparable time period before the placement. Similarly, a child who has been receiving some form of individual help from a clinician, teacher or parent, might be expected to show the effects of that treatment and a comparison of changes over time on the basis of formal assessments would be an appropriate way of obtaining relevant information.

The ideal way to evaluate some form of special teaching help is to compare the changes which occur over two periods of time, only one of which is associated with intervention, such as a special placement or a particular kind of therapy (see Figure 6.1).

Clearly, in order to obtain this kind of information it is necessary to conduct three assessments under similar conditions so that they are directly comparable and spaced at equal time intervals. If such a procedure is to be successfully executed, it is likely to require careful planning and substantial time commitment.

However, when this approach is used with single children or with small groups, it may still not be possible to attribute any observed changes in the child's language to the effect of the intervention. Other factors may also have played a part. For example, the child's home experiences may have changed during the same period, thus helping or hindering language development, or the fact that the child is older during the second time period may influence language performance.

In addition to this 'before-and-after intervention' approach, there are other experimental designs which have been specially developed for teachers and therapists working in therapeutic settings. One popular technique is to measure a child's ability with respect to a number of relatively discrete aspects of language and then to target specific areas for intervention. The areas which do not receive intervention can then serve as a basis for comparison with the targeted areas after a suitable period of time has elapsed (see Table 6.1). If the intervention is effective, the areas specifically addressed by the teaching programme should show greater signs of improvement than the areas not targeted for intervention.

In this kind of evaluation of change over time, it is argued that it is easier to attribute changes directly to the planned intervention, since it is unlikely that other experiences to which the child might be exposed would produce the same pattern of differential progress across different aspects of language.

Developing strategies for teaching

One of the principal reasons for conducting a detailed assessment of a child's language is to determine the most effective way of helping that child. This raises the question of exactly what kinds of experience are likely to be most helpful to a child who is experiencing difficulties with language and communication. At some point it is necessary for someone to provide clear guidelines regarding how others should interact with that child in order to promote learning and developmental changes most effectively . The question of how best to structure a child's learning experiences invites the

Figure 6.1 The role of assessment in evaluating the effectiveness of remedial interventions

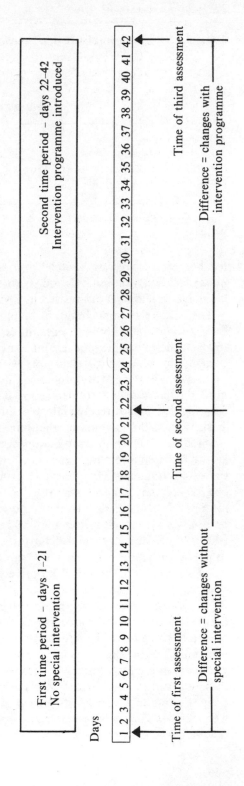

Table 6.1 Comparison of multiple baseline measures before and after intervention

	% of all utterances	
	Before intervention	*After intervention*
Asking questions*	5	12
Answering questions	7	6
Making statements	3	5
Responding to statements*	12	23

*Areas targeted for remedial teaching.

teacher or therapist to switch from the focus on linguistic description, presented in Chapters 1, 2 and 3, to the concern about explanations of language development discussed in Chapters 4 and 5.

Therapeutic recommendations involve moving beyond a description and interpretation of the child's difficulties, and expressing a commitment to a theoretical framework concerning how changes can be initiated or accelerated. This chapter will deal only with issues relating to description and assessment, leaving a discussion of different approaches to intervention until Chapters 9 and 10. However, it is possible to make some general comments about the ways in which descriptions of a child's language difficulties can contribute to planning intervention.

First, it is appropriate for those working with a child to try to communicate at the right level; this means introducing language structures with which the child is already familiar and trying to ensure that the content of conversations is appropriate to the child's ability to understand and to her interests. It also means creating opportunities for interaction, either verbal or non-verbal, which reflect the child's command of the functional characteristics of language (for a description of language structure, content and function, the reader is referred to Chapters 1, 2 and 3). While it is true that a sensitive adult will respond intuitively to a child's language and make numerous adjustments to his or her own language in a way that will reflect the child's strengths and weaknesses, it may nevertheless be helpful to make these explicit in a written assessment so that intuitions can be further refined on the basis of objective information.

Second, since intervention is often directed at the areas of relative weakness in a child's linguistic abilities, it may be helpful to identify what these are and to what extent they are likely to impair the child's ability to communicate in a variety of settings. If a child has a number of areas of weakness, it should be possible to organise these in terms of their significance for functional communication. Alternatively, for a child with generally delayed language, it may be necessary to generate a set of priorities solely in terms of the communicative situations which the child has to deal with on a daily basis.

Third, an assessment should identify those areas of language and communication in which the child has relative strengths. This provides useful information for anyone who needs to address the child as part of a daily routine or anyone who seeks to engage the child in conversation informally. It may also be desirable to use existing, well-established language and communication skills as the basis for teaching weaker or less well-established skills. For example, in discussing the way in which normal children develop language, Slobin (1973) has suggested that new functions are first learned using existing language forms or structures and, conversely, new forms or structures are first used to express well-established functions. This simple 'bootstrapping' approach to language suggests a specific strategy by which teachers and therapists might capitalise on areas of relative competence in order to assist a child in those areas where she is experiencing difficulty.

Theoretical issues in language assessment

Interpreting assessment information

The underlying rationale for any psychological or linguistic assessment is that it provides objective evidence which can be appropriately interpreted and evaluated. Most assessment procedures are developed in order to provide a particular kind of interpretation and because of this the criteria against which the child's language will be evaluated are implicit in the procedure. An interpretation of a child's language will be derived from some comparison between the child's actual language and a descriptive framework incorporated within the assessment procedure. Because the basis for making comparisons is not always made explicit, it may be helpful to discuss two kinds of descriptive framework which are frequently employed in assessment procedures.

First, it is possible to generate descriptions of the kinds of language which would be helpful to a child in particular situations. For example, it might be suggested that a child with severe learning difficulties would benefit if she were able to communicate simple requests, such as asking for a drink or indicating a need to use the toilet. The precise mechanisms employed for signalling these needs might be determined on the basis of the child's existing behavioural and linguistic abilities, without reference to the conventional forms used to express such requests or to 'normal' communication strategies. For an older child with articulation difficulties, it might be suggested that communication would be enhanced if the child's speech were more easily intelligible. Therapy designed to increase clarity of articulation might therefore involve teaching a child to make phonemic contrasts which are not normally associated with phonological development (Ingram 1976).

Such situationally based or functional descriptions are clearly important in determining the focus of any therapeutic intervention, but they also have limitations. For example, on the basis of an approach concerned with the adequacy of communication in different situations, all children and many adults might be assessed as having language difficulties. A normal child of 3 is far from being a completely effective language user, and yet it would be inappropriate to target that child for therapy. Some other form of comparison is therefore necessary to indicate the *extent* to which a child is experiencing difficulties.

Second, many assessment procedures are based on an implicit comparison between the language of the child being assessed and the language of normally developing children of a similar age. Here, it is assumed that the severity of any language problem is indicated by the extent to which a child's language differs from that found among other children of a similar age. This line of reasoning then raises the question of what might be regarded as an accurate description of the language of ordinary children at different ages. After all, normal children, who are not identified as having language problems, show considerable variation with respect to the overall speed of language development and in terms of the relationship between the structural, semantic and functional features (Brown 1973; Lieven 1978; Nelson 1973).

Developmental norms

Developmental norms are an attempt to provide an indication of the ages at which one might expect ordinary children to show evidence of certain skills or abilities. Since children vary with respect to the ages at which they demonstrate any particular behaviour, norms represent an 'average' obtained from an examination of the developmental changes occurring in a large number of children. Data from a large sample will show the earliest age at which a child would be expected to gain control of a particular aspect of language, and the age by which 90 per cent or 95 per cent of non-handicapped children might be expected to show evidence of the same ability. If children who have already been diagnosed as suffering from some specific handicapping condition are included, the data will show the expected age delay before this group matches the performance of the normally developing children.

Significant age norms may be identified on the basis of the age at which most children first demonstrate a particular linguistic skill. For language skills which are first seen to occur in children of very different ages, it may be more helpful to choose the age by which a given percentage (for example, 50 per cent) of the total sample has shown evidence of that skill. However, the average figure would need to be interpreted in the knowledge that substantial age variations were in fact a part of the 'normal pattern'. For more detailed information on the age norms for a number of structural, semantic and functional features, the reader is referred to Bloom and Lahey (1978) and Miller (1981a).

Any subsequent comparison of an individual child with the age norms will indicate the extent to which that child's performance is consistent with the performance of most other children and, if there is a discrepancy, an indication of the time-gap involved.

One obvious problem in establishing and using age norms is that, for any given child, it is not easy to be precise about when any specific skill has been mastered. A child's linguistic performance may vary from day to day and even from hour to hour. Detection of small but important changes may also be dependent upon the knowledge and sensitivity of the adult observer. For example, if we were to ask 'When do children first become able to use single words?' the immediate response might be: 'It depends on what you mean by single words. Do you want to count idiosyncratic words, phonologically constant forms or only utterances which are clearly recognisable as conventional words?'

Since children's linguistic performance varies across situations, it is particularly important that the conditions associated with the collection of the data for the age norms are repeated as closely as possible when an individual child is assessed. How far this is possible depends to a great extent on the quality of the instructions accompanying the assessment procedure. However, even when this is achieved, there may still be problems in interpreting what this information means.

Structure, meaning and function in language assessment

The first three chapters suggested that there are three main levels of linguistic description; structure, meaning and functional characteristics. Structural descriptions are concerned with the realisation of meaning through the organisation of speech sounds and subsume grammatical descriptions at the level of phonology, morphology and syntax. Descriptions which focus on meaning are concerned with the way in which conceptual understanding is expressed in language and functional descriptions are concerned with the relationship between language and the social context in which it occurs. Speech-act theory offers a way of integrating these different levels of description and, in doing so, emphasises that any utterance is amenable to description and analysis at each of these levels.

As ordinary, non-handicapped children develop, the three aspects of language are co-ordinated, to a considerable degree, so that changes in one are associated with changes in the other two. Similarly, difficulties with respect to one of these aspects of language are likely to be associated with difficulties in the other areas. While it is true that different assessment procedures usually focus on one or other of these different aspects of language, this is a reflection on the recent history of psycholinguistic research and ought not be taken to imply that assessment is best carried out by focusing on discrete areas. Indeed, the development of a set of assessment procedures which integrate structural, semantic and functional descriptions of language is perhaps the next major focus for clinical research. In the meantime, the task for the teacher or therapist is to examine all aspects of the child's language, using whatever devices are available, with the objective of generating an assessment which reflects both strengths and weaknesses in the three areas, and indicates the extent to which difficulties identified in each of these areas may or may not be interrelated.

Competence and performance

One of the major distinctions between the different approaches to language description already discussed concerns the extent to which it is deemed appropriate to regard language behaviour as being a reflection of an underlying knowledge base. Traditional behavioural formulations have regarded spoken language as the minimal units for any form of analysis. Increasingly detailed levels of analysis might therefore be concerned with the patterning of sounds within words or, alternatively, with the relationship of words to other words or of words and sentences to the surrounding context (Skinner 1957). In direct contrast to this emphasis on the *surface* features of language, Chomsky (1959) argued that the complexity of grammar indicated that language users have a sophisticated understanding of a rule system and that any description must be concerned with a speaker's knowledge of these rules. According to Chomsky's formulation, speech and, indeed, writing are examples of **language performance.** In contrast, the knowledge of the rule system, which an individual needs in order to be able to produce and understand grammatical sentences, is referred to as **language competence.** This differentiation of competence and performance is necessary, since ordinary speech is frequently ungrammatical, while adults and children are well able to demonstrate knowledge of linguistic rules by distinguishing between grammatical, anomalous and ungrammatical word strings (Chapter 7). Thus, what people seem to know about grammar is not always reflected in the language they use. Chomsky's explanation for this apparent contradiction is that, during the process of production, grammatical knowledge is imperfectly translated into speech because of memory constraints and fluctuating attention.

The competence–performance distinction is maintained in contemporary approaches to language description (see Chapter 1). It is also reflected in both the nativistic and the interactionist accounts of language development (see Chapter 5).

The approaches to gathering linguistic information described in the next chapter are all based on the assumption that it is possible to sample a child's language and that, under certain conditions, this will provide a useful indication of the child's linguistic ability in other situations. Such an assumption requires the invocation of additional processes to explain precisely how what a child does or does not do in one setting might be related to the child's performance in a different setting.

Conventionally, this problem has two solutions. The first is to argue that the elicitation procedures used in language assessment provide examples of language behaviour, which is determined by the child's previous learning experiences within similar situations. Any inferences regarding the applicability of the assessment information to other settings will be based upon the notion of generalisation – that is, an analysis of the inferred or observed similarities between the stimulus conditions obtaining in the assessment procedure and those which are present in other naturally occurring settings.

The second solution is to regard linguistic knowledge or competence as a characteristic of the individual child. It is then assumed that if the child demonstrates a knowledge of the rules for producing or comprehending language in one setting, that knowledge will be transported with the child to any other setting and will be available for deployment in communicative interactions.

These two explanations of the relationship between language produced in assessment settings and language in other everyday situations suffer from fairly obvious limitations. In the first explanation there is too little attention paid to the role of the child as the mediator between environmental stimuli and language use. Conversely, in the second account, there is too much emphasis on individual knowledge and too little emphasis given to the way in which individual abilities vary as a function of the social and physical context. In spite of these criticisms, these two explanations are frequently implicit in the conduct of language assessments. Part of the reason for this is that they make the interpretation of information derived from assessments unproblematical. For example, if language difficulties identified from an assessment can be described in terms of a functional analysis, and an environmental deficit, remedial procedures might be directed at rearranging the contingencies in the child's natural environment. Alternatively, if language problems are seen in terms of the child's limited understanding of the rule system, this, in turn, might lead on to a programme of intervention designed to teach the child more about the rules assumed to underlie language use. This could be carried out in the school, the clinic or the child's home. Since the assumption is that the child will carry around any new linguistic knowledge, there will be no need to take any account of the environment within which the teaching takes place.

One reason why these two interpretations are commonplace is that, until recently, there has been no clearly articulated theoretical position which offered a viable alternative. However, there is now a growing body of research literature which emphasises the interdependence of both individual and social influences on language use (Austin 1962; Searle 1969; Vygotsky 1962, 1978).

Within this framework, language may be conceived of as a process which arises from the social interaction of individuals; it is neither a skill possessed by individuals nor simply a reflection of environmental influences. Of course, individuals do become fluent in the exercise of language within a number of very different contexts and some of these may not, at first sight, appear to be social. For example, writing a letter or reading a book may appear to be solitary activities in which individuals exercise personal skills. But in order for these activities to be meaningful, they must be understood as communicative processes between people, and the individuals concerned must be able to construct social contexts within which their reading and writing activities can have meaning.

This interactionist approach to language description has resulted in an emphasis upon functionally based descriptions (see Chapter 5). It is therefore important to examine methods of language assessment in terms of the interaction between individual abilities and contextual influences on performance.

Chapter seven

Sources of linguistic information

Introduction

Normally developing children often seem to be inexhaustible sources of spoken language; they seem to relish their developing abilities and to use them on every possible occasion. However, the situation immediately becomes more complicated when an attempt is made to determine precisely what language a child is capable of producing, how much a child understands, and, if the child appears to be experiencing difficulties, just where these difficulties lie.

The central problem is that it is only ever possible to sample a child's language over a fixed period of time and within a finite number of situations. However, development is never static, and therefore an assessment at one point in time is an artificially frozen 'snapshot' of a dynamic process.

Second, when making an assessment, information about what a child is able to do in one situation must necessarily form the basis of inferences about what a child might be able to do in other situations. For example, we might draw the inference that a child who is able to name a picture of a boat, while looking at a picture book with her mother, will be able to name it on any other occasion; the child 'knows the meaning of the word boat'. However, it will never be possible to test the validity of this conclusion, since 'knowing the meaning of a word' implies being able to use that word in an infinite number of possible situations. It may be that the child only recognises a particular picture in a particular book as an appropriate context for the word 'boat'; or she may be able to recognise sailing boats but not canoes and motor boats. Thus, one of the problems of language assessment becomes how to make a fair estimate of the child's language ability, given evidence from a very restricted set of situations.

There are two ways in which researchers and clinicians have attempted to solve this problem. The first involves designing special procedures for eliciting language from a child and the second involves sampling the language produced by the child under ordinary, everyday settings. Elicitation procedures make it possible to examine a very broad spectrum of linguistic abilities in a systematic manner over a relatively short period of time. However, they are limited in that they create artificial contexts which may not provide a good basis for predicting performance in other settings. Second, elicitation procedures suffer from difficulties in interpreting what 'no response' means. On the one hand, it may be indicative of the absence of a particular linguistic ability while, alternatively, it may be explained by influences unrelated to linguistic ability, such as lapses in attention, boredom or a failure to understand instructions.

Sampling language from a range of everyday settings overcomes the problem of the artificiality of elicitation procedures. However, the information collected will be determined by the situations and activities in which the child is engaged during the period of time being sampled. Some linguistic abilities may not be detected, not because the child is not able to demonstrate them, but simply because the occasion did not arise where they were required. This chapter will consider a number of elicitation strategies before turning to the procedures for collecting language samples in everyday settings.

Elicitation procedures

An elicitation procedure is designed to provide a child with the opportunity to respond to a specific set of stimuli; the relationship between a stimulus and the child's response is then taken as an indication of the child's mastery of a particular aspect of language. There are two types of elicitation procedure; the first involves the child in making a non-verbal response to a verbal stimulus and is used as a measure of the child's comprehension of spoken language. The second requires the child to make a verbal response to either a verbal or a non-verbal stimulus and is used as a measure of the child's ability to produce spoken language.

Eliciting stimulus	Child's response	Language area sampled
Verbal	Non-verbal	Comprehension
Verbal or non-verbal	Verbal	Production

Elicitation procedures for language comprehension

Elicitation procedures which measure a child's comprehension of spoken language generally only require a relatively simple response. This might involve the child in selecting a picture or an object from an array to match the word or words spoken by the teacher or therapist. For example, in the British Picture Vocabulary Test, the child is required to point manually or to eye-point to indicate her selection from a set of pictures. This simplifies the response aspect of the task and makes it more likely that errors will be the result of difficulties in understanding the verbal stimulus, rather than problems in signalling what has been understood. Balanced against these advantages is the limitation that a pre-selected array inevitably increases the chances of the child guessing the correct answer. Given a two-choice array, there is a 50 per cent possibility of a correct response occurring by chance, while with a four-choice array there is only a 25 per cent chance of a random response being correct.

Some comprehension elicitation procedures involve the child in manipulating simple toys. For example, during the administration of the Reynell Developmental Language Scales, the child is told, 'The doll sits in the chair. Show me the doll in the chair' and, 'The spoon goes in the cup. Show me the spoon and the cup.' When using these procedures, there is obviously the danger that the materials themselves will invite the child to perform certain actions (the spoon naturally goes in the cup), irrespective of whether or not the child understands the instructions. On the other hand, instructions which require the child to perform unusual or bizarre actions may simply result in hesitation or confusion, even though the child may have understood the language used.

With items concerned with grammatical relations, the verbal stimulus may be more complex and the choices presented in the stimulus array will be designed to reflect specific aspects of grammatical knowledge. For example, M. Harris (1986) describes a strategy for assessing a child's understanding of number markers. Four different number markers were presented in sentence pairs:

Demonstratives: 'This sheep jumped'; 'These sheep jumped.'
Regular nouns: 'The girl jumped'; 'The girls jumped.'
Auxiliary verbs: 'The sheep is jumping'; 'The sheep are jumping.'
Third-person regular present tense verbs: 'The sheep jumps'; 'The sheep jump.'

Each sentence was presented in conjunction with two pictures, one of which depicted the singular version of the sentence and one the plural. The child's task was to point to the picture which correctly depicted what was described in the sentences.

Elicitation procedures for language production

Perhaps the simplest procedure for eliciting spoken language is to require the child to imitate a model provided by the adult. This has the advantage of establishing a high degree of control over the target utterance and, if the child is co-operating, it is possible to make a direct comparison between the utterance the child was attempting to produce and what the child actually said.

Unfortunately, imitation makes special demands upon the child's pragmatic skills and may not, therefore, always provide an accurate indication of the child's ability to produce language spontaneously (Ingram 1974) or of the child's underlying linguistic competence (Slobin and Welsh 1973). Moreover, the effects of imitation on performance seem to differ with respect to phonological abilities and grammatical abilities.

Ingram reported that for children with phonological disorders, imitation tasks lead to fewer errors compared to spontaneous speech. He suggests that whereas spontaneous speech invokes the child's own realisation rules, imitation does not. Fraser *et al.* (1973) also argued that grammatical errors were less frequent and less systematic within an imitation task, compared to an activity in which a child was required to match a sentence to a picture and say the sentence. Like Ingram, they concluded that imitation is predominantly a perceptuo-motor task which is not influenced by the child's understanding of meaning.

In contrast to these results, Slobin and Welsh found that a child was able to imitate one of her own utterances immediately after she had produced it spontaneously, but that errors occurred when the child was asked to imitate the same utterance some minutes later. They suggest that production is supported by conceptual knowledge and the intention to communicate. In the absence of intentional communication, as is the case with imitation tasks, the child is restricted to a linguistic analysis of the target utterance without any contextual support. Slobin and Welsh argue that this actually makes imitations of phrases and sentences more complex tasks than spontaneous production. On this basis imitation tasks ought to be regarded as giving a conservative estimate of the child's grammatical knowledge.

Consistent with this interpretation is the finding that some errors in imitation are a result of the child trying to understand the meaning of the target utterance and then encoding the meaning according to the child's own grammatical system. For example, Slobin and Welsh report a child being asked to imitate, 'This is the giant, but this one is little' and saying, 'Dis one little, annat one big.'

Thus, while imitation tasks appear to provide a simple and direct way of assessing a child's linguistic ability, the interpretation of children's performance on imitation tasks is far from simple. It may be possible to target specific phonemes to assess articulation but the child's performance is likely to be somewhat better than during spontaneous speech. On the other hand, requiring the child to reproduce phrases and sentences may lead to a lower level of performance as the child seeks to make sense of the adult constructions and in doing so reinterprets them through her own emerging system of grammatical rules.

In addition to imitation, there are a number of other procedures designed to give the teacher or therapist some degree of control over the child's language production. These include sentence-completion tasks, the use of puppets and role playing (Miller 1981b).

The main advantage of elicitation procedures is that they give a relatively high degree of control over areas of linguistic ability which are being assessed. Furthermore, because the child is provided with simplified situations which have been specifically designed to help the child understand what is required, it might be argued that elicitation procedures should provide an optimal measure of performance. Balanced against this is the problem that these procedures are likely to involve the child in unusual activities with strange people; they may not, therefore, provide an accurate picture of what children are able to do under more natural and relaxed conditions. Of particular importance is the fact that all these procedures impose considerable constraints on the pragmatic and conversational aspects of the child's language production, and as yet little is known about how this may interact with measures of grammar and meaning. Whatever measures are derived from a structured task, we are still likely to be left wondering how they relate to the language the child uses in everyday settings and it is to a consideration of procedures for sampling naturalistic language production that we now turn.

Naturalistic language samples

The rationale for trying to obtain verbatim records of children's speech in naturalistic settings is that it provides the best indication of what language a child actually uses in ordinary, everyday settings. In the past, samples of children's language have been collected using a diary approach where examples of children's utterances, together with a description of the surrounding context, were simply written down over a period of weeks or months (Miller 1981a). This is a time-consuming activity and obviously susceptible to human fallibility. However, diaries kept by parents can produce valuable information and also help parents to see themselves as active partners in the assessment process. Miller suggested that parents focus on five aspects of language and communication:

1 the sounds and words the child produces;
2 whether or not the child's sounds or words are imitations;
3 whether or not the child's words are addressed to another person;
4 why the child said a word or phrase;

5 what is happening in the immediate surroundings when the word is produced.

Since the advent of electronic recording, examples of children's language in ordinary settings can be made using audio or audio-visual recorders. Consequently, the language of the child and others addressing the child can be coded or transcribed. The procedure for collecting language samples in this way can be considered under four headings: recording equipment; sampling children's language; observer effects; and transcription.

Recording equipment

Although video recordings may have a strong appeal, in so far as they appear to capture a more complete picture of any speech episode, they have major disadvantages in that they are highly obtrusive, they usually need to be manned and they are relatively cumbersome if the child has to be followed around. Tape recorders, on the other hand, are relatively small and can therefore be placed in position where they will not attract much attention. Furthermore, if necessary they can be left unattended. The major disadvantage with audio recorders is that a great deal of contextual information is not recorded and therefore, unless some other method of recording the context, such as note-taking, is employed, it may not be possible to recover a 'rich interpretation' of the child's language. The decision to use a video recorder or an audio recorder will depend upon a number of considerations, including the reason for making the recording, the data which the teacher or therapist hopes to recover and the resources available for making recordings and for coding and/or transcribing.

Recordings of one child with one adult may be made using a domestic tape recorder and a standard microphone. However, if it is necessary to follow the child around from one room to another, or if it is desirable to record a child with other children or with more than one adult present, then it is advisable to use a radio microphone which can be attached to the child's clothing. This will ensure that a relatively good recording of the child's language will be obtained, together with a fair amount of the language of the other people. If it is particularly important to record the language of two or more people in a group (for example, a teacher and a pupil in a classroom), then it is better to use two radio microphones transmitting on different frequencies and with the two signals fed through a sound mixer before being recorded. A cheap alternative to a radio microphone that produces acceptable recordings of one speaker is to use a small tape recorder attached to a tie-clip microphone. In either case, it will be necessary to attach a small microphone somewhere below the child's chin and to provide some arrangement for the child to carry around the radio transmitter or the small tape recorder.

Sampling children's language

Before any recording is undertaken it will be necessary to obtain the co-operation of the child's parents and teachers. This ought not to present any problems, although it is probably a good idea to emphasise the importance of the child's language and to try to reduce any anxiety or embarrassment that adults might feel at the prospect of being recorded. It is also worthwhile explaining that the recording is intended to capture the child's natural language and that the adults should try to behave as normally as possible and should not make any special efforts to get the child to talk.

The main questions regarding sampling are: under what conditions and for how long? Rather than simply sampling at random, it is helpful to make some preliminary enquiries among the child's parents or teachers regarding the kinds of situations in which she is most likely to talk. Alternatively, it may be considered appropriate to make a series of short recordings in different settings and compare the results. A number of researchers (Hughes *et al.* 1979; Wells 1981) have reported that the amount of talk by children and their caretakers varies, both in respect of the time of day (more talk first thing in the morning and early afternoon) and as a function of their familiarity with the process of being recorded (less talk on the first day, compared with subsequent days). This last point indicates that it is useful to introduce at least one dummy-run to familiarise children and their caretakers with the procedure prior to making the recordings to be used for analysis.

While it is true that the longer the period of time over which the child's language is sampled, the more representative that sample will be of the child's underlying linguistic knowledge, in practical terms the length of any recording will be constrained by the time available for transcription and coding. In general, it is reasonable to assume that a simple transcription in traditional orthography (that is, without using phonemic symbols or a phonetic transcription) will take between four and six times the length of the original recording. Fortunately, there are now a number of assessment instruments designed to utilise spontaneous speech samples, and some of these suggest coding utterances direct from a tape without the need for transcription.

Observer effects

The goal of collecting naturalistic language data is, by definition, to capture a sample of the child's language as it occurs under ordinary, everyday conditions. Inevitably, the very fact that someone has decided to try to record the child's language makes this ideal unattainable. With modern recording equipment and careful preparation, so that all the participants have been acclimatised to the recording procedure, the intrusive effects of recording can be considerably reduced. However, one dilemma remains. In order to be able to understand the child's language, it is usually necessary to have a detailed knowledge of the context within which that language occurred. This can be most easily achieved by an observer who is present while the recording is being made and who can make a full transcription within a few hours. But the presence of an observer is likely to be even more intrusive than the recording equipment, and thus any transcription will fail to reveal natural language.

A number of solutions have been put forward to try and overcome this problem. The most implausible of these simply involves telling the adult caretakers to carry on as normal and to 'do what you would normally do'. In spite of the confidence and frequency with which researchers report this technique, it is easy to imagine the constraints on the behaviour of both adults and children which occur during periods of recording:

> The mother was instructed to remain in two adjoining rooms with the child, to ignore the observer, and to avoid having visitors, telephone calls, or the television on during the observation. The observer, equipped with a cassette tape-recorder, earphone and coding sheets, stationed himself so that he could observe the mother–child interaction in either of the two adjoining rooms.
>
> (Forehand and Peed 1979, cited in P. J. Harris 1986:173–4)

An alternative is to try and utilise the participating adults as observers who might subsequently be able to provide sufficient contextual detail to support interpretations of the transcribed speech. This involves either going through the transcript with the child's caretakers and inviting comments and interpretations on specific utterances, or playing the recording back and making detailed notes about movements and activities of the participants during the recording period. Although this procedure removes the contamination of the observer, it is far from clear to what extent adults are able to reconstruct the context of their previous linguistic encounters with children, and how far *post hoc* interpretations regarding what was said and what was meant are subject to distortion.

These limitations and practical difficulties do not remove the value of recording children's speech in relatively natural settings; they do, however, emphasise that it is extremely difficult to obtain objective and accurate information on which to base an assessment of a child's linguistic abilities.

Transcription

The purpose of preparing a transcript is to present, in print, as complete a record of the taped material as is required for the particular assessment: 'It provides the foundation of all subsequent analyses and, as such, its importance cannot be over estimated' (Crystal 1984). At one extreme, it is possible to try to commit everything on the tape to paper. This would include at least the following:

1 a transcription of everything the child said, using phonemic symbols to represent non-conventional pronunciations and unintelligible vocalisations;
2 a gloss in traditional orthography of the observer's interpretation of what a child intended to say;
3 a transcription of any adult utterances;
4 a detailed account of the non-linguistic context surrounding each utterance.

Crystal (1984) makes a strong case for providing a detailed transcription of the language of all those who are candidates for assessment. He argues that, given our present state of ignorance regarding the classification of linguistic disorders, descriptive detail is necessary, both as a prelude to intervention and in order to increase our basic understanding of language development. Since language is a coherent system, it is important not simply to focus upon specific areas which, at first glance, suggest errors, but to examine the whole system in the expectation of discovering interrelationships between the different levels of linguistic functioning. To this end, he recommends that transcripts be used as the starting-point for the generation of assessments which address structural, semantic and functional language characteristics.

In spite of this ideal, for most of us time is short and the benefits of an exhaustive transcription of recorded speech must be balanced against other professional commitments. It may, therefore, be expedient on certain occasions to utilise taped material in a more selective manner. For example, an assessment of a child's command of phonology may focus on the child's use of certain problematic contrasting phonemes, and it may only be necessary to transcribe phonemically those words in which particular contrasts normally occur. Similarly, if there are good reasons to target the assessment of the child's command of specific grammatical structures or certain functional aspects of language, it may be sufficient to scan a tape for examples of these structures or functions, or for contexts in which they might reasonably be expected to occur. It may also be helpful to consider analysing transcripts using well-established procedures. A selection of these is considered in the next section.

Procedures for the analysis of transcripts

Mean Length of Utterance

In Chapter 1 it was suggested that Mean Length of Utterance (MLU) measured in morphemes provides a useful summary of the normal child's

Figure 7.1 Conventions for transcription of naturalistic speech

Layout

These transcripts need to be written on A3 paper, using one side only. The page is divided into three columns measuring approximately 6 inches, 6 inches and 4 inches. Column 1 is used for the teacher's utterances; Column 2 is used for the children's utterances; and Column 3 is used for comments on context or any additional information which will help to convey perceived meaning. Utterances will usually follow in sequence, left to right. Successive utterances by one speaker will begin on new lines in the appropriate columns. Each utterance begins on a new line.

Indicate target child by child's initial in brackets at beginning of each utterance. Other children may be indicated by distinctive letter or initial in brackets or, where discrimination between other children is not possible, by (X). If more than one adult is involved, use T1, T2, T3, etc., as necessary.

Segmenting utterances

The main unit of analysis is the utterance. Utterances may be defined in relation to grammatical marking, intonation, pauses and conversational turns. While it is difficult to provide a good definition of an utterance, most people have a good subjective appreciation of what constitutes a separate utterance, and it is possible to obtain high inter-rater reliability. The following guidelines should be used in cases of uncertainty:

1 Elliptical and incomplete clauses should be counted as separate utterances, e.g. 'In the morning', 'I thought I'd —', 'Perhaps'.
2 'Yes' and 'no' are treated as utterances unless they simply reinforce the positive or negative meaning of the utterance which follows without intonation or pauses to indicate distinctiveness, e.g. 'Yes, I can' (= one utterance), 'Yes, I'll be ready in five minutes' (= two utterances).
3 Clauses introduced by 'and' should be treated as separate utterances *unless* the 'and' expresses a *logical* relationship between clauses and intonation and pauses confirm the 'single-utterance' interpretation. Where 'and' links two clauses in which one constituent is deleted in the second clause (e.g. 'Tomorrow John is going swimming and I'm going fishing') transcribe as one utterance.
4 'Mm', 'oh', 'ssh', 'well', etc., are treated as separate utterances when they have specific functions of responses, commands, or exclamations. Otherwise, they should be included in the utterances they introduce.
5 'Look' is counted as a separate utterance when it is a command to pay attention to something particular, such as what the child is doing. When it is an emphatic device linked to a clause (e.g. 'Look, I've told you already . . .') 'look' is not counted as a separate utterance. Again, intonation and pauses may help to disambiguate specific items.

Conventions for transcribing

1 In general, standard English orthography will be used for transcription. However, phonetic symbols may be helpful in the following cases:

  (a) where one or more words are clearly heard as a string but no meaning can be attached;

(b) where a word such as a preposition or article would normally be expected but the sound does not allow discrimination to be made, e.g. 'Sweet /a/ you Mummy' (where /a/ could be 'to' or 'for'). Always enclose phonetic symbols between diagonal slashes.

2 Where intended meaning may not be apparent from the transcription, always provide an interpretative gloss.

3 Pauses to be identified with dots (....) where one dot equals one second. This can easily be achieved by counting 'one and, two and, three and', etc. For longer pauses a digit may also be included, e.g. '...10...' (= 10-second pause).

4 Alternative interpretations of words or phrases are to be included in round brackets ( ) immediately after the word(s) to which they apply.

5 Unintelligible utterances are to be indicated by * where the number of asterisks corresponds as closely as possible to the number of words which cannot be interpreted.

6 Where both participants speak together, indicate overlapping portions of each utterance with one-line underlining.

Punctuation

?	Used at end of any utterance where interrogative (questioning) meaning is intended.
!	Used following utterance considered to have exclamatory intention.
'	Used for contractions and ellision of syllables.
CAPS	For any part of utterance which receives unusually heavy stress to carry emphasis or contrastive meaning.
⌒	Slur mark indicates unbroken intonation contour where a pause or clause boundary might otherwise indicate the end of an utterance.

Source: Based on Wells and Harrison (1979).

mastery of grammatical structure. Brown (1973) provided the first set of guidelines to be widely adopted for the calculation of MLU, thus making it possible to use this measure as a basis for comparing language performance across children. The instructions for calculating MLU listed below are those originally proposed by Brown with some minor adjustments introduced by Chapman (1981).

The Mean Length of Utterance is found by dividing the number of morphemes, in a consecutive sequence of utterances from a speaker, by the total number of utterances. Thus, the longer the utterances are on average, the higher will be the MLU. At this point it may be noted that there is no completely satisfactory definition of 'an utterance'. However, listener's intuitions based upon such cues as pauses, intonation and stress contours and turns within a conversation are normally reliable. Morphemes may be identified on the basis of the following rules.

1 Begin with the first page of the transcript and count the first 50 utterances which fulfil the following conditions:

Figure 7.2 Example of transcribed audio recording of adult–child conversation.

Jamie is a 9-year-old child with Down's Syndrome. The recording was made with a radio microphone during an ordinary school day. In this brief extract, Jamie is sitting on the floor and the teacher is trying to persuade him to come and sit down at a table to look at some picture cards.

Teacher's Utterances		*Children's Utterances*	
(T)	We'll have a look at some cards		
(T)	Have a look at some cards with me?		
		(c)	Ye'
(T)	Um		
(T)	'Cos you're a very good boy, aren't you?		
		(c)	Ye'
(T)	You can work very hard		
		(c)	I Know
		(c)	****
		(c)	**fire*
(T)	Should you throw * in the fire?		
		(c)	Ye'
(T)	Ah		
		(c)	I * tomorrow
(T)	Have another one tomorrow		
		(c)	**** (to tie it/look?)
(T)	Where are you going tomorrow then?		
(T)	Where are you going tomorrow then, Jamie?		
		(c)	Ye'
(T)	Where are you going?		
		(c)	*Shopping*
(T)	*Shopping*		
		(c)	**
(T)	Where?		
		(c)	Aberdare
(T)	To Aberdare . . .		
	How are you going to Aberdare?		
		(c)	**
(T)	That's Dominic, Alexandra and * going		
		(c)	* Picnic
(T)	You're going for a picnic		
(T)	Where?		
		(c)	Aberdare
(T)	In Aberdare Park		
(T)	You're lucky	(c)	Yer
		(c)	** come ** picnic
(T)	I,		
(T)	Yes,		
(T)	I'd love to come and have a picnic . . .		
		(c)	How far
(T)	How far what?		
		(c)	Ye'
(T)	Claire and Dominic and Alexandra too		
		(c)	Ye'
(T)	All right then		
(T)	We'll have a look at some cards now		
		(c)	****
(T)	We'll have a look at some cards now, all right?		
		(c)	Um
		(c)	*

Note: Figure 7.1 provides a summary of the main procedures involved in making a transcript of an audio recording of a child's language. An extract of a transcribed recording of a teacher with a young mentally handicapped child is given in Figure 7.2.

Table 7.1 Stages in early grammatical development: MLU and Upper Bound

	MLU	Upper Bound
Stage 1	1.0 – 2.0	5
Stage 2	2.0 – 2.5	7
Stage 3	2.5 – 3.0	9
Stage 4	3.0 – 3.5	11
Stage 5	3.5 – 4.0	13

Source: Brown (1973).

(a) Use only fully transcribed utterances.
(b) Include all full repetitions, but not hesitations and stutters preceding a final pronunciation of a word.
(c) Do not include fillers, such as 'mm', 'oh', but do count 'no', 'yeh', and 'hi', as separate morphemes.

2 Count as single morphemes:

(a) Compound words such as 'birthday' and 'milkman'.
(b) Irregular past tense verbs.
(c) Diminutive forms such as 'doggy' and 'mummy'.
(d) All auxiliaries such as 'have', 'can', 'will', 'would', 'must'.
(e) Catenatives such as 'gonna', 'wanna', and 'hafto'.
(f) Inflections such as possessive (s), plural (s), third-person singular (s), regular past (ed) and progressive (ing).

A second measure which Brown and his colleagues found useful was the length of the longest utterance in a speech sample, referred to as the 'Upper Bound'. Together, Brown argues, these two measures provide a reasonably accurate picture of grammatical complexity until MLU reaches 4.0 (Brown 1973).

MLU was used by Brown as a basis for dividing early language development into a series of stages. As he admits, the divisions are arbitrary, but they have the advantage of making it possible to refer easily to the level of grammatical complexity in a speech sample, and to group children on the basis of language complexity. It is mainly for these reasons that MLU and the stages identified by Brown have subsequently found such wide acceptance among academic researchers and practitioners (see Table 7.1). However, it is worth emphasising that the stages and the measures on which they are based are derived from a grammatical description and that, in the case of children with language difficulties, it cannot be assumed that structurally based measures are predictive of functional skills (Blank *et al.* 1979).

Taking this approach one step further, Miller (1981a) has provided a table which details the relationship between age and MLU to be expected in

Table 7.2 Predicted MLUs for normally developing children

Age (within 1 month)	Predicted MLU	Predicted MLU range
18	1.31	0.99 – 1.64
21	1.62	1.23 – 2.01
24	1.92	1.47 – 2.37
30	2.54	1.97 – 3.11
33	2.85	2.22 – 3.48
36	3.16	2.47 – 3.85
39	3.47	2.71 – 4.23
42	3.78	2.96 – 4.60
45	4.09	3.21 – 4.97
48	4.40	3.46 – 5.34
51	4.71	3.71 – 5.71
54	5.02	3.96 – 6.08
57	5.32	4.20 – 6.45
60	5.63	4.44 – 6.82

Source: Miller (1981a)

normally developing children for each three-month interval from 18 months to 5 years of age (see Table 7.2). Since chronological age and MLU do not correspond perfectly, the table includes an indication of the range of MLU scores to be expected in children developing normally. This gives the range of MLU scores which accounted for the middle two-thirds of the 123 children studied at each age level. In other words, a child with an MLU which falls below the bottom of this range is relatively unusual in so far as her MLU is lower than about 85 per cent of ordinary children. In conjunction with other evidence, this kind of statistical information can be extremely useful in communicating with parents and other professionals, and in making decisions about further assessment and in designing treatment programmes.

Miller comments that in the case of children with learning difficulties, including mentally handicapped children, it may be helpful to calculate mental age using a development test or a standardised test of intelligence and to compare the MLU predicted by chronological age with that predicted using the child's mental age. In particular, use of mental age will indicate the extent to which the child's language is in step with other aspects of social and cognitive functioning.

Language Assessment Remediation and Screening Procedure (LARSP)

This procedure was first introduced by Crystal and his associates in 1976 to provide a structure for the analysis of spontaneous speech transcripts obtained from either children or adults. It aims to provide the teacher or therapist with a profile which represents strengths and weaknesses in respect of syntactic skills, although some consideration is also given to discourse skills (initiations versus responses) and functional speech characteristics, such as the use of commands, statements and questions. Crystal *et al.* recommended that the procedure is applied to spontaneous speech samples of about 30 minutes' duration, although there is no reason why this should not be varied. The analysis begins once the sample has been transcribed.

Analysis is designed to determine how advanced any adult or child is in respect of learning the grammatical rules for the generation of complex sentences.

> The aim of the exercise, then, is to hypothesise a set of syntactic stages through which children pass in their progress towards the adult language, and to classify the structures and categories which operate at each stage, thus providing a *syntactic profile chart* of development.
>
> (Crystal *et al.* 1976:61; original emphasis)

The stages described by Crystal are different from those described by Brown (1973) and are determined by the level of grammatical complexity evident in the transcribed utterances.

Stage 1: Sentences composed of single elements.

Stage 2: Sentences composed of two elements. These may be analysed in terms of sentence structure and in terms of their phrase structure.

Stage 3: Sentences composed of three elements. These may be analysed in terms of sentence structure, phrase structure and clause structure.

Stage 4: Sentences composed of four elements or more, analysed in terms of sentence, clause and phrase structure.

Stage 5: Sentences incorporating recursion – for example, by using co-ordinating conjunctions such as 'and' or 'so'.

Stage 6: Evidence of the full range of grammatical sentences.

At each stage, LARSP seeks to provide a means of establishing how far the child's utterances are consistent with normal development, and to what extent there are gaps in the child's understanding of grammar or evidence of abnormal constructions, which might impair subsequent developmental progress. In order to obtain a profile which summarises the child's grammatical strengths and weaknesses, it is suggested that the teacher or therapist carry out a total of eight scans of the transcript. Each scan deals with separate aspects of the analysis and is recorded on a profile summary sheet:

Scan 1: Identification of unanalysable utterances (for example, those that are unintelligible, those that are onomatopaeic sounds and obviously deviant sentences), incomplete utterances and syntactically ambiguous utterances.

Scan 2: Identification of spontaneous utterances versus responses. Responses are further classified into those which are full, major sentences, elliptical sentences and minor sentences. Spontaneous utterances are divided into those which are 'novel' and those which are self-repetitions.

Scan 3: Identification of sentence connectivity.

Scan 4: Analysis of sentence structure.

Scan 5: Analysis of clause structure.

Scan 6: Analysis of phrase structure.

Scan 7: Analysis of word structure.

Scan 8: Analysis of syntactical problems.

There is no doubt that LARSP provides a useful approach to the description and analysis of linguistic disability. However, there are a number of constraints which are likely to influence anyone considering its use. First, although it may not take very long for a trained and experienced therapist to analyse a transcript using LARSP, the procedure itself is relatively technical and is likely to take some time to learn from scratch (Connolly 1979). Second, LARSP places considerable emphasis on grammar, with relatively little attention to phonology, semantics or functional characteristics of language. While this may not present a problem if the child's difficulty is perceived as one of understanding syntax, it does emphasise the point that, although LARSP is very detailed, it is not necessarily the best assessment for every child. A third point is that the profile indicates the child's ability to control aspects of the emerging adult grammatical system and therefore makes the assumption that, for children, language learning is about the acquisition of that adult system. Chapter 1 discussed the criticisms of this kind of approach and the available research evidence. While this issue is as yet undecided, it is certainly not one which should be forgotten. On the positive side, LARSP does make it possible to summarise an enormous amount of information in a highly principled way, and to generate useful hypotheses about strengths and weaknesses which have direct implications for remedial intervention strategies.

Developmental Sentence Analysis

This is another method of making a gramatically based analysis of recorded speech samples. In fact, Lee (1966, 1974) suggests two related strategies; one referred to as Developmental Sentence Types (DST) is designed to help the teacher or therapist classify pre-sentence utterances, while Developmental Sentence Scoring (DSS) is a method of quantifying the 'grammatical load' which is carried by complete sentences.

Lee suggests that this analysis requires a sample of at least 100 different utterances recorded during a single session. If a child is not able to meet this criterion, then the method is not appropriate. The analysis begins with the

Figure 7.3 Examples of Developmental Sentence Types

Word class	One word	Two words	Three words
Noun	'car', 'daddy'	'a car', 'daddy ball'	'my big car'
Designator	'here', 'these'	'here car', 'what these'	'it my truck'
Descriptive item	'big', 'pretty'	'car there', 'it big'	'car over there'
Verb	'eat','walk'	'hit ball', 'sit chair'	'eat the cookie'
Vocabulary item	'yes', 'hey'	'in car', 'not here'	'in the car'

Source: Adapted from Lee (1974).

separation of the child's speech into separate utterances and, in the case of DSS, into separate sentences. A minimum of 50 complete sentences from the total corpus of 100 utterances is needed for Developmental Sentence Scoring.

The analysis for Developmental Sentence Types involves classifying each utterance in respect of number of words and grammatical category. The grammatical categories selected are shown in Figure 7.3.

From these examples, it can be seen that while the classification of single-word utterances is relatively straightforward, this process becomes much more problematic with two- and three-word utterances. However, Lee has taken considerable trouble to provide detailed instructions and many examples to help clarify this issue. She has also provided some normative information based on a study of 40 normally developing children between the ages of 2 years and 2 years and 11 months.

A similar approach is adopted for the analysis of complete sentences (DSS), with the addition of a quantitative scoring system. Each complete sentence can be scored for the inclusion of nine possible grammatical features. Apart from the first item, which is solely concerned with whether the whole sentence conforms to the rules of the adult grammar, each grammatical feature is assigned a score which reflects its developmental complexity. For example, main verbs – such as 'I *see* you' and 'He *is* coming' – score one point; irregular past verbs – such as *ate* and *saw* – score two; while the use of *have* with a past tense verb ('I've eaten') scores seven points. The eight grammatical features which Lee scores are shown in Figure 7.4, with examples of highest and lowest scoring items. In addition to these categories, Lee suggests that one point be added, to the total score, for every utterance which meets all the grammatical criteria for acceptable adult sentences. The mean Developmental Sentence Score (DSS) is derived by adding the total sentences score for a sample of 50 utterances and dividing the total by 50.

Figure 7.4 Developmental Sentence Scoring

Sentence point:	One point for correct adult grammar	
	Lowest scores	*Highest scores*
Indefinite pronouns or noun modifications	'it', 'this'	'last', 'second', 'third'
Personal pronouns	'me', 'mine'	'own', 'oneself'
Main verb	'I see'	'should have been sleeping'
Secondary verb	'I wanna see' ('I want to see')	'swinging is fun'
Negative	'not mine'	'they aren't big'
Conjunction	'and'	'I know where to go'
Interrogative reversal	'were they there?'	'wouldn't he have been going?'
'Wh' question	'what is he eating?'	'whose car is that?'

Source: Adapted from Lee (1974).

As with the Developmental Sentence Types, Lee provides normative data, from 160 children of normal intelligence between the ages of 2 years 0 months and 6 years 11 months. Indications of language delay may be estimated by comparing actual DSS scores with age group means.

Not surprisingly, Lee reports strong positive correlations between MLU measured by Brown's (1973) formula and DSS scores, and between MLU and the frequency of complete grammatical sentences in a language sample.

While both LARSP and Developmental Sentence Analysis are well-established procedures for assessing a child's command of grammar from transcripts of naturalistic recordings, they are both restricted in the extent to which they provide the teacher or clinician with systematic information on other aspects of a child's linguistic ability. It is therefore necessary to consider other methods of analysing spontaneous speech samples.

Classification of language uses

Building on the work of Halliday (see Chapter 3), Tough (1976, 1977) has provided a set of broad descriptive categories for classifying young children's language uses, together with illustrative strategies 'by which the child reveals the purpose of his talk' (Tough 1976:81). The framework set out in Figure 7.5 is provided by Tough as a guide for teachers when identifying uses of language 'which they are probably already fostering, either intuitively or with some deliberation'.

The seven functional categories presented in Figure 7.5 have been derived empirically from classroom observations and for this reason it is not clear how they match up with Halliday's interpersonal, ideational and textual

Figure 7.5 Children's uses of language

1 Self-maintaining language
  Strategies:
    Referring to physical and psychological needs and wants: 'watch me',
      'watch what I can do'
    Projection of self and self-interests: 'you're hurting me'.
    Justifying behaviour or claims: 'I can have it 'cos I asked first'
    Criticising others: 'I don't like your building, it's silly'
    Threatening others: 'if you don't give it to me I'll hit you'

2 Language for directing behaviour
  Strategies:
    Monitoring own actions: 'turning it around, the lorry's going round'
    Directing the actions of self: 'turn it – it's hard – turn it a bit – a bit and
      take it off like that'
    Directing actions of others: 'you take the lorry over there'
    Collaborating in action with others: 'you cut the paper and I'll stick'

3 Language for reporting past and present experiences
  Strategies:
    Labelling the components of a scene: 'thats a car, there's a bus and
      that's a lorry'
    Referring to detail: 'the little red bus has a little door'
    Referring to incidents: 'that boy's got some bricks and he's piling them
      up'
    Referring to a sequence of events: 'he's put a load on and he's taking it
      over to a building'
    Making comparisons: 'this lorry is bigger than the red bus'
    Recognising related aspects: 'when it goes fast it crashes'
    Making an analysis using several of above features: 'there's three little
      lorries and two big ones but they won't all go in the garage, and that
      one's too big, it'll have to stay outside'
    Extracting the central meaning: 'we're pretending it's an accident'
    Reflecting on the meaning of experiences: 'I like playing with lorries,
      but I don't like that boy banging mine – he's spoiling it'

4 Towards logical reasoning
  Strategies:
    Explaining a process: 'when you break your arm they put something on it
      like a bandage'
    Recognising causal and dependent relationships: 'if the bridge is low
      boats can't go under'
    Recognising problems and their solutions: 'this box isn't big enough to
      make a garage so I'm going to make it with blocks'
    Justifying judgements and actions: 'I'm cutting this box to make doors
      'cos we need doors to put the cars in'
    Reflecting on events and drawing conclusions: 'I don't think we'd
      better take the clock to pieces, we couldn't put it back together'
    Recognising principles: 'I want a bike but I can't have one because it's
      too dangerous on our road'

5 Predicting
   Strategies:
   Anticipating/forecasting: 'I'm going to paint a picture when I've finished my milk'
   Anticipating the detail of actions and events: 'I'm going to make some tarts with jam in, some red and some yellow ones'
   Anticipating a sequence of events: 'I'm going to put some more bricks on that tower and then I'll put this flag on'
   Anticipating problems and possible solutions: 'that brick won't be long enough to go over the road, I'll go and find a piece of wood'
   Anticipating and recognising alternative courses of action: 'we could make a bridge over with a box or we could have a long rope or get a ladder'
   Predicting consequences: 'that propeller will fall off if you can't stick it properly'

6 Projecting
   Strategies:
   Projecting in to the experiences of others: 'he's driving fast in his car and it'll be all windy and cold'
   Projecting into the feelings of others: 'I think he's frightened his mother will be cross'
   Projecting into the reactions of others: 'he'll come and get all the bricks back if we take them'
   Projecting into situations never experienced: 'I would like to be a rabbit living in that cage'

7 Imagining
   Strategies:
   Developing an imaginary situation based on real life: 'I'm the captain of this boat and I don't want you to sail it'
   Developing an imaginary situation based on fantasy: 'there a witch and that's her cat'
   Developing an original story: 'the little boy wanted his mummy but the baddies took him away and he was frightened and he cried'

Source: Tough (1976)

functions (see Chapter 3). However, they have been widely used by Tough and by many of the teachers she has worked with and thus, from a practical point of view, they seem to have been well tried and tested by practitioners.

In spite of the considerable popularity of Tough's framework, she has not subjected the specific strategies to a rigorous examination of reliability and, when other researchers have attempted to replicate her work, they have not always been able to demonstrate good agreement between different observers (Wells 1979). In some ways this is not surprising, given the similarity between many of the strategies described. For example, is the utterance 'It's raining and we'll get wet' an example of reporting and recognising related aspects of experience, or is it an example of recognising causal relationships under logical reasoning? Thus, while Tough's work may provide some interesting ideas for dealing with functional aspects of spontaneous speech, it may be less than entirely satisfactory as a means of obtaining reliable and objective assessment information.

Cognitively based language assessment

While Tough has attempted to provide a set of categories which reflect a broad range of language functions, Blank and her colleagues (Blank 1973; Blank and Franklin 1980; Blank *et al.* 1978) have focused on the relationship between language and higher-level intellectual processes. In particular, they are concerned with those aspects of language which are implicated in observation, identification of attributes, classification, anticipation, and inductive and deductive reasoning (Blank *et al.* 1978). They provide a set of descriptive categories, many of which are similar to some of those presented by Tough. However, Blank's categories differ in two distinct ways. First, they represent a putative developmental sequence which reflects the child's gradual mastery of language for dealing with abstract ideas and, second, they have been shown to generate high levels of inter-observer agreement (Blank and Franklin 1980) (see Table 7.3).

Developmental charts and checklists

Developmental charts and checklists are an attempt to provide a simple, non-technical procedure for gathering information about a child's language. The charts are composed of a list of items, each of which describes a specific linguistic skill or ability. The items may be grouped into sections dealing with similar aspects of language – for example, items concerned with vocabulary – or they may be ordered in terms of a putative developmental sequence.

The teacher or therapist is required to indicate whether or not each item characterises the target child. In some charts a distinction is made, in terms of the reliability of the child's performance, so that the practitioner is required to indicate whether the child regularly demonstrates the particular skill or only sometimes. Thus, the child's language is not sampled directly but, as it were, by proxy in terms of what the teacher or therapist is able to recall of the child's performance under everyday conditions. The accuracy of the assessment therefore depends upon the observational skills of the person completing the checklist.

In practical terms, a checklist may take only a very short time to complete, providing that the teacher or therapist is familiar with the child being assessed. Checklists are not appropriate for people who do not have intimate knowledge of a child over a period of some weeks. Similarly, checklists completed by a teacher may not provide reliable information with respect

Table 7.3 Coding utterances on a scale of 'abstraction'

Sample processes	Examples of utterances
Level 1 Matching experience	
(a) Identifying objects by sight, sound, or touch	that's a car' (upon hearing a car)
(b) Imitating utterances of other speakers	'it's all right' (after someone has just said that phrase)
(c) Labelling actions or events	'she's sitting.'
(d) Employing social routines	'bye-bye'
(e) Requesting attention	'Mommy'
(f) Requesting desired objects	'I want a cookie'
Level 2 Selective analysis of experience	
(a) Noting attributes	'I want a blue ball'
(b) Noting possession	'this is daddy's letter'
(c) Noting location	'it's in the drawer'
(d) Comparing objects	'this doll is prettier than this one'
(e) Identifying the function of objects	'what can you use to cut things?'
(f) Integrating objects, actions, and events	'she is sitting on the grass'
Level 3 Reordering experience	
(a) Sequencing material or events	'I'll put this one first and then this one second'
(b) Defining objects or events by exclusion	'what else could we do besides go to the park?'
(c) Role-taking	'what would you say if you were a tiny rabbit?'
(d) Establishing conditional relationships (that are not causally related)	'he finished his lunch, so he can have a cookie'
(e) Talking about language (metalinguistics)	'I wonder if you can tell me what *shortcake* means?'
(f) Formulating a generalisation about a set of events (similarity)	'they're all so soft' (touching cotton, wool, a blanket, and velvet)
(g) Describing social conventions	'it's impolite to sing at the table; the table is a place for conversations'
Level 4 Reasoning about experience	
(a) Formulating a solution to a problem	'how could we find out if the store is open?'
(b) Justifying a decision	'you only need one spoon of syrup 'cos it's a small glass'
(c) Identifying the causes of an event	'the bus is going slow 'cos there's too much traffic in the way'
(d) Explaining the construction of objects	'why is the wheel made of rubber?'
(e) Explaining the inference drawn from an observation	'you can tell the puppies are sad 'cos of their long faces'

Source: Blank and Franklin (1980).

to the child's use of language at home and information provided by a parent, on the basis of the child's abilities at home, ought not to be taken as an indication of the child's performance in other settings.

Checklists may be used not only to determine a child's current level of functioning, but also to establish the focus for subsequent intervention. While some checklists may simply identify a list of 'useful linguistic skills' which may serve as a selection menu with few constraints on the sequence in which separate items are taught, those which are based on a developmental sequence place strong constraints on the selection of teaching objectives. If the items truly reflect a developmental sequence, then, it is argued, the items immediately following the last items ticked, for a given child, provide the best focus for intervention. The rationale for this is that intervention cannot replace natural developmental processes, but only complement them; it is therefore necessary to ensure that structured attempts at intervention and 'natural developmental processes' are working in unison.

The value of any checklist will be determined by the quality of the items employed. Item quality can be summarised briefly. First, those items which make it difficult to recognise specific abilities in a child will be of less value than those which provide descriptions that can easily be applied. Second, if a checklist claims to provide a developmental sequence, the validity of this claim will affect the utility of the scale in practice. Third, for any checklist which claims a developmental sequence, the larger the 'developmental space' between items, the less the checklist will discriminate levels of linguistic ability, and the less accurate it will be. If the checklist is to be used as a basis for intervention, large 'developmental gaps' between items will require that the teacher or therapist is able to devise suitable intermediate objectives to bridge the gap between items. Other factors influencing the developmental space between items are the sensitivity and knowledge of those completing the checklist, and the conditions under which they are able to observe the target child. Examples of language items from three checklists are given in Figure 7.6.

Figure 7.6 Examples of commercially produced checklists

A. Gunzberg Primary Progress Assessment Chart of Social Development

This chart is divided into 'Self-help', 'Communication', 'Socialisation' and 'Occupation'; only part of the 'Communication' section concerned with expressive communication is shown here. The person completing the chart is required to indicate whether the skills listed are performed easily or frequently.

Throaty noises
Coos
Mmmm or ssss sounds
Polysyllabic vowels – iii, rrr, etc.
Two syllables – da-da, ba-ba, etc.
One clear word
Three to four clear words
Incipient jargon (many intelligible words)
20 single words

Two-word combinations – 'Daddy go', 'bye car', etc.
Three-word sentences – 'want a drink', etc.
Pronouns – 'me', 'my'
Refers to himself by his own name
Uses names of familiar objects
Constántly asks questions – 'what's that?' 'what's this?'
Refers to himself as 'I'
Uses question form 'why . . .?'
Expresses feelings, desires, problems verbally
Able to tell a story, relates experiences in a coherent way
Gives full name on request

B. The Vineland Adaptive Behaviour Scales (Interview Edition, Survey Form)

The Vineland is divided into the following sections: 'Communication', 'Daily Living Skills', 'Socialisation', 'Motor Skills' and 'Maladaptive Behaviour'. Only part of the section concerned with communication is shown here. The person completing the checklist is required to indicate for each item listed: 'Yes (usually)', 'Sometimes' or 'Partially'; 'No (never)', 'No (no opportunity)' or 'Don't know'.

Raises arms when caregiver says, 'Come here' or 'Up'
Demonstrates understanding of the meaning of 'no'
Imitates sounds of adults immediately after hearing them
Demonstrates understanding of the meaning of at least ten words
Gestures appropriately to indicate 'yes', 'no' and 'I want'
Listens attentively to instructions
Demonstrates understanding of the meaning of 'yes' and 'okay'
Follows instructions requiring an action and an object
Points accurately to at least one major body part when asked
Uses first names or nicknames of siblings, friends or peers, or states
    their names when asked
Uses phrases containing a noun and a verb, or two nouns
Names at least 20 familiar objects without being asked
Listens to a story for at least five minutes
Indicates a preference when offered a choice
Says at least 50 recognisable words
Spontaneously relates experiences in simple terms
Delivers a simple message
Uses sentences of four words or more
Points accurately to all body parts when asked
Says at least 100 recognisable words
Speaks in full sentences
Uses 'a' and 'the' in phrases or sentences
Follows instructions in 'if–then' form
States own first and last name when asked
Asks questions beginning with 'what', 'where', 'who', 'why' and 'when'
States which of two objects not present is bigger
Relates experiences in detail when asked

C. Early Language Training Programme

This language training programme provides a detailed assessment instrument in the form of a checklist. It includes the following sections: 'Non-verbal Communication', 'Comprehension' and 'Production'. The section on production is sub-divided into: 'Motor Movements', 'Speech Sounds and Babbling', 'Vocabulary', 'Single Words', 'Two Words', 'Three Words' and 'More Complex Syntax'. Only part of the section on assessing language production is reproduced here.

Two words:
1   Can the child use any words regularly as pivots (e.g. 'ball *gone*', 'teddy *gone*', '*all gone* milk', '*all gone* teddy')?
2   Test whether the child can combine two words using:
    i. Subject and verb (e.g. 'Mummy eat', 'car go')
    ii. Verb and object (e.g. 'eat dinner', 'wash hands')
    iii. Descriptive word plus object
       (a) Concrete (e.g. 'big car', 'little car')
       (b) Abstract (e.g. 'good girl', 'naughty girl')
       (c) Colour (e.g. 'red car', 'blue cap')
       (d) Number (e.g. 'two books', 'one biscuit')
    iv. Process words (e.g. 'run *quickly*')
    v. Possessive words describing objects (e.g. 'Daddy shoe', 'my chair')
    vi. Words to imply location (e.g. 'teddy car')
3   Test whether the child can use:
    i. Negative forms
       (a) Non-existence (e.g. 'no ball – where I expected it to be')
       (b) Rejection (e.g. 'no ball – I don't want the ball')
       (c) Denial (e.g. 'no ball – it isn't a ball')
    ii. Recurrence words (e.g. '*Jump again*', '*more* peanut')
    iii. Introducer words
       (a) Statement (e.g. 'see boy')
       (b) Command (e.g. 'look car')
       (c) Greeting (e.g. 'hello dog')
    iv. Question words
       (a) What? (e.g. 'what this?')
       (b) Where? (e.g. 'where teddy?')
       (c) Which? (e.g. 'which book?')
       (d) Who? (e.g. 'who this?')
       (e) When? (e.g. 'when go?')
       (f) Why? (e.g. 'why go?')
       (g) How? (e.g. 'how often?')

Source: Gunzberg (1973); Sparrow *et al.* (1984); Clements *et al.* (1983).

In summary, language checklists may provide a very practical and relatively quick form of assessment which can be used for a variety of purposes described at the beginning of Chapter 6. They also have the advantage of being able to integrate the assessment of structural, semantic and functional aspects of language by including a variety of different kinds of items, or by employing items which examine more than one aspect of language performance. Perhaps most important of all, checklists draw upon the knowledge of people who have experience of the child under ordinary, everyday conditions. They are therefore designed to indicate to what extent and in what ways the child uses language in naturalistic settings.

However, their utility is constrained by a paradox which arises from their underlying rationale. To be useful to the 'non-expert' professional, they must include items which are easily understood and which translate easily from relatively casual observation of the child. Such items are used extensively in both the Gunzberg Progress Assessment Charts and the Vineland Adaptive Behaviour Scales – for example, 'Constantly asks questions', 'Listens to a story for at least five minutes' (see Figure 7.6, A and B). However, such items are liable to some variability in terms of how they are applied by different people and, furthermore, they convey little in terms of specific information about a child's command of language. The alternative would be to provide a set of much more specific items which relate directly to specific language skills. Examples of this approach are evident in the checklist provided with the Early Language Training Programme (see Figure 7.6, C). While these items closely reflect developmental research on the child's mastery of two-word utterances, it seems unlikely that even an experienced therapist or teacher would be able to complete the checklist without spending a considerable amount of time with each individual child being assessed. Specificity and detail are bought at the cost of ease of understanding and speed of completion.

At least one study has found a positive and statistically significant relationship between maternal ratings of children's command of specific vocabulary items and performance on a formal language test (Cunningham and Sloper 1984) and this provides some support for the validity of checklist assessments. On the other hand, very few checklists have been systematically evaluated in relation to the formal criteria which are normally applied to language tests (see Chapter 8). Checklists are seldom employed to assess phonological skills, but are much more frequently applied to grammatical and functional language abilities which may be relatively difficult to elicit during a formal assessment session.

Chapter eight

Standardised tests of children's language

Introduction

In line with the continuing strength of the psychometric tradition within clinical and educational psychology in Britain, and more especially in the United States, the largest category of language assessment instruments is formal tests. While language charts are specifically concerned with the way in which a child uses language on a day-to-day basis, language tests are much more concerned with what a child can do or say under optimal conditions.

All tests rely upon some combination of the elicitation strategies described in Chapter 7. To the extent that tests provide a standard form for the administration of these strategies, they are referred to as 'standardised tests'. In addition to employing specific elicitation procedures, some tests seek to quantify the data obtained so that numerical comparisons can be made between individuals and with respect to the same individual at different points in time. While some tests provide summary scores which reflect success and failure on different items, other tests make it possible to derive a numerical score for the whole test which reflects an individual's test performance relative to that of other individuals. These kinds of tests are often referred to as 'normative tests', since they involve comparisons with scores from a 'normal' group of children.

The numerical score may be either an age equivalent or a standardised score. Both of these are derived from the performance of large numbers of children on the same test. The age equivalent indicates the age at which a sample of children without identifiable language handicaps obtain the same score as the target child. Thus, a child aged 8 years experiencing language difficulties might perform on a particular language test at the same level as a group of ordinary children of 6 years of age. This information may help to give an impression of the severity of the child's difficulties, with respect to the areas of language sampled in the test, and an indication of any change in performance over time.

Standardised scores

Standardised scores are derived from the distribution of scores for children of a similar age to the target child. Tests are constructed so that, for any item, some children will succeed and some will not. Similarly, for any group of items which are intended to measure the same aspect of linguistic functioning, there will be a range of scores for children of a similar age (see Figure 8.1). The technical process by which items are selected and tried out on a large group of children is referred to as the process of **standardisation** and the group of children is referred to as the standardisation **sample.** (This procedure provides a second meaning for 'standardised test'.) A sample is simply a group of individuals selected from a much larger group. The larger group may be all the children in a county, all the children in a country or any other clearly defined **population.** If the sample is carefully selected, then the pattern of scores obtained by the sample ought to provide a close match for the pattern of scores which would be obtained if the whole population of children were to be tested. It should then be possible to select any single child from the population (whether or not that child was included in the standardisation sample), and, after testing, compare her score to the pattern of scores obtained from the standardisation sample. By comparison with the scores from the sample, the child's performance can then be judged as high, low or average, and, by inference, high, low or average in respect of the population at large.

Unlike the construction of age equivalents, in the generation of standard scores it may help to include children with linguistic difficulties in the standardisation sample, since the test's items will be designed to discriminate these children from children who are not experiencing language difficulties. Inclusion of children with known language difficulties will ensure that items which most effectively identify language difficulties are included in the test.

Many tests develop a system of numerical scoring which makes it possible to make precise comparisons between the scores obtained by different individuals. This is done by taking the distribution of scores for children in the standardisation sample of a given age, and imposing on this a numerical scale which has clearly defined characteristics. The new scale will assign an arbitrary mean score to those children with average scores, and children performing above and below the mean will be assigned higher and lower scores on the new scale. Any new children in the original population (from which the standardisation sample was selected) can then be tested and, on the basis of their age and test performance, they can be given a test score which reflects their performance relative to the standardisation sample.

This gives rise to a number of advantages for the teacher or therapist. First, if a number of subtests are used as part of a larger test, the conversion of the subtest scores to a single standard scale will assist in the interpretation

Figure 8.1 Responses of a sample of 50 children to a test item measuring language skills (imaginary data): mean score = 7.0

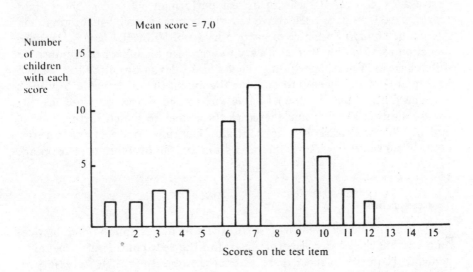

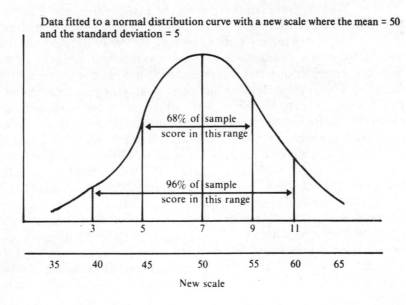

Data fitted to a normal distribution curve with a new scale where the mean = 50 and the standard deviation = 5

68% of sample score in this range

96% of sample score in this range

New scale

of the subscale scores. It is obviously much easier to compare scores if they are all represented on a single scale, rather than on four different scales with different distributions and different mean values. Second, it is possible to derive a single overall measure of test performance from all the subtest scores, once they have been converted to a common scale of measurement. Third, the common practice of using a mean of 50 or 100, and a standard deviation of 15 points, makes it easy to compare a child's performance on different tests. Fourth, providing the standard deviation of the test scale is known, it is relatively easy to estimate the extent to which a child's score is extreme (either high or low) in relation to the scores obtained by the standardisation sample, and therefore the extent to which further testing and possible intervention is appropriate. The importance of this inform-ation is considered again in the discussion on the evaluation of language tests.

Test evaluation

Because of the claims made by test constructors in relation to the numerical scores which can be derived from tests and the very considerable technical demands required to meet these assessment objectives, it is necessary to evaluate language tests against a number of well-established criteria (McCauley and Swisher 1984). Some of these criteria are described below.

Choice of target group

First, as already indicated, normative tests are those tests which are des-igned to facilitate comparison between the performance of the child being tested and the distribution of scores from a large sample of children. It is therefore necessary for the tests to include information regarding the size and nature of the standardisation sample so that the teacher or therapist may judge whether or not it is reasonable to use the distribution of sample scores as a basis for evaluating the performance of particular individuals. For example, it may not be appropriate to use a test standardised on a sample of children in North America to evaluate the performance of a child in Britain. The reason for this is that the linguistic, social and educational environments of the two countries may be so different as to provide diff-erent opportunities for language learning. If a British child scored relatively poorly in a North American test, this could only be interpreted in terms of the child's ability relative to that of North American children. It would not be clear whether the child's low performance was associated with poor linguistic ability in relation to British children, or whether it simply reflected the different experiences available to children in Britain and the USA. In addition to the nationality of the children included in the standardisation sample, it is also useful to know whereabouts in a particular country they live, their socioeconomic status and the extent to which the sample was screened for children with linguistic, sensory or learning difficulties (McCauley and Swisher 1984).

Reliability

Any instrument used in language assessments needs to provide **reliable** measures. A reliable measure is one where variations which occur between one occasion of use and another are due solely to variations in the characteristic being measured. Unfortunately, all language tests are subject to some degree of unreliability. There are two main sources of measurement error which reduce reliability. The first is concerned with differences in the way in which the test is administered. It is extremely difficult for any practitioner to administer a test in exactly the same way on two occasions, even if the same child is being tested. Additional variation is likely to creep in when different children are tested at different times of the day and possibly in different locations. These factors will affect the **external reliability** of the test.

Another source of variation comes from the interaction of the test items with the child's linguistic ability. Linguistic ability cannot be measured directly, but only via elicitation procedures which attempt to make visible a certain aspect of a child's language. Any elicitation procedure is itself subject to a degree of variation in terms of how successfully it stimulates a child to make a particular response. Naturally, during the process of test construction, those items which are particularly unreliable are excluded. A completely reliable item would be one which, on every occasion that it was administered, correctly differentiated between those children who do and those who do not have a particular linguistic ability. In practice, no items are completely reliable and, as a consequence, any test will be subject to some degree of **internal reliability** error.

Because the reliability of a test is so important, it is usual to quantify it in some way. External reliability can be measured by comparing the test scores obtained by one tester working with the same group of children on two separate occasions separated by a short time interval. The interval must be long enough to avoid any carry-over practice effects between the first administration and the second, but sufficiently short so that it can be assumed that there will have been no change in the real underlying abilities of the children concerned. This is called test–retest reliability. Another way of measuring external reliability is to compare the scores obtained by different testers working with the same group of children. This is referred to as **inter-tester** reliability.

To measure internal reliability, it is necessary to compare two sets of test items. Some tests are constructed to give two versions; thus, there are two separate tests made up of different but equivalent items. A comparison of the scores achieved by a group of children on the two different versions of the tests would provide an indication of the internal reliability of the test. On tests which do not have parallel forms, it may be possible to create two separate tests by selecting alternate odd and even test items. The scores obtained by a group of children for the odd items can then be compared with the scores obtained by the same children for the even-numbered items. Whether parallel forms or a split-half method is used, the agreement between the scores is used as a basis for an overall measure of agreement.

A statistical procedure called **correlation** is frequently used to calculate the agreement between two sets of figures. In the case of reliability estimates, correlations are calculated from the two sets of scores obtained from inter-rater, test–retest or split-half comparisons. Correlations are expressed in terms of a figure between 0 and 1, with 0 indicating no agreement between the scores and 1 indicating perfect agreement. The precise interpretation of correlation co-efficients depends upon the size of the datasets employed, but, as a rule of thumb, a correlation of 0.7 indicates that approximately half of the variation in the set of test scores is attributable to real variations in the attribute being measured. The rest of the variation is due to unspecified error. On this basis, it may be assumed that reliability estimates ought to exceed 0.7 if a test is to be regarded as providing 'reliable' scores.

Validity

An assumption underlying all tests is that they actually provide measures which reflect the abilities they purport to test. Thus, it is assumed that a test of linguistic ability actually measures language as opposed to some other characteristic. While such an assumption may seem so obvious as to be hardly worth mentioning, it is important that tests are able to substantiate their implicit claim to validity.

There are various ways of defining validity, only some of which can be quantified. **Face validity** reflects the extent to which the test items appear to be concerned with the abilities in question. When tests are given to adults, it may increase co-operation if a test has high face validity. However, for tests which are designed for children, face validity is of relatively little importance. Of much greater significance is **construct validity** – that is, the extent to which the test items are consistent with contemporary linguistic theories, and how far results are interpretable within the conceptual framework provided by those theories. The descriptions of children's language in Chapters 1, 2 and 3 provide the basis for an evaluation of the construct validity of any language test. Tests which are not based upon adequate linguistic descriptions must be regarded as lacking in construct validity.

Content validity is concerned with the test's content – that is, the way in which the items, both singly and together, provide information which is relevant to the linguistic abilities in question. The content validity of individual items may be determined by inspection by someone with expertise in the area of language assessment. Even for a practitioner who does not claim to own such expertise, it is important to consider the extent to which items seem to call upon the linguistic abilities at which the test is directed. This will improve the tester's familiarity with the test and gradually lead to an accumulation of knowledge of testing in general. An alternative approach to measuring content validity involves the use of correlational procedures to determine the extent to which performance on each item is associated with the overall test score. A good test would be one in which each item has a high correlation with the overall test score, since this would indicate that all the items tap into the linguistic ability which the test purports to measure. However, it is also possible for items to correlate too highly with the total score. The argument here is that a high correlation between an item and the overall test score means that the item contributes little new information which is not already tapped by other items. This procedure is referred to as **item analysis.**

The most objective forms of test validity are derived from comparisons between the way in which children perform on a language test and some other independent measure of language ability. This may simply involve calculating correlations between two sets of test scores. If the new test is found to correlate highly with an old, established test, this may be used as evidence in favour of validity. However, if the old test is obviously defective – for example, if it is based on out-of-date linguistic theories and thus lacks construct validity – this measure of **concurrent validity** will not be very meaningful. Measures of concurrent validity must therefore be examined in order to determine whether the comparison measure is, in itself, a valid measure of the linguistic ability in question. An alternative to concurrent validity involves comparing a test score at one point in time with another measure of language performance obtained sometime subsequently. This indicates the extent to which the language test is able to predict how a child's language will change over time and is referred to as **predictive validity**.

Distribution of scores

In addition to the information with respect to reliability and validity, McCauley and Swisher (1984) suggest that, for the proper interpretation of test scores, the test user must have information regarding the spread of scores obtained from the standardisation sample. This is necessary to interpret the significance of scores which may occur above or below the mean. For example, if a child scores 40 on a test with a mean standardised score of 50, is this an average score, a poor score or a very poor score? This can only be evaluated with respect to the distribution of scores obtained by the standardisation sample (see Figure 8.2). If the scores are spread so that a relatively large proportion of the sample attained a score of 40, then scoring 40 does not distinguish the child as having any particular difficulties. On the other hand, if the scores of the standardisation sample were such that only a very small proportion – say, 5 per cent – scored 40 or less, then a child with this score may be identified as being in need of further, more detailed assessment.

The spread or distribution of the test scores (and therefore the significance of scores which are above or below the mean) is indicated by the standard deviation, or SD. The smaller the SD in relation to the mean, the more scores cluster around the mean with relatively few high or low scores. Alternatively, a high SD indicates that more scores from the sample were substantially higher or lower than the mean. The shape of frequency distributions for sets of scores with relatively high and low SDs is shown in Figure 8.2. From Figure 8.1 it can be seen that, for all tests with symmetrical distributions of scores (known technically, and rather confusingly, as 'normal distributions'), any score which differs from the mean by two or more standard deviations will be unusual and therefore worthy of further consideration.

Appendix: review of commonly used tests of children's language

There are many tests of children's language which have been developed and marketed over a number of years. A large number of these are reviewed by Longhurst (1977) and McCauley and Swisher (1984). Here, only a small selection of those tests which are in current use in Britain will be described. Since different tests are designed to assess different aspects of linguistic ability, they will be considered under four categories: tests of articulation or phonological ability; tests of vocabulary; tests of grammatical ability, including morpho-syntactical rules; and, finally, tests of more general aspects of psycholinguistic ability.

Articulation tests

The Edinburgh Articulation Test (EAT)

The EAT (Anthony *et al.* 1971) is designed as a screening procedure for children whose articulation of English consonants is retarded or otherwise abnormal. In addition to the exclusion of vowels, it makes no attempt to assess other aspects of phonological skill, such as rhythm and intonation (Grunwell 1982) although these have been identified by Crystal (1984) as significant sources of phonological disabilities.

The test was designed to assess children's production of consonants as they appear in English words. This indicated the need to consider consonant production in the following contexts:

Figure 8.2 Distributions of test scores

A. Distribution of standardised sources: mean = 50; SD = 10

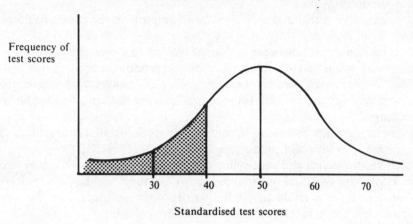

Standardised test scores

B. Distribution of standardised scores: mean = 50; SD = 5

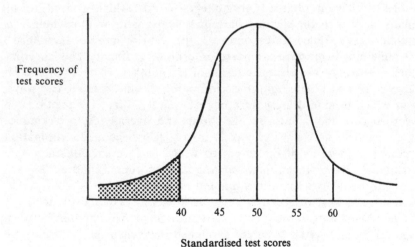

Standardised test scores

Note: Shaded portion of curve shows proportion of standardisation sample with scores below 40. In A this is approximately 16 per cent, while in B it is approximately 2.5 per cent.

149

1 Word-initial position – for example, can the child pronounce the 'f' in 'finger'?
2 Monosyllabic words' final consonants – for example, can the child pronounce the final 't' in 'boat'?
3 Word initial consonant clusters – for example, can the child pronounce the 'br' in 'bridge'?
4 Monosyllabic word final clusters – for example, can the child pronounce the 'lk' in 'milk'?
5 Medial consonants between accented vowel and unaccented vowel in disyllabic words – for example, can the child pronounce the 'r' in 'garage'?
6 Medial consonant clusters between accented vowels and unaccented vowels in disyllabic words – for example, can the child pronounce the 'ng' in 'finger'?
7 Final consonants following accented vowels in disyllabic words – for example, can the child pronounce the final 'l' in 'pencil'?
8 Medial consonants and post-syllabic consonants in disyllabic words – for example, can the child pronounce the 'pl' in 'apple' or the 't' in 'battle'?
9 Consonants in possible trisyllabic words – for example, can the child pronounce the 'l' in 'elephant' or the 'm' in 'umbrella'?

A selection of commonly used naming words which incorporated consonants in the appropriate contexts was tried out with 130 normal children and 57 children of average or above-average intelligence who had already been identified as having retarded phonology. Words which proved to be unreliable as stimuli for eliciting particular consonants were excluded, as were children who failed to respond to 15 per cent or more of the items.

The remaining items were compared in terms of 'Difficulty' and 'Discrimination'. Difficulty was defined in terms of the numbers of children at each age level getting each item right. Discrimination was measured in two ways, each of which produced a measure of test validity. First, the relationship between success and failure on each item and overall test performance produced an item analysis with a correlation of 0.935. Second, discrimination was examined in terms of the extent to which performance on each item differentiated between the normal and language-disordered children. At each age level, those items which discriminated between the normal and speech-delayed subjects were regarded as being valid measures of articulation.

The test items were subsequently standardised on 510 children between the ages of 3 and 6 years. Analysis indicated that when the children were grouped into six-month age bands, the difference between the scores from each age band was significant ($p < 0.05$). This confirms the ability of the test to discriminate between the performance of ordinary children of different ages. The raw scores were then standardised to a scale with a mean of 100 and a standard deviation of 15. The authors suggest that any child who achieves a score of less than 85 should be regarded as in need of further assessment and, possibly, structured intervention. Estimates of reliability indicate that any test score can be regarded as within approximately 6 points of the 'real' score 95 times out of 100.

The procedure for administering the EAT is to elicit a series of 68 non-imitated words from the child in response to a set of pictures. This normally takes between 10 and 15 minutes. Normative scoring involves marking the child's performance on each item as correct or incorrect and converting this to a standardised score or an age equivalent. Further quantitative analysis may be carried out for consonant structure, liquid confusion, lengthening, palatisation and order of acquisition of consonants, although this requires the test to be tape recorded and can be successfully completed only by someone with a sound knowledge of phonemic analysis.

The Goldman–Fristoe Test of Articulation

Whereas the EAT relies upon a single elicitation strategy (word naming in response to a picture stimulus), the Goldman–Fristoe test (Goldman and Fristoe 1969) sets out to examine a range of different phonemes in both imitative and 'conversational' contexts. The 'Sounds in Words' part of the test uses a picture-naming approach to elicit words which contain the relevant phonemes; whereas the EAT focuses exclusively upon consonants, the Goldman–Fristoe test claims to sample all consonants (except 'measure'), all vowels and the majority of English diphthongs. The sounds /h/, /w/, /wh/, /y/ and the final voiced /th/ are omitted from the test because of their relative low frequency of occurence. The test claims that the sounds are presented in a developmental sequence, although no data is presented to support this.

Since a child's ability to produce a particular sound will vary according to the speech context (Ingram 1976), the Goldman–Fristoe test samples speech sounds in three positions within words (initial, medial and final) and also as they occur in sentences. The sounds in sentences subtest involves the child being told a story which is illustrated with pictures. The child is then required to retell the story, using the pictures as a guideline, in the expectation that the child will repeat the key words which contain the target phonemes.

The third elicitation strategy employed by the Goldman–Fristoe test is designed to provide an indication of the child's optimal performance when given both visual and oral support. It is suggested that this might indicate those sounds which will be most suitable as a target for subsequent intervention. The procedure works by asking the child initially simply to imitate a single sound – for example, /suh/. For each item, the child is allowed a number of opportunities to produce a correct imitation. If the child succeeds here, then the word (for example, 'sun') is modelled in a sentence and the child is given a number of opportunities to produce a correct imitation. Success with this form of presentation is then followed by opportunities for repetition of the sound in a complete sentence, 'I had sun in my eyes.'

Whereas the test designers suggest that a teacher without specialist knowledge might give the test as a screening device to identify the existence of articulation problems, the analysis of the nature of the errors and the appropriate forms of intervention ought to be left for an expert in phonological analysis. Qualitative analysis can be described in relation to the following parameters:

1 The position of a phoneme in a word (initial, medial or final).
2 Putative simplification strategies (see Chapter 1), such as substitution, omission, distortion or addition of phonemes.
3 The consistency of the child's phonological errors in single words and in sentences.
4 The distribution of errors in relation to the frequency with which sounds occur in English.
5 The place and mode of articulation difficulties – for example, are errors predominantly concerned with nasal sounds ('thi*ng*'), plosives ('*p*each') or fricatives ('*th*ese')?
6 The extent to which the pattern of articulation errors reflects the difficulties experienced by 'normal' children and might therefore be considered as part of a developmental sequence.

The Goldman–Fristoe test reports test–retest reliabilities of between 94 per cent and 95 per cent for the 'Sounds in Words' and 'Sounds in Sentences' subtests. Inter-rater reliability ranges from 86 per cent to 92 per cent and intra-rater reliability (agreement for the analysis of errors from a single test made by the same tester on different occasions) is 91 per cent. No information is available on the reliability of the third subtest, designed to examine the child's optimal performance.

The validity of the Goldman–Fristoe test is based on the authors' selection of the specific items and the fact that the 'Sounds in Words' subtest samples all but one of the consonants found in English. The 'Sounds in Sentences' samples a smaller set of sounds 'most likely to be misarticulated', and the third, 'Optimal Performance', subtest examines those sounds 'known to be misarticulated'. This a-priori selection of sounds for more detailed analysis clearly restricts the scope of the test, particularly as no evidence is presented to support the selection of sounds for the two subtests.

Comparison of the EAT and the Goldman–Fristoe test

Both of these tests depend, to a great extent, upon the use of pictures to elicit key words from a child. Children who, for any reason, have difficulty in recognising or naming pictures are therefore likely to have difficulty with both these tests. In terms of sampling the sounds necessary for speaking

English, the designers of each of the two tests have taken slightly different approaches which reflect different priorities. The EAT provides a more extensive assessment of consonants and consonant blends than does the Goldman–Fristoe test, but the latter is more systematic in that, for each consonant included in the test, articulation is examined with respect to three word positions and with respect to production within sentences. Thus, the consonant/dz/is sampled in all three word positions in the Goldman–Fristoe test ('*j*ump', 'py*j*amas', 'oran*ge*') but only in the third position ('gara*ge*', 'brid*ge*') in the EAT. A number of consonant blends – including /nk/ ('mon*k*ey') /nz/ ('win*gs*') and /ns/ (pen*c*il') – appear in the EAT, but not in the Goldman–Fristoe. On the other hand, the blends /bl/ ('*bl*ue'), /dr/ ('*dr*um'), /fl/ ('*fl*ag') and /skw/ ('*squ*irrel') are sampled in the word-initial position in the Goldman–Fristoe test, but do not appear in the EAT.

On the basis of these observations, it is not possible to say whether or not one of these tests provides a more useful assessment tool than the other. This will depend upon the purpose of the assessment and how much is already known about a particular child. An experienced speech therapist might find it useful to employ the EAT as an initial screening device, while reserving the Goldman–Fristoe for a more detailed assessment prior to devising a programme of therapy. Teachers who do not possess the necessary skills for a qualitative analysis of phonological errors are encouraged, by the designers of Goldman–Fristoe, to use the test as a way of gathering systematic information about children whose articulation gives cause for concern. In contrast, the EAT, while using a very similar strategy for both elicitation and scoring, is recommended for use only by qualified speech therapists.

Vocabulary tests

The British Picture Vocabulary Test (BPVT)

The BPVT (Dunn *et al.* 1982) is a revised version of a well-established North American test which has been restandardised on a sample of British children. It measures the extent of an individual's receptive vocabulary by requiring a subject to select one picture from a set of four in response to a verbal stimulus. The test subject may respond by gesture or eye pointing. Standardised scales are available for children as young as 2 years up to adulthood at 17 years 11 months.

The test designers recommend the test can be used for a variety of purposes and with different categories of children. For pre-school children, it is suggested that the BPVT might be used as a screening instrument to identify children who may require some form of special or compensatory provision, and as a way of indicating a child's readiness for reading. In view of the importance of language in education, the authors also suggest that the BPVT might be used to assess scholastic aptitude, although it seems unwise to rely solely on one test for this purpose. The wide age range covered by the

BPVT, and the use of gestural responses, means that it may be particularly useful with children who experience difficulties with spoken language, including those who stutter, autistic children and children with cerebral palsy. The test does, however, require a level of hearing sufficient to discriminate between single words and the capacity to recognise pictorial representations of objects.

The British standardised scales were obtained by giving 424 test items to 1,401 subjects aged 2 years to 16 years. Each item is made up of a plate displaying four pictures, three of which are distractors. Final selection of the plates to be included in the test was determined by a number of criteria: the percentage of subjects getting an item correct had to increase with the age of the children; the distractors at each age should attract responses, but not correlate with the total score; and the final items needed to be evenly spread across the ability range. A set of 32 items meeting these criteria were selected for a short form of the test, and a larger set of 150 items was included in a long form of the test. A much larger standardisation sample of 3,334 children was then tested with the short form of the test to provide the normative scales. Test scores can be converted to standardised scores (mean=100; standard deviation=15) to age equivalents or to percentile ranks.

Split-half reliability for the BPVT is reported as between 0.75 and 0.85 for items in the short form, and between 0.70 and 0.95 for items in the long form. Item reliability for all items varies from as low as 0.28 to 0.78. On the basis of these figures, the authors suggest that any test score can be regarded as falling within seven points of the true score for the short form, and within five points of the true score for the long form of the test. The content validity of the test is argued on the basis of the range of vocabulary items included, while, for construct validity, the authors rely upon the widely accepted practice of using vocabulary items in intelligence tests, and the justification for this practice put forward by Binet and Simon in 1905, and by Terman in 1916. The concurrent and predictive validity of the BPVT is based mainly on the extensive research which has been conducted with the Peabody Picture Vocabulary Test (PPVT), and particularly the high correlations obtained when scores of the PPVT have been compared with scores from standardised intelligence tests.

Although the BPVT is a language test, it covers only a relatively narrow range of strictly linguistic abilities – that is, comprehension of single vocabulary items. At the same time, successive items on the test do not measure changes in a child's linguistic ability so much as the development of conceptual abilities which underlie the acquisition of abstract vocabulary items. The value of the BPVT in terms of the assessment of language is likely to be greatest when it is used in conjunction with other forms of assessment, so that a comparison between different aspects of linguistic and cognitive functioning is possible.

Tests of Grammar

The child's increasing mastery of grammar has proved to be the most attractive domain for test developers. Numerous tests are available to assist in the systematic assessment of a wide range of grammatical abilities, only a small selection of which are presented here.

Word Order Comprehension Test (WOCT)

This test (Fenn 1979) was designed to determine whether a child who is able to understand single words can also understand the relationships which are expressed by different forms of word order. The test requires the child to select one of a pair of pictures to go with a stimulus sentence. The child's response may be either manual pointing or eye pointing. The stimulus may be expressed orally, through signs, or in writing. Since the test requires a knowledge of single words, but sets out to assess syntactical knowledge independently of vocabulary, a separate list of the words used is included.

The test consists of nine sets of items and each set has two practice items and ten test items. Each set deals with the separate domains – for example, 'on', 'under', subject and object nouns, object pronouns, indirect object nouns and prepositional phrase nouns. For instance, in the third set (subject–object nouns) the child is presented with a sentence – such as, 'The duck is splashing the frog' – and is required to select from two pictures, one of which shows a duck splashing a frog, and the other a frog splashing a duck. The different sets might therefore be regarded as providing criterion-referenced information with respect to specific grammatical sub-skills. It is suggested that each subtest is scored separately and no overall test score is obtained. Since for each item there is a 50 per cent chance of a correct response simply by guessing, children with scores of 8 or less on any set are regarded as in need of retesting, while very low scores (0–1) indicate that the child is systematically misunderstanding the meanings to be derived from word order.

The WOCT does not provide age norms, but it has been piloted with groups of normal and handicapped children, aged between 4 and 5 years 5 months, from lower social class backgrounds. Success for the normal children ranged from 82 per cent to 100 per cent, and Fenn suggests that, as a rule of thumb, a child who fails the test should be regarded as functioning below the level of the normal 4- to 5-year-old. Data from 100 deaf and mentally handicapped children showed considerable variability and performance was not related to scores from the Reynell Developmental Language Scales (see below) or the Peabody Picture Vocabulary Test (see above). This suggests that this test has identified a linguistic skill which is distinct from the linguistic abilities required for success on these other tests.

This test is concerned with a specific aspect of linguistic ability and does not provide either standardised or age equivalent scores. There is no information regarding the reliability of the test items and the validity of the test depends upon the interpretation afforded the separate subtests. However, on this criterion, content validity and construct validity would appear to be high. These comments suggest that the test is unlikely to be useful as a screening instrument but, when used in conjunction with other tests or with children who have already been identified as having language difficulties, it may assist in the generation of a balanced assessment of a child's strengths and weaknesses. If a child is found to be weak in one or more of the areas covered by the subtests, this information may provide a valuable guide for designing a programme of intervention. The flexibility of both the mode of eliciting a response and the response itself suggests that the test may be particularly suitable for children with handicaps which make comprehension or production of speech difficult.

The Northwestern Syntax Screening Test (NSST)

As the name of this test implies, it is designed to be used as a screening device to identify children between 3 and 8 years of age who require further assessment and possible intervention (Lee 1969). The test sets out to examine the child's command of a range of syntactic forms in terms of both comprehension and production. These include 'behind'/'under', 'on'/'in', 'he'/'she', 'is'/'are', 'their'/'his', 'play'/'plays', 'this'/'that', 'jumps'/'jumped', as well as interrogatives and agent–object contrasts. For the comprehension items, the tester speaks the two stimulus sentences – for example, 'The cat is behind the chair'; 'The cat is under the chair' – and then requires the child to 'Show me the cat is under the chair' from a set of pictures. For the expressive items, the tester asks the child to repeat two sentences ('The baby is sleeping'; 'The baby is not sleeping') and then to say the sentence which goes with the picture indicated by the tester. Any variations from the target sentence are counted as errors, and it is suggested that these are recorded so that they can be analysed prior to intervention. However, the reader is reminded of the difficulties of interpreting errors in imitation tasks described in Chapter 6.

The test was standardised on 344 children, aged between 3 years and 7 years 11 months, who were 'presumed by their teachers to have no handicapping conditions which would contribute to atypical language development' (Lee 1969: 7). The children came from middle- and upper-middle-income homes where 'standard American dialect was spoken' (ibid.) Lee recommends that any child who scores below 2 standard deviations from the standardised mean should be identified for further assessment, although no reason is given for this. She suggests that children who score low on both comprehension and production may be immature or mentally retarded, although no explanation is provided as to what she might mean by these terms. Children with low comprehension scores but high expressive scores are seen as having possible emotional problems, or as suffering from echolalia. Once again, there is no elaboration of the reasoning behind these diagnoses. Lee does, however, report that a group of 18 children, who had already been identified as having delayed language, showed a wide gap between comprehension scores which were in the 'low–normal range' and expressive scores which were 'very low'.

No evidence is presented regarding the reliability of this test and there is no discussion of validity. Validity can therefore be assessed only on the basis of the items which are included. The sentence pairs are designed to reflect important grammatical contrasts but, without information regarding how the particular contrasts were selected and how far they are representative of the grammatical skills available to children of this age, it is impossible to determine how useful they are as test items.

Finally, although the test has been standardised, the sample of children used differs in important respects from British children. This raises questions regarding the extent to which the standardised scores provide a useful basis of comparison for children born and brought up in this country.

Test for Auditory Comprehension of Language (TACL)

The TACL (Carrow 1973; Carrow-Woodfolk 1985) is designed to assess four distinct areas of grammatical knowledge. These are form classes and function words (nouns, adjectives; verbs, prepositions, etc.), morphological constructions (e.g. noun + noun + derivational suffix 'er'; verb + verb + derivational suffix 'er'), grammatical categories (such as gender and number pronoun, number and noun, tense of verb) and syntactical structures (e.g. imperative mood, noun and verb agreement, modification). During the test, the child is required to indicate a choice from a selection of pictures in response to a verbal stimulus.

Carrow claims that for normal children the test scores increase with age and that it differentiates individuals with known disorders, including deaf children and those with articulation difficulties, from ordinary, non-handicapped children. A study of the test's predictive validity showed that test scores correlated (0.79) with the subsequent progress of dysphasic children. On this basis, it is suggested that the test offers a valid way of screening for linguistic disorders. Carrow also suggests that, for children scoring below their chronological age equivalent, the separate subtests can provide useful qualitative information. Test–retest reliability is reported as 0.94 when children were retested within one week, while an item analysis indicated an overall measure of test consistency of 0.77.

The test's revised norms are based on test scores obtained from 1,003 American children aged between 3 and 10 years. While this sample was designed to provide a cross-section of American children, and thus included children of black, Anglo and Mexican parents, it is unlikely that the resultant norms provide an accurate basis of comparison for British children. The test scores can be expressed as standardised scores, age equivalents or as percentile ranks.

Test for Reception of Grammar (TROG)

Like the TACL, this test (Bishop 1982) is designed to measure children's comprehension of a range of grammatical devices. It can be administered to children between the ages of 4 and 13 years, and is recommended as being particularly suitable for children suffering from specific language disorders, deafness, mental retardation and cerebral palsy. As with the other tests described in this appendix, the child is required to select, by gesture or eye pointing, one of two pictures in response to a sentence spoken by the examiner. Since this provides the opportunity for the child to score correctly 50 per cent of the time simply by guessing, each grammatical contrast is presented in blocks of four items and the child is required to get all four items correct to pass on any block.

The test sets out to assess a wide range of grammatical understanding, including grammatical categories such as noun, verb and adjective; negatives; singular and plural personal pronouns; reversible active verbs; personal pronouns; singular and plural noun inflections; comparative adjectives; reversible passive sentences; 'in'/'on'; post-modified subjects; 'X but not Y' constructions; 'above'/'below'; 'not only but also' constructions; the relative clause; 'neither X nor Y' and embedded sentences. Tense is not included as it was found too difficult to test within this framework. For each pair of sentences the 'incorrect' picture contains either a grammatical distractor (e.g. 'He is sitting in the tree' vs. 'She is sitting in the tree', for a picture of a girl) or a lexical distractor ('He is sitting in the tree' vs. 'He is swinging in the tree'), and it is suggested that the extent to which a child shows sensitivity to one or other of these kinds of distraction may be useful in terms of assessment and the planning of intervention.

The TROG has been standardised on a sample of non-handicapped British children aged between 4 years and 12 years 11 months. Children whose parents were non-native speakers of English, or who had resided in a non-English-speaking country for more than six months in the previous three years, were excluded. Test scores can be compared directly with the scores obtained by normal children of the same chronological age. A qualitative analysis of the various subtests can be used to identify specific difficulties with grammar and as an indication of whether the child is progressing in the same way as most normal children, or whether there are signs of deviant patterns.

Since no empirical data is presented, the validity of the TROG depends upon an analysis of the test items and the elicitation strategies employed. In general, the items appear to be well selected to reflect a broad range of grammatical abilities. A split-half reliability carried out on the data from children in the standardisation sample between the ages of 4 years and 8 years 11 months produced correlations of between 0.64 and 0.84 for the different items. Unlike the TROG and the NSST, the TACL has been standardised on British children and therefore age-based comparisons are likely to be much more useful for this group.

The Language Imitation Test (LIT)

The principal innovation associated with this test (Berry and Mittler 1984) is that, instead of pointing in response to a word or sentence, the child is required to imitate a sentence spoken by the adult. This strategy is based upon the work of Slobin and Welsh (1973), and upon the authors' own extensive research regarding the imitative abilities of mentally handicapped children. No test materials other than the scoring sheet are required. The authors suggest that the LIT is a test which is particularly suitable for use with severely and moderately mentally handicapped children.

The test is made up of six subtests covering the following areas:

1 sound imitation (items taken from the EAT);
2 word imitation;
3 syntactic control of active declarative sentences;
4 syntactic control of questions, negatives, passives and passive negative sentences;
5 word organisation control (imitation of telegraphic sentences with all functors deleted);
6 sentence completion.

Although the test has not been standardised, it does provide the possibility of numerical scoring on a scale from 0 to 173. The authors provide a rule-of-thumb guide to interpreting these scores. It is also suggested that the six areas provide important qualitative information with respect to a child's command of grammar and have particular relevance to the planning of intervention.

The validity of the LIT is based upon the existing research which supports imitation as an index of a child's knowledge of grammar and the high correlations obtained when scores on the LIT were compared with other measures of language production. The authors also claim that the test measures are closely related to the teacher's ratings of a child's language. Repetition of the test with a single group of children showed stability in the scores for each subtest, with the overall correlation co-efficient being 0.975. The authors also report that a group of 12 teachers were taught to score the LIT with 90 per cent accuracy.

Although this test does not provide the statistical and normative data for making comparisons with the performance of ordinary children found in

Figure 8.3 Verbal communication processes underlying the RDLS

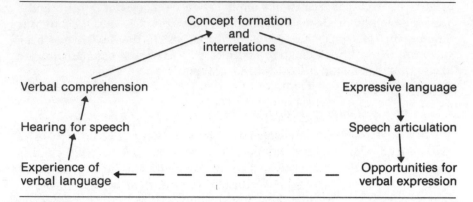

some other tests, the use of imitation as an elicitation strategy makes it a valuable assessment tool for children who are unable or unwilling to co-operate with other testing procedures.

Tests of general psycholinguistic ability

The Reynell Developmental Language Scales (RDLS)

The RDLS (Reynell and Huntley 1985, 2nd revision) provides separate measures of language comprehension and language production which may be used independently or together to provide a comparison of a child's relative strengths and weaknesses in the two areas. It sets out to cover the normal stages of language development between the ages of 1 and 5 years, although it is intended principally as a clinical tool for children with delayed and deviant language. Two scales are provided for assessing language comprehension, one of which is specially modified so that only eye pointing is required.

The test is based upon an explicit model of the processes thought to be involved in verbal communication (See Figure 8.3). Comprehension is seen as being dependent upon the ability to hear essential speech sounds, the ability to recover meaning from sound sequences and to interpret meanings in terms of abstract concepts and relations. Speech production is seen as relying on the reverse process – that is, the ability to translate abstract ideas into speech sounds and to articulate those speech sounds in such a way that they are comprehensible to other people. Whereas the other tests so far reviewed have been concerned with specific aspects of linguistic ability, the RDLS is much more concerned with the way in which the child's increasing mastery of language is associated with conceptual development and more sophisticated problem-solving skills. The different items are specially selected to reflect the child's increasing command of an abstract symbol system which can be used for manipulating abstract concepts and relations.

The comprehension scales begin with items concerned with the extent to which a child associates a word or phrase with affective or situational meaning, and proceed to a point where 'ideational content goes well beyond the concrete evidence' – for example, 'The little boy has spilt his dinner; what must he do?' The majority of the test items require a chid to respond to a question or an instruction by pointing to, or manipulating, a variety of household objects and models. For example, in Section 3 the child is asked 'Where is the dog?' 'Where is the man?', while in Section 8 the child is asked to 'Put the pigs behind the man.' After the age of 5 years it is suggested that language increasingly becomes a tool for higher intellectual functions and therefore is difficult to assess independently of other cognitive processes.

The expressive scale begins with an examination of the child's use of words to express emotional states and in response to specific situations – for example, 'ta' on taking something – and proceeds to explore the child's command of simple vocabulary items through picture naming and in response to requests for definitions – for example, 'What is a shop?' The final part of the language expression scale calls upon the child to describe pictures where scoring is determined by the number of ideas expressed.

The test has been standardised with 636 British children aged between 6 months and 6 years. Children whose first language was not English were excluded from the sample. Any test score can be converted to an age equivalent (a language age) for comparison with the child's chronological age and, if appropriate, the child's mental age. Separate figures can be obtained for expressive and comprehension scales. Split-half reliability for the expressive scales is reported as being between 0.84 and 0.96, while for the comprehension scales it varies between 0.60 and 0.96 on Scale A, and between 0.46 and 0.95 on Scale B.

Various measures of test validity are presented in the test manual. The comprehension scale (A) correlates positively with the expression scale, although this is much higher for the youngest children (0.67) than for the oldest (0.32). This is interpreted as being indicative of the different functions which are served by comprehension and production with increasing age. Concurrent validity is based upon the high positive correlations between RDLS scores and scores obtained from the Stanford, Binet and Wechsler intelligence tests and the Illinois Test of Psycholinguistic Abilities (see below). Scores from the RDLS also correlated with performance in the Wechsler Intelligence Scale for Children (WISC) and the Word Reading Test after age 3 years, thus providing support for the test's predictive validity. These figures give strong support for the view that the RDLS measures a child's increasing control of language for cognitive functions, but there is little evidence of the test's ability to identify specific areas of language functioning or its sensitivity to changes in a child's command of specific language forms or other language functions.

The test may be used as a screening device, although it is relatively time-consuming to administer compared with other tests. It is also likely to provide valuable information when used with certain children and in conjunction with other tests of language. The use of the test as a prelude to intervention will depend very much on the extent to which it is regarded as important to direct remediation at the specific linguistic functions which this test addresses.

The Illinois Test of Psycholinguistic Abilities (ITPA)

Over the years the ITPA (Kirk *et al.* 1968) has become one of the best known and most widely used of all language tests. Like the RDLS it is based on an explicit model of language production and comprehension. Using Osgood's (1957a; 1957b) theoretical views as a starting-point, Kirk *et al.* set out to provide an instrument to assess three dimensions of linguistic functioning: level of organisation, channel of communication and process (See Figure 8.4). Organisation is divided into the representational level, which employs symbols to carry meaning, and the automatic level, where behaviour is highly organised and integrated but less susceptible to voluntary control. 'Channel' refers to the medium by which messages are received or transmitted: comprehension of language may take place through auditory (hearing) or visual channels (reading print or signs), and production may be mediated via vocal (speaking) or motor (writing or manual signing) systems. Processes are described as being concerned with reception (comprehension), expression (production) or organisation.

Although all the logical combinations of levels of organisation, channels and processes create the possibility of 16 subtests, only eleven subtests are actually included. These are as follows:

Representational level
  Receptive process (decoding):
    auditory reception ('Do dogs eat?');
    visual reception (the child is shown a geometric
    shape and required to select one from an array).

  Organising process (association):
    auditory vocal association ('A fish has . . .?');
    visual motor association (the child is required to find
    a match for one object from an array).

  Expressive process:
    verbal expression (the child is requested to describe a
    picture);

Figure 8.4 Three-dimensional model of the ITPA

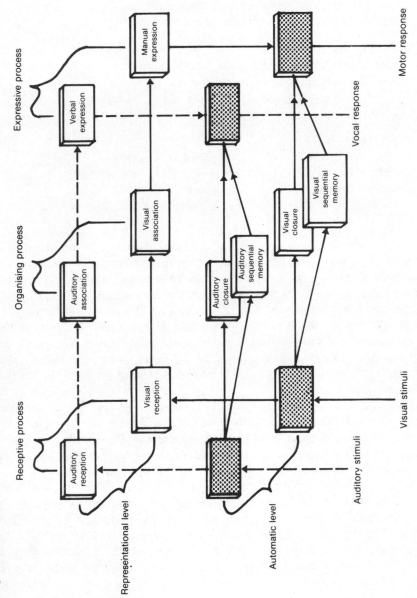

Source: Kirk et al. (1968)

manual expression (the child is requested to 'Show me what we do with a . . .').

Automatic level
Closure:
grammatical closure (the child is required to complete unfinished sentences);
visual closure (the child is required to identify a common object from an incomplete representation).

Sequential memory:
auditory sequential memory (the child's ability to recall a random sequence of numbers);
visual sequential memory (the child's ability to repeat a sequence of non-meaningful figures from memory).

Supplementary subtests:
auditory closure (the child is required to identify a word when only parts of it are spoken, e.g. 'tele — one');
sound blending (the child is required to identify a word when its syllables are pronounced with half-second intervals).

The test was originally standardised on 1,000 children aged between 2 and 10 years from schools in Illinois. Subjects with IQ scores below 80 and over 100 were excluded, as were children with serious sensory or physical handicaps and black children. Although the test is intended to delineate specific abilities and disabilities in children so that remediation may be undertaken, it is clear that the restrictions placed upon selection of the standardisation sample limits the value of the standardised scores for the purpose of comparison (Weener *et al.* 1967). Furthermore, the absence of a British standardisation raises problems for the use of the test with British children.

From a separate analysis of reliability, Weener *et al.* (1967) comment that while measures of internal consistency (item analysis) are high, the test-retest reliabilities for the separate subscales are low. The standard errors of measurement for many of the subtests are also unacceptably high, indicating that obtained scores might vary considerably from 'real' scores.

While it may be agreed that the different subtests assess different aspects of linguistic functioning, there is considerable controversy concerning whether this is a complete or representative set of subtests, and whether they do in fact tap the processes described by Osgood (1957a, 1957b). The original validation of the test was carried out using 86 subjects, ranging in age from 7 years 4 months to 9 years. Concurrent validity was determined by comparing scores on the ITPA with scores on existing language tests and the linguistic portions of achievement tests. Predictive validity was examined by comparing the ITPA scores with measures from the other language and achievement tests obtained after a time-lapse. The concurrent validity co-efficients varied from 0.03 to 0.65, and the predictive measures ranged from – 0.19 to 0.53.

While different interpretations may be offered of these low correlations, the fact remains that the ITPA has only limited empirical support for its validity. Weener *et al.* conclude that the data from the studies of internal validity show that the test does not adequately integrate the eleven subtests, nor does it explain the relationship between the subtests or between subtest performance and other relevant behaviour.

In a review of 39 studies which used the ITPA or one of its subtests as a criterion for language improvement, Hammill and Larsen (1974) found little evidence to support the view that the psycholinguistic constructs measured by the ITPA responded to existing training methods. However, two factor-analytic studies (Hare *et al.* 1973; Newcomer *et al.* 1974) provided general support for the concept of levels, processes and the auditory–vocal modality distinction. Only the visual–motor modality was not substantiated.

Kirk *et al.* (1968) argue that the test can be used in two ways: first, to compare a subject's overall score with the age-group norms from the standardisation data; and, second, to compare the subtest score with the overall mean score. Here, it is suggested that a score of +10 or –10 points should be regarded as a discrepancy and worthy of further assessment. Weener *et al.* conclude that, although the overall score does provide a reliable measure, it is of questionable validity. The reliability of the individual subtests is regarded as 'too low for adequate prediction and diagnosis from individual profiles' (Weener *et al.* 1967: 377). In the intervening two decades since Weener *et al.* published their review, little has happened to improve the acceptability of the ITPA and, in terms of the developments which have occurred in linguistic theory and our knowledge of children's language acquisition, a great deal has happened further to undermine its theoretical foundations.

Discussion of language tests

Having briefly described ten tests of language, it is now possible to compare them on a range of criteria. The criteria included here may be divided into two: first, those which are concerned with the content and manner of administration of the test; and, second, those which are concerned with their technical sophistication and adequacy. While the former provide information regarding whether a test might reasonably be expected to facilitate the assessment of particular individuals and for particular purposes, the latter give information regarding the nature and quality of any information which is derived from the test. For ease of reference by practitioners who may wish to use these criteria to evaluate tests for specific purposes, the tests described and the criteria are presented in the form of a table at the end of this chapter (see Table 8.1, pp. 168–9).

Content and administration

Does the test measure comprehension or production or imitation?

This will influence the teacher's or therapist's decision regarding whether or not the test is likely to be useful for a particular child and for a particular purpose.

What kind of elicitation procedure is employed? What kind of response is the child required to make?

These two criteria will determine the extent to which it is felt that the test can provide a meaningful assessment of children who may have additional articulatory, sensory or physical disorders, as well as possible linguistic difficulties. For example, a child who has difficulty perceiving pictorial materials may be expected to have considerable difficulties with any test which uses pictures as part of the elicitation procedure *for reasons other than poor linguistic ability*. Similarly, a test which requires a response to a spoken word or sentence should be used only for children who have reasonably good speech perception.

Test measures

Has the test been standardised? What were the characteristics of the sample, and from which population (sample frame) was the sample selected?

This information is important if a child's test score is to be compared with information from the standardisation sample in order to make judgements about relative severity of a linguistic problem or language delay. In cases where the standardisation sample is drawn from a different population from that of the child being tested (for example, the sample is North American children and the child to be tested is British; the sample comprises children from a different age group from that of the child being tested), it is inadvisable to make judgements based on comparisons with the standard-isation data. Where certain categories of children have been excluded from the standardisation sample, it is necessary to exercise extreme caution when using the test with any children from those categories. Finally, it is necessary for the standardisation sample to be sufficiently large to provide a fair reflection of the variation to be expected in the population. McCauley and Swisher (1984) recommend that 100 be regarded as a minimum number for an adequate sample. In Table 8.1 information on sample size, chronological age, sample frame and exclusions is included where these factors are described in the test manual or other publications.

Has the test been shown to be reliable?

This is a very basic requirement of any measuring device. If the test has not been *shown to be reliable* in empirical studies, then there is no guarantee that any information obtained by using the test will provide an *accurate* reflection of any child's ability. Information on two types of reliability is discussed here. Internal reliability or consistency is concerned with the extent to which the individual test items provide measures that are accurate reflections of the overall score. It indicates that the test items themselves are accurate. However, since tests are always used by different people in different settings, it is also necessary to know something about the extent to which the same tester may achieve stable scores, when the test is given to the same person on different occasions, or the extent to which the scores from different testers would be comparable if they were to test the same individual. This is referred to as 'external reliability'.

Has the test been shown to be valid?

This information is necessary if the test user is to be confident that the linguistic abilities which the test purports to measure are indeed the abilities that are actually measured. While many tests may have high face validity – that is, they may *look* as if they measure a particular linguistic ability – this is not a sufficient justification for using test data as a basis for clinical or educational decision-making. Test validity can be determined in different ways. 'Construct validity' (C1) refers to the extent to which the test results are interpretable within the framework of contemporary linguistic theory. 'Content validity' (C2) refers to the extent to which individual items can be shown to be measuring the same underlying skills or abilities. 'Concurrent validity' (C3) is the agreement between the test scores and some criterion measure at the same point in time, while 'predictive validity' (P) refers to the agreement between test scores and some criterion measure obtained some-time later.

Does the test provide quantitative or qualitative scores?

This is a particularly important criterion, since the kind of information recoverable from a test will constrain the ways in which the test can be used. Quantitative scores may be more appropriate for research purposes, for evaluating the effectiveness of different forms of therapy, for screening large numbers of children, and for identifying whether or not a particular child is experiencing difficulties which warrant further assessment and possibly some form of placement or remediation. Qualitative measures, on the other hand, are of more use for conveying information to parents and other

Table 8.1 Evaluation of language test: summary table

	Description			Scoring		Standardisation			Reliability [4]	Validity [5]
	Comprehension or production	Elicitation procedure	Response mode	Quantitative	Qualitative	Sample	Country	Characteristics		
Articulation tests										
Edinburgh Articulation Test	Production	Pictures	Single words	Age norms[1] Confidence limits[2] Standardised scale[3]	Yes	N=510 Age=3–6yrs	UK (Scotland)	Pupils at ordinary schools	Internal	C_2
Goldman–Fristoe Test of Articulation	Production	Pictures and imitation	Single words and sentences	Age norms	Yes	No information	USA	Pupils at ordinary schools	External	C_2
Vocabulary tests										
British Picture Vocabulary Test	Comprehension	Spoken word plus pictures	Point or gesture	Age norms Confidence limits Standardised scale		N=1,401 Age=2–16yrs	UK	Pupils at ordinary schools	Internal and external	C_1, C_2, C_3
Test of Grammatical ability										
Word Order Comprehension Test	Comprehension	Spoken sentences and pictures	Point or gesture	Age norms	Yes	N=50 Age=4–5½yrs	UK	Normal and moderately handicapped children	No information	No information
Northwestern Syntax Screening Test	Comprehension and production	Spoken sentences, pictures and imitation	Point or gesture; speech	Standardised scale	No	N=344 Age=3–7.11yrs	USA	Only normally developing children	No information	No information

Test for Auditory Comprehension of Language	Comprehension	Spoken sentences and pictures	Point or gesture	Age norms Confidence limits Standardised scale	Yes	N=1,003 Age=3-11yrs	USA	Randomly selected	External Internal	C_1, C_2, C_3 P
Test for Reception of Grammar	Comprehension	Spoken sentences and pictures	Point or gesture	Age norms	Yes	N=2,112 Age=4-12.11yrs	UK	Excluded all handicapped and second language users	Internal	No information
Language Imitation Test	Comprehension and production (i.e. imitation)	Imitation of model	Speech	Numerical	Yes	N=108 Age=N/A	UK	Severe learning difficulties	External Internal	C_2, C_3
Tests of psycholinguistic abilities										
Reynell Developmental Language Scales, 2nd edn	Comprehension and production	Instructions, models/toys, pictures	Manipulate models; speech production	Age norms Standardised scale	No	N=363 Age=6mths-6yrs	UK	Excluded immigrants	Internal	C_2 C_3, P
Illinois Test of Psycholinguistic Abilities	Comprehension and production	Various	Various	Age norms Standardised scale	Subtests profile	N=1,000 Age=2-9yrs	USA	Extremes of IQ, handicapped and blacks excluded	Internal	C_2

Notes: Information refers to details published in the test manual and not to subsequently published validation or reliability studies.

[1]'Age norms' indicates that test includes procedures for making age comparisons with standardisation group.

[2]'Confidence limits' indicates information on standard error of test measurements.

[3]'Standardised scale' indicates scale based on standard deviation units.

[4]Reliability: 'internal reliability' reflects item consistency; 'external reliability' reflects test-retest or split-half reliability.

[5]Validity: C_1 = construct validity; C_2 = content validity; C_3 = concurrent validity; P = predictive validity.

professionals, and are essential as a basis for detailed planning or remedial strategies.

Two forms of quantitative scoring are considered here: age norms, and standardised scores. In addition, since no test is completely accurate (that is, all tests have a reliability co-efficient of less than 1), it is desirable to have information regarding the level of confidence which a test user can have in any obtained score. This is usually given in the form of the probability that any obtained score will be within a given range of the true score. For example, 95 per cent probability that any score will be within +5 or −5 points of the 'true' score.

Qualitative scores are of two kinds. First, there are scores which are simply the quantitative scores from a set of separate subtests. Where the subtests can be shown to be reliable and valid, such subtests scores may provide a useful profile of the child's ability in a variety of areas. Second, qualitative scores may be obtained from a descriptive analysis of the child's performance across a range of subtests or across different items. Once again, it is necessary that the separate items should be demonstrably reliable and valid, since specific interpretations may well be based not on the accumulation of correct and incorrect responses, but on the child's pattern of scores. An important criterion for the use of tests involving a qualitative assessment is that the test user is fully familiar with the theoretical basis of the test and is competent to translate variations in test performance across items into valid generalisations about a child's linguistic ability and, if necessary, into recommendations for treatment. Qualitative assessments depend to a greater extent than quantitative scoring on the skills of the person administering and interpreting the test.

Part four

Approaches to Language Teaching

Chapter nine

Strategies for improving language learning: the behavioural approach

Introduction

At its broadest, language intervention is any attempt to improve the linguistic functioning of individuals who are recognised as experiencing some form of language impairment. The way in which we might describe and therefore understand language impairment raises numerous issues which are considered in Chapters 7 and 8. This chapter and Chapter 10 deal specifically with the theory and practice of language-based interventions. Such interventions vary from the informal and unstructured approaches which might be employed by well-meaning relatives and caregivers, to the more structured and carefully planned approaches which are more likely to be developed and implemented by trained professionals. The focus here will be on the latter, although some consideration will be given to the ways in which individuals without any formal training can provide effective help for children with language disabilities.

The aims and objectives of language teaching

Language intervention may be initiated in order to influence the child's command of language in two ways: first, it may be aimed at providing language which is better suited to the child's needs within a particular setting. For example, a child who experiences difficulties in having conversations because she rarely asks for opinions or information from others, may be taught how and when to ask questions. Similarly, a developmentally younger child who is undergoing toilet training, may be taught a word to indicate 'I want to go to the toilet now!' Here, the aims of the intervention are to help the child deal more effectively with different aspects of the environment, and the language which forms the focus of the intervention is selected accordingly. This is often termed a 'functional' approach and it is closely related to functional descriptions of language outlined in Chapter 3.

Another quite different aim for intervention is to help the child make developmental progress. Here, development is the unfolding sequence of linguistic skills which are displayed by ordinary children without linguistic impairments. The aim of intervention would be to help the child learn those aspects of language and communication which would ordinarily appear next in the developmental sequence. Thus, for a child who is able to produce negative sentences, but invariably places the negative at the beginning of the sentence ('No Daddy go work' for 'Daddy isn't going to work') the next developmental step, and hence an appropriate target for intervention, would be to produce sentences with the negative in the appropriate place in the sentence (e.g. 'Daddy no go work'). However, note that the negative is still expressed by 'no' rather than the more acceptable adult form 'is not', since this represents a more advanced developmental stage.

This example suggests that a focus for intervention which is developmentally appropriate, need not necessarily result in the child having greater control of her environment; that is to say, it may not be functionally relevant. And, by the same token, teaching objectives, which are selected solely in terms of the child's perceived needs, may not fit neatly into a developmental sequence. Whereas functional objectives are derived from a clear description of the child's behaviour in particular settings, developmental objectives are derived from the literature on language development of normal children. This is most easily accessible from the developmental charts and checklists which are available either independently as assessment instruments or as part of a language-teaching programme (see Chapter 7).

Teaching methods

No matter how well chosen the objectives for intervention might be, they are of little value unless the methods by which they are taught to the child are effective. There are two important parameters which need to be considered in relation to any statement about teaching methods: what are the characteristics of the individuals who are being taught? What is the nature of the material which they are required to learn?

Characteristics of the children

Children may experience language disorders for a variety of reasons and there is a considerable disagreement regarding the extent to which aetiology is a sound basis for predicting either the specific deficits exhibited by individuals, or the teaching methods that are most likely to be effective. Indeed, there is controversy over the very existence of certain diagnostic categories (Crystal 1984). However, it is clear that the child's characteristics will have a major influence both on the choice of teaching method and its likely outcome.

From a developmental perspective, the child's general cognitive level will provide a guide to the existence of underlying knowledge which is considered necessary for the acquisition of certain linguistic skills. For example, a number of studies have indicated that children are unlikely to begin using productive two-word combinations until they have acquired cognitive abilities associated with the end of Piaget's sensori-motor period (Corrigan 1978; Kahn 1975). Where a child has yet to reach this stage, it is probably unwise to attempt to teach anything more advanced than production and comprehension of single words, and it may be profitable to concentrate on the kinds of sensori-motor and social experiences which are thought to underlie the acquisition of grammatical forms and different language functions (Bricker and Bricker 1973; Mclean and Snyder 1978). While some researchers (Cromer 1974; Slobin 1973) have made a strong case for cognitive abilities being regarded as necessary, but not sufficient for later language development, it is as yet unclear as to whether it will be possible to show a close relationship between specific cognitive abilities and the attainment of more advanced grammatical or functional language skills.

The child's ability to attend to and retain new information will place constraints on how much can be taught at any one time, and the optimal intervals between sessions. It will also indicate whether learning is more or less successful using certain modalities – for example, whether visually presented material is more likely to be retained than orally presented material.

Finally, the child's cognitive level will influence decisions about the most appropriate kinds of activity that might form the basis of intervention. For example, if a play-based approach is to be used, a developmentally young child might be interested in toy dolls and animals, while for an older child computer games might be more suitable. The child's general behaviour and ability to co-operate will determine how easy it is for the teacher or therapist to establish a good rapport with the child and whether or not it is desirable to initiate behavioural training prior to beginning work on language *per se*. Some children appear to have little interest in communication and may even find social interaction unpleasant. With these children, it may be necessary to spend a considerable amount of time in gradually establishing social contact and evolving simple forms of non-verbal communication before tackling specifically linguistic forms of communication.

Most children who acquire language have normal vision and hearing. Deficits in either of these senses are likely to have important repercussions for the language-learning child (Conrad 1979; Fraiberg 1977; Wood *et al*. 1986). Children who are congenitally blind seem to follow the normal pattern of language development, albeit at a somewhat slower rate than children with normal vision (Fraiberg 1977). Children who are born with impaired hearing, or who lose their hearing before they have acquired language, experience considerable delays in acquisition and subsequently display language in which the pattern of errors is quite different from those found in the language of normal children at a similar stage (Bishop 1983).

There are, therefore, grounds for arguing that, while loss of vision results in some language delay, significant hearing impairment gives rise to deviant forms of language. In terms of intervention, both visual and auditory sensory deficits place severe constraints on the kinds of experience which may be regarded as beneficial for language learning. The interaction between sensory impairment and strategies for intervention is dealt with in more detail in Chapter 11.

Spoken language is possible in humans because of the physiological characteristics of the mouth, tongue, lips and larynx (Lenneberg 1967). If there is a structural abnormality in any of these areas or if there is impaired motor control, then the capacity for speech may be impaired or eradicated. Appropriate exercises may assist an individual in improving motor control or in compensating for physiological malformations which inhibit speech, and, in some cases, corrective surgery may help. Since this is essentially a question of physiologically based difficulties which hinder speech production, it is not a central concern of this book. However, teachers and therapists should bear in mind that problems with language production, and articulation difficulties in particular, may have a physiological basis which would not be amenable to the types of intervention described here.

All theories of language acquisition emphasise the importance of experience for the language-learning child. Unfortunately, it is difficult to be more precise than this. Children who have insufficient exposure to language clearly suffer language delay (Clarke-Stewart 1973) and the greater the level of deprivation, the greater the impairment. For example, Curtiss (1977) describes the case of a child without any apparent congenital deficits who had been deprived of normal human contact since infancy and, at the age of 10 years, was unable to communicate using conventional language. However, it is impossible to quantify exactly what constitutes enough exposure for a child to become a proficient language user, and some children learn language from what might appear to be very impoverished experiences (Heath 1983).

In spite of this lack of precision, it is important to recognise that a child's linguistic ability reflects previous opportunities to hear language and to be involved in conversations on a daily basis. The existence of additional cognitive or sensory difficulties may exacerbate the problem and, in some instances, it may be difficult to determine to what extent an unsupportive environment is created, at least in part, by a difficult or unresponsive child. For many children with language difficulties, the inability to communicate easily and effectively seems to create problems for those around them, and *ad hoc* strategies for correcting perceived problems may actually have the opposite effect and actually reduce the opportunities available to the child for learning about language. Where the child's background is suspected of having a major role in language delay, it is necessary to consider ways in which environmental compensation may be introduced – through the school or the home or, in the case of younger children, through placement in appropriate pre-school facilities.

Language characteristics

The second issue which directly affects the design of language intervention strategies concerns the nature of language and its relationship to other aspects of psychological functioning. In Chapter 4 it has already been suggested that behavioural psychologists view language as subject to the same laws of learning as other behaviours. This view has a number of implications. First, it suggests that descriptions of language do not need to be concerned with anything more than the words that are spoken, the context in which utterances occur and the responses that follow; there is no need for any account of communicative intentions, underlying representations or linguistic knowledge. Second, since language behaviours are learned like any other behaviours, the methods that are likely to be successful in language intervention are the same as those that are successful in teaching other skills – specifically, these involve reinforcement, shaping, modelling, prompting and chaining.

An alternative view of language is presented by developmental psychologists and linguists working within a sociocognitive framework. Here, language is viewed as part of a communicative process which cannot easily be separated from the cognitive and social abilities that are essential for human communication (Mead 1934; Vygotsky 1962, 1978). Since language is acquired in conjunction with other related social and cognitive abilities, it makes little sense to plan for intervention unless full account is taken of these other abilities. Opportunities for language learning should therefore be presented in situations where there are also opportunities for the development of other, associated, social and cognitive abilities. Furthermore, since language is seen as part of a process for achieving communicative ends, intervention strategies should be directed at improving the *means* by which linguistic and communicative ends are attained, rather than teaching specific language forms as ends in themselves. Since there is no clear understanding of the ways in which language and communication develop naturally, the best strategy for assisting children to learn about how to use language is to provide language-impaired children with the kinds of experience that are associated with language learning among normal children and to 'tune up' or enhance those features of the environment which research has indicated as being most supportive of developmental progress.

In the rest of this chapter and in Chapter 10, different approaches to language intervention are described in more detail. This is followed by Chapter 11, which considers the ways in which intervention strategies may be modified to meet the needs of particular groups of children.

The behavioural approach

The behavioural approach to language intervention can be traced directly to Skinner's (1957) analysis of language development and the functional analysis presented in *Verbal Behaviour* (Blackman 1984). A number of specific approaches have been developed within the behavioural framework and these are often referred to by slightly different names – for example, *target teaching*, *structured teaching* and *teaching to objectives*. In spite of small differences, these approaches can be considered together, in so far as they share a common theoretical framework and they all place considerable emphasis on three features of any intervention programme. First, teaching objectives are specified in terms of directly observable behaviours; second, the sequence of teaching steps and the criteria for success at each stage are specified in advance by the language therapist; third, teaching involves encouraging the child to perform those behaviours specified in the programme by the manipulation of environmental contingencies.

The approach can most easily be described in terms of the specification of the behaviours which are to be taught and, second, the procedures by which the behaviours can be most efficiently trained (Ruder 1978).

Identifying objectives

Programme planning would normally begin with a functional assessment of the child's existing strengths and weaknesses. As described in Chapter 3, this includes an account of the relevant antecedent stumuli or cues, the child's typical response and the environmental events which follow as a consequence of that response. Such a description is designed to provide valuable insights into the factors which serve to reinforce and maintain a child's language, and the reasons why the child's performance is not improving as rapidly as might be expected. For example, it might be that the child's caretakers always respond to relatively simple forms of language and thereby reduce the incentive for the child to express her needs in more complex and more precise forms. Once the child's current level of performance has been established in relation to cues and consequences, it is then possible to consider what might be reasonable language objectives.

There are three sources of information which can assist the teacher–therapist in the selection of target behaviours. First, a functional analysis of the child's communicative needs, within a given setting, can indicate the kinds of language that will assist the child in dealing with ordinary social encounters. For example, is the child in a class where she is expected to be able to follow simple instructions? Or does the child have to express personal needs such as choosing what to eat from a menu? If these tasks are considered too difficult because the child does not possess the linguistic skills for dealing with them, then a description of precisely those language behaviours which would enable the child actively to participate in these exchanges would provide appropriate teaching objectives.

Second, the teacher–therapist might draw upon descriptions of adult language as a basis for establishing teaching objectives. The argument for this approach is that it is not sufficient to teach a child rote responses for dealing with set situations; instead, the child needs to be taught something of the language system. Since a great deal of time and effort will go into the teaching programme, it is important that the child is taught to speak as a grown-up right from the start. The alternative of introducing age-appropriate language would be regarded as inefficient, since as the child gets older she will constantly have to be taught new ways of speaking. Furthermore, a considerable amount of research has been carried out on adult language and it is arguable that the descriptions which exist for adult language are more accurate and complete than those which exist for the language of children.

The third approach is to look for descriptions for the language which would be used by the non-language-disordered child at the same chronological age. Once again, it is suggested that the child needs to be taught more than superficial rote responses, but here the argument is that the best way to help a child to understand language as a system for expressing thoughts and intentions is to try and mimic the pattern of development found among normally developing children; age-appropriate language may lead to some highly optimistic goal-setting, but it sets the child in the right direction and avoids the anomalous situations of setting up objectives for language-disordered children which are far in excess of the abilities demonstrated by ordinary children of a similar age.

Just as the behavioural approach calls for the child's existing level of performance to be described in relation to antecedent and consequent environmental events, so it also requires that the same kind of description be applied to teaching objectives: the objective is specified in relation to the events which would normally indicate when the response should occur and what reinforcing events would normally follow. The gap between the child's existing repertoire of language behaviours and the teaching objectives determines the size of the teaching problem. While it is conceivable that this gap might be very large, time constraints of the language therapist, and the need for the child, her parents and other caregivers to see goals being met, determine the practical limitations of teaching goals. It is generally advisable that goals are selected which are likely to be achieved in a matter of days or weeks, rather than months or years.

Sequencing teaching steps

While some teaching programmes may require only that the child increase the frequency with which certain utterances or responses occur, more often the objectives call for the teaching of new words and sentences which do not already appear in the child's speech or new ways of using language. This is achieved by a behavioural procedure known as 'shaping'. This involves selectively reinforcing successive approximations to the target utterance. In order that the therapist or teacher can have a clear idea of which responses constitute an improvement in terms of moving towards a better approximation of the target response, the target utterance is usually broken down into a sequence of teaching steps. Thus, if the target utterance for a child, who produced only single-word utterances, was the three-word utterance 'Me want drink', this might be broken down into the following steps:

(a) 'Me want';
(b) 'Want drink';
(c) 'Me want drink'.

The course of learning is thus defined in advance by the sequence of learning steps, and responses that do not conform to this sequence will be treated as errors. Even if the child spontaneously produced a two-word utterance – such as 'Have drink' or 'Want eat' – which was not part of the teaching programme but nevertheless conveyed something of the meaning expressed in the teaching objectives, a strict adherence to behavioural principles would require that the child should not be reinforced for that response. While this may at first sight seem unreasonable, it is clear that the whole behavioural approach relies upon the skill of the teacher–therapist in selectively reinforcing only those reponses which lead to the teaching objectives. Freedom for the teacher–therapist to interpret what may or may not count as a legitimate response would, it is argued, inevitably result in confusion for the child and much slower progress.

Since behavioural responses are typically highly variable, it is usually considered desirable to specify the frequency of a response in the presence of a specific stimulus as a measure of success at each stage of the learning sequence. For example, for a child being taught to answer simple questions, a criterion of eight out of ten correct answers on two successive days might be regarded as an acceptable indication of success. The antecedent stimuli might be specified in relation to the grammatical and content features of the questions (for example, 'wh' questions concerning activities which had occurred that day), and the nature of the reinforcers which maintained the behaviour (for example, immediate verbal praise and a chance to play a computer game following eight correct answers).

Clearly, the choice of the teaching objective in relation to the child's existing repetoire of linguistic skills, and the way in which this is broken down into a sequence of teaching steps, will be crucial to the outcome of the programme. If the learning steps are too large, then the child may not be able to make progress. Similarly, it is possible for the programme to create additional problems by requiring the child to produce responses which are particularly difficult. For instance, in the example used above, it is likely that most children would find the word 'squash' much more difficult too articulate than 'drink', and that 'dink' would be an easier option still. Imposition of the more difficult word, or too strict an adherence to correct articulation, would introduce unnecessary problems and slow the child's progress.

In the same way that there are three sources of information to assist in the selection of teaching objectives, so too there are different ways in which to translate teaching objectives into a sequence of learning steps. First, learning steps may be derived from a logical analysis of the behaviours which are involved in producing the teaching objectives (e.g. Guess *et al.* 1974). For example, Guess *et al.* suggest that if a child is unable to vocalise and does not imitate, it is necessary to teach vocal imitation behaviours as a basis for subsequent teaching of words and phrases. While this approach is likely to generate a teachable sequence which will result in the child producing the required behaviours, there are numerous difficulties. Among these are that the programme is likely to be so lengthy that it may never be applied in practice (Guess *et al.* 1974) and, second, that there is considerable doubt as to whether such a teaching sequence can ever produce more than mindless parrotting responses.

The second source of information for a teaching sequence is provided by formal descriptions of adult grammar. For example, a programme based upon Chomsky's generative grammar would seek to analyse the teaching objective into its phrase-structure and transformational components and then use this as a framework for structuring a teaching sequence. The rationale for this approach is that the teaching steps will help the child to have some insight into the underlying structure of the language system. The problem with this is that, as Chapter 1 indicated, while transformational grammar (and any other description of adult language) may provide an elegant set of rules which characterise the language, it does not necessarily describe the way in which individuals understand language or, indeed, the best sequence of steps for teaching language.

The third approach – and one which is most commonly employed by programme designers – is to look to the sequence of language abilities which characterise the development of ordinary children. Much of the research that has been carried out on non-language-disordered children is concerned with the best way of describing the development of linguistic abilities, and it is this work which forms the basis of many teaching sequences (Harris 1984c). The advantage of this approach is that the curriculum that is offered to language-disordered children represents a natural sequence and is therefore seen as being consistent with normal developmental trends. The underlying assumption is that disordered children acquire language in the same manner as normal children except at a different speed (Miller and Yoder 1974). While this issue is as yet unresolved (J. Harris 1986; Zigler and Balla 1982), there are futher complications which arise from the adoption of developmental sequences for planning learning sequences.

The first of these is that there are a variety of descriptive frameworks that can be employed, and each gives rise to very different language-teaching sequences. For example, characterisation of early multi-word utterances in terms of pivot–open structures would suggest teaching two distinct categories of single-word utterances and then various two-word combinations (Jeffree *et al.* 1973; Willbrand 1977). On the other hand, a semantic-relations approach would indicate that language instruction needs to be related to the non-linguistic context and to the child's activities immediately prior to speaking (Miller and Yoder 1974). Functional descriptions would suggest other, quite different, teaching sequences. A complete developmental training sequence would therefore require the integration of structural, semantic and functional aspects of language at each stage; unfortunately, the available evidence from research on ordinary language-learning children is at present inadequate for this purpose.

The second problem with this approach is that it separates developmental descriptions of language from any account of the causal processes which may be implicated in developmental change. While developmental descriptions may be useful in terms of telling us *what* develops, they are severely restricted if separated from associated descriptions of *how* language develops. Linking such descriptions with a behavioural approach assumes that the behavioural teaching techniques can replace ordinary developmental processes. Interestingly, this claim is defensible only if it is also assumed that the descriptions provide a definitive account of any given aspect of language performance. Since the teaching strategy is intended to change behaviour, it is necessary for the sequence of behavioural objectives, derived from the accounts of the normal child's language, to provide a *complete* characterisation of language performance at any stage of development. Even if this were possible, it would result in an extraordinarily long and complex teaching sequence and one which would be continually growing in response to new discoveries about children's language.

If it is not accepted that such behavioural descriptions provide definitive accounts of language performance – that is, if it is claimed that such descriptions provide only markers which chart the course of more profound underlying cognitive developments – then the rationale for building a language curriculum from behavioural principles becomes considerably weaker. The view that descriptions of normal language development give us an accurate picture of underlying change does not imply that those same underlying changes can be achieved simply by establishing a behavioural repertoire which, in certain respects, mirrors the developmental sequence (Harris 1984a).

Against this argument may be presented the view that developmental sequences are employed as the best way of identifying teaching objectives which are not defined simply in terms of behaviour, but which are sufficiently flexible to incorporate other aspects of contemporary descriptions of language development (Seibert and Oller 1981). This then raises the question of the value of teaching strategies specifically designed to focus on behaviour in teaching objectives which cannot be reduced to behavioural descriptions.

From these criticisms, it may appear that the behavioural approach has little to offer; in fact, this is far from the truth and intervention for language-disordered children has gained much from the application of behavioural technology. Nevertheless, in terms of future developments and the ways in which research is being translated into practice, it remains true that there are considerable differences between the behavioural teaching approach and contemporary research on children's language acquisition, and these differences have important implications for the design of language intervention programmes.

Teaching methods

The most important feature of behavioural approaches to teaching is that pre-selected responses are followed with desirable consequences or rewards in the expectation that those responses will increase in frequency. Gradually, through the reinforcement of successive approximations specified in the sequence of learning steps, the child's responses will be shaped until they match the teaching objective. Among the advantages claimed for this approach is that it requires the child to be actively involved and to produce relatively frequent overt responses. Furthermore, the concept of mastery learning or self-pacing means that the child must perform to a pre-specified standard at each stage before moving on to subsequent steps (Costello 1977). The criterion for moving from one learning step to the next is thus determined by the language therapist. The child controls progress only in terms of how quickly she is able to meet the criteria for success laid down by the therapist at the beginning of the programme.

Reinforcers are those contingent events which have the effect of increasing the frequency of occurrence of the responses they follow. The range of potentially reinforcing events is therefore infinite and is likely to vary considerably from child to child. The reinforcers, which are used in structured teaching situations, are those which are effective for individual children and are easily manipulated by the therapist. In the majority of cases, food, drink or sweet rewards are highly effective, although they may be regarded as inappropriate for health or aesthetic reasons. Social reinforcers – such as verbal praise, smiling, stroking and hugging – are more natural and therefore more acceptable and, in many instances, just as effective as food or sweets. Preferred activities can also be effective, especially when they are linked to a **token system**.

This involves the child being awarded points or tokens for correct responses. At the start of training, the tokens will be paired with either tangible reinforcers or preferred activities so that, over a period of time, the token attains reinforcing properties. Subsequently, tokens can be employed to strengthen behaviours during a teaching session, without the disruption which might accompany the use of preferred activities, or some tangible reinforcers such as food or drink. At the end of the teaching session, or when a specified number of tokens has been accumulated, the child is able to exchange them for the opportunity to engage in the preferred activity or for tangible reinforcers. This ensures that the reinforcing property of the tokens is maintained at a high level.

Unless the teacher or therapist already knows the child, it is generally advisable to seek advice from the parents or other caregivers regarding the kinds of reinforcers that might be effective for the child and acceptable to those who look after her. Alternatively, a period of observation (with younger children) or an informal interview (with older children) may indicate likely reinforcing events. The effect of reinforcing events can, however, be confirmed only be trying them out in a teaching situation.

While the use of reinforcers is an essentially simple procedure, it is important that simple guidelines are closely adhered to:

Be clear about **what behaviours** are candidates for reinforcement.

To begin with, reinforce the behaviour on **every** occasion.

Reinforce **immediately** after the behaviour has occurred (any delay will reduce the link between the reinforcer and *that* behaviour).

Record the initial frequency of the behaviour prior to introducing the reinforcer and then again while the reinforcer is being used; this will indicate whether the behaviour is occurring more frequently.

Further reading on behavioural approaches to teaching is available in a variety of textbooks; for example, see Blackham and Silberman (1975), and Martin and Pear (1988).

Various additional techniques are available to assist the teacher in eliciting responses which can be reinforced at each stage of the programme. The most widely used of these is **modelling**, in which the teacher, another adult or a child produces a model of the target utterance. Modelled utterances may also be reinforced and the child may be encouraged to observe and try to discriminate between reinforced and non-reinforced utterances (Leonard 1975). When modelling is paired with a prompt for the child to produce a similar response, which is then reinforced, the procedure is referred to as **imitation training**. A study carried out by Connell (1987) suggested that, while modelling alone is just as effective as imitation training for normal children learning an artificial grammatical rule, children with language delays perform better when required to imitate the modelled response.

In order that a child is able to learn when a particular response is called for, various **prompts** or **cues** may be devised. These may be physical –

touching or stroking the child when she is required to speak – or verbal prompts. For example:

Teacher: you say 'ice cream'.

Child: Ice cream.

A more subtle verbal prompt is the unfinished sentence. For example:

Teacher: Here is a picture of a boy with a ball. The boy is kicking the . . .

Child: Ball.

A prompt is used to help the child become aware of the appropriate contexts and timing for different responses. In order that the child does not simply learn to respond to the prompt and ignore other naturally occurring cues, it is essential that prompts are gradually reduced, either in intensity or in frequency, with the expectation that the child will eventually respond appropriately without them.

In many cases, particular language forms are taught in relation to particular referents. Thus, noun labels are generally taught in relation to pictures, models or life-size exemplars. Like prompts, these stimuli may initially be selected because they are capable of evoking a particular response, although they may not represent all naturally occurring varieties of a class of referents or even the most common examples. Thus, the child who is taught the word 'car', using a picture of a 1935 Austin, would be severely limited unless she was able to generalise the response 'car' to a wide variety of referents which nevertheless meet the defining characteristics of 'car'. The speed and extent of appropriate **stimulus generalisation** will vary across children and in relation to the aspects of language being taught. It is therefore important that any teaching programme should be organised so that the child is systematically exposed to stimuli which are increasingly representative of naturally occurring referents.

While the emphasis here has been on increasing the frequency of desirable responses, and gradually teaching the child new responses, it is sometimes considered desirable to reduce the frequency of utterances which contain errors or are considered undesirable for other reasons. The simplest strategy is to ignore the inappropriate response in the expectation that responses which are not regularly reinforced will, eventually, become less frequent – this is referred to as **extinction**. Where non-reinforcement or extinction is difficult to maintain or seems to be having little effect, other procedures may be introduced. Verbal reprimands represent the introduction of moderately aversive stimuli contingent on the production of the inappropriate response. This needs to be operated with extreme caution to avoid the possibility of becoming locked in a teaching cycle which focuses on the child's errors, to the exclusion of the correct and appropriate utterances. Too free a use of reprimands may also alter the child's perception of the teacher or therapist, so that he or she is seen as generally aversive and to be avoided. This in turn may reduce the power of social reinforcers delivered by that person.

If a child is earning tokens or points for correct responses, then it is relatively easy to penalise the child by removing points or tokens contingent upon incorrect responses. This **response-cost** procedure may be extremely effective, particularly if it is introduced in the context of a game and providing the balance of gains and losses is calculated in advance so that the child always has a good chance of being able to earn sufficient tokens or points to be exchanged for reinforcers.

The last strategy which may be useful in dealing with inappropriate responses involves the removal of all potentially reinforcing stimuli. The easiest way of achieving this is to move the child to a separate room which has minimal furnishing and decoration. For this reason, it is referred to as **time out from positive reinforcement**, or simply **time out**. Usually, it is only necessary to exclude the child for a matter of minutes, but to avoid the possibility of the time-out room becoming a 'sin-bin' for dealing with problematic children, the precise duration of any time out should be specified in advance and clearly documented during the course of the programme. This is an intrusive procedure which is likely to be very upsetting for the child; it should therefore be used only in extreme cases and only in consultation with a qualified psychologist.

While these procedures focus on penalising the child in some way when an inappropriate response does occur, it is also possible to introduce positive reinforcement after a set period of time during which an inappropriate response did not occur. For example, if a child persistently called out for attention while the teacher was working with other children, the teacher might decide to provide the child with lots of attention only after a period of three minutes had elapsed without the child calling out. This is called **differential reinforcement of zero levels of responding** or a DR0 schedule.

The problem with all these techniques is that while they may be effective in communicating to the child that the previous response was in some way inadequate, they do not help the child to learn a more appropriate response. For this reason, a procedure known as **differential reinforcement of alternative responses** (DRA) is particularly helpful in that it combines techniques of reducing the strength of one behaviour with those for increasing the strength of another behaviour. Here, the teacher–therapist is required to identify an appropriate response which is incompatible with the incorrect or inappropriate response. While the inappropriate response may be reduced through any of the procedures described above, at the same time an alternative response is modelled and reinforced. For example, consider the case of a child who persistently misuses personal pronouns so that instead of saying, 'He is walking', she says, 'Him is walking.' In this case the DRA procedure would involve the teacher–therapist in saying, 'No, that's not right' (reprimand); 'Say: "He is walking" ' (model); 'What is he doing?' (prompt). If the child responds appropriately, the teacher–therapist would reinforce the child with praise or some other reward.

Summary of procedures involved when implementing a behavioural language-teaching strategy

- Functional assessment. This may be carried out in the child's natural environment to establish what demands for communication are made of the child. Alternatively, the child may be assessed using some form of normative comparison to determine her level of ability in relation to normally developing children.
- Identification of language objectives. These will be expressed in terms of what the child is expected to say or do, the cues which indicate when it is appropriate to speak or act, and the consequences which will maintain the appropriate level of responding.
- A description of learning steps. This will trace the sequence of behaviours the child needs to learn in order to move from the existing level of ability to performance of those behaviours described in the objectives. Learning steps may be derived from logical analysis of the task demands, descriptions of adult language performance or developmental sequences.
- Decisions regarding the use of modelling, prompting and shaping procedures.
- Decisions regarding the use of reinforcers to increase the strength of behaviours. For example, is the child likely to respond to social reinforcers or will it be necessary to use primary reinforcers such as food and drink initially? Is it worth setting up a token economy system?
- Decisions regarding the use of procedures to decrease the strength of behaviours: extinction, time out, response cost, differential reinforcement for absence of a particular response (DR0), differential reinforcement of alternative responses (DRA).
- How will the child's performance be recorded prior to the introduction of the programme and while teaching is in progress?

Evaluation of behavioural approaches

There is little doubt that behavioural approaches are extremely effective in teaching individuals to perform new behaviours (Garcia and DeHaven 1974; Snyder *et al.* 1975). However, there are two reasons why behavioural strategies ought not to be regarded as a panacea for children's language problems. The first is that there is still considerable uncertainty regarding the extent to which language which is learned within a highly structured training session provides the child with skills which can be usefully employed in other settings. This is frequently referred to as the problem of **generalisation**, although it may properly be regarded as three related problems.

1 Do the specific responses learned in the training session employed carry over or generalise to other settings?
2 Are the responses learned in the training sessions when the child is with other people besides those involved in training?
3 Where behaviours which, ordinarily, are governed by a linguistic rule are taught, is there evidence that the rule is applied to language forms (morphemes, words, phrases, etc.) other than those which were employed in the training session? For example, if a child is taught the plural /s/ marker for 'boys', 'toys' and 'drinks', is the rule spontaneously extended to other words in the child's vocabulary such as 'girls', 'balls' and 'biscuits'?

The answer to the first two questions is that generalisation does not occur unless it is identified as a programme target and specific steps are taken to assist the child in transferring behaviours to other settings (Hughes 1985). In the case of the third question, there is still considerable disagreement. It seems unlikely that teaching a restricted range of surface structures will inevitably lead to language-disordered children inferring the abstract linguistic rule from which those structures are derived. However, Connell (1982) has recently conducted a study in which he successfully taught four language-disordered children (aged 3 years 4 months to 4 years 2 months) to use a number of grammatical rules associated with the correct use of the sentence subject. The teaching procedure involved a relatively complex combination of modelling, imitation and reinforcement of successive approximations which were specifically selected to highlight the way in which grammatical subjects function in sentences. In this study, not only was the grammatical rule generalised to language forms besides those used in the teaching sessions, but this understanding was applied in non-teaching settings. In spite of this optimistic result, it is worth remembering that this is but one study carried out with only four children; much more research needs to be carried out before the problems associated with generalisation can be dismissed.

The second problem for behavioural approaches is concerned with the separation of language content from linguistic and communicative processes. From the behavioural standpoint, language is but a class of behaviour; since it is assumed that the learning of all behaviour is subject to the same general principles, it makes sense to separate issues about structuring content from questions about how that content can be best taught. Learning theorists have joined linguists and child psychologists in the debate regarding how language can be best described, and what constitutes the best basis for structuring a teaching sequence, while at the same time assuming that whatever description is finally accepted will be amenable to behavioural programming. This has led to a variety of different types of language description – including generative grammar, semantic relationships and, more recently, functional descriptions – being embraced as frameworks for structuring learning objectives.

During the last 20 years or so, those working clinically within a behavioural framework have moved away from early ideas about language being studied in context and the importance of language as part of a social process (Mead 1934; Skinner 1957). Instead, language has increasingly been treated as a disembodied subject which has to be presented to the learner much like any subject is presented to a child at school. And just as the organisation and structuring of the school curriculum is seen as the key to successful teaching (Lawton 1983) so the issue of linguistic description has dominated the research literature on language intervention.

Behavioural descriptions have made it possible to see language as a set of skills, while grammatical descriptions focus on language as personal knowledge of linguistic rules; in both cases, language is seen as something which an individual *does* or *has*. The teacher is seen as having a skill or possessing knowledge which is either shared with or passed on to a pupil. In each case, language is conceived of as an entity rather than as a process. From this perspective, it makes sense to seek optimal conditions for sharing or passing on the skills or the knowledge necessary for using language, since the subsequent performance of the pupil will be largely determined by how successfully this is done; in optimal conditions, with a well-structured programme and an attentive pupil, the child should absorb the lesson content and thereafter be in possession of more knowledge or better skills. Most importantly, the emphasis has shifted from a concern with how language has functional significance in the natural environment (see Skinner 1957), to how knowledge or skill can be transmitted from the teacher to the learner. And as a result, those aspects of language which are concerned with function and use seem to have been ignored.

The only theory that actually treats language as a problem external to the individual and, in a sense, dislocated from other aspects of social functioning, is that put forward by Chomsky. In contrast, Skinner in *Verbal Behaviour* presents linguistic categories that are based on social and communicative functions. Similarly, more recent sociocognitive theories of language development emphasise that language is not *something*, but rather a part of a broader communicative process. The young child is not learning about a discrete subject called *language*; instead, the child is being drawn into a increasingly complex set of social and communicative processes, and linguistic knowledge is essentially an understanding of how to achieve interpersonal goals using a conventional system of communication. From this theoretical perspective, structured teaching using behavioural techniques is unlikely to succeed, since those techniques confine the teacher and child to a rigid and artificial set of social interactions which are considered consistent with didactic instruction. The child's understanding of linguistic processes – about the ways in which language can be used in social situations – will be limited to the circumscribed and one-sided interactions which are possible within an instructional setting and are unlikely to be of any value in naturalistic settings.

Rees (1978) provides a telling illustration of this problem when she quotes from a paper by Geller and Wollner (1976). A 10-year-old language-disordered boy had been taught to produce 'wh' questions.

> After having been trained in the therapy room with appropriate stimuli to ask 'who is it?' 'what is it?' and 'where is it?' the clinician decided to test Jeffrey's ability to use these questions in a more natural, real-life situation. Jeffrey was told that he and the clinician were going for a walk, and he was reminded to ask questions when he got outside. At this point, Jeffrey opened the door, stepped outside the building, and announced to no one in particular – 'who is it?' 'what is it?' 'where is it?'

Here, the child seems to have mastered the lesson content in that he is able to produce specific structures; but he has clearly failed to learn anything about the social context in which it would be appropriate to use these phrases.

Incidental teaching

In response to these criticisms, some researchers have sought to introduce behavioural teaching strategies into naturally occurring conversations within everyday settings. This approach is referred to by different names including **incidental teaching** (Cavallaro and Poulson 1985), **interactive language instruction** (Cole and Dole 1986) or **milieu teaching** (Cavallaro 1983). Here, the emphasis is on following the child's lead and making use of ordinary objects and events as reinforcers (Warren and Kaiser 1986). As with behavioural teaching in more structured settings, the teacher–therapist specifies in advance of teaching the target responses which will be reinforced, although these may in fact be defined in terms of response categories – for example, nouns, or three-word utterances – rather than specific behaviours. A scale of prompts is also devised so that the teacher may modify the amount of teaching support that is offered in response to the child's changing level of performance during the teaching session. For example, Cavallaro (1983) identified the following conversational prompts, listed in order from those providing least support and most freedom to those which give the child most help, but also impose the greatest constraints regarding an appropriate answer:

1 Focusing the child's attention – for example, 'Hey, look at this [book].'
2 Asking an open-ended question – 'What kinds of book do you like to read?'

Table 9.1 Incidental teaching compared with direct instruction

Incidental teaching	Direct instruction
Sequence of language goals is determined by child during teaching session.	Sequence of learning steps is determined by teacher–therapist in advance.
Reinforcement arises from naturally occurring events.	Reinforcement specified in advance.
Modelling is the primary teaching method.	Elicited imitation is the primary teaching method.
The natural context provides language referents, i.e. what stimulus is talked about.	Referent materials are pre-selected – talk is focused on these.
The child is encouraged to initiate language production.	The child's language is teacher-directed.
The child's response rate is generally low.	The child's response rate is generally high.
The child is seen as actively involved in abstracting linguistic rules.	The child is seen as learning specific language behaviours.

Source: Adapted from Cole and Dole (1986).

3 A request for verbalisation – for example, 'Tell me about this book.'
4 Partial prompt – 'Is it a book of stories?'
5 Full prompt – 'It's a detective story.'

Every effort is made to capitalise on the child's own interests and desires and adult co-operation is made dependent upon pre-specified linguistic responses. For example, a child who indicated non-verbally that she wished to watch the television might be required to verbalise the request, with a structure which reflected the teaching objectives, before being allowed to switch on the TV. The opportunity to watch television would then serve as a natural reinforcer for the preceding response. The differences between incidental teaching and direct instruction methods are summarised in Table 9.1.

In a recent review of incidental teaching methods, Warren and Kaiser (1986) indicate that they have been found to be effective with children suffering from a variety of language disorders, and when used to teach a range of different language objectives. Different studies have reported increases in child-initiated responses and at least modest gains in language measures such as vocabulary size. Of particular interest, in view of the limitations of direct teaching methods, is the finding that language learned in this way does seem to generalise to situations beyond those in which the teaching took place. However, Warren and Kaiser also recognise the limitations of the available research evidence and they suggest that more evidence is needed to confirm the effectiveness of incidental teaching. In particular, they argue that the existing studies have not successfully demonstrated that incidental teaching results in improved social uses of language or that the new forms and functions which are learned generalise to new settings faster when this approach, rather than other more traditional approaches, is used. Thus, while incidental teaching seems to be a very promising extension of behavioural methods, empirical questions still remain with respect to generalisation and the social/interactive aspects of language functioning.

Finally, incidental teaching does not represent a single method of teaching so much as an attempt to introduce the principles of behavioural teaching into the natural environment. There is therefore a continuum which runs from didactic teaching, in an environment which has been designed to optimise instructional objectives, to an interactive style of teaching, in which the teacher attempts to apply behavioural principles while working in a messy and uncontrolled natural environment. While the 'laboratory' environment may favour the implementation of a number of sophisticated behavioural procedures and therefore lead to effective learning, it is also likely to promote the kinds of interaction which are unrepresentative of the child's everyday social experiences. In contrast, the natural environment may be ideal from the point of view of teaching the child language which will have immediate relevance to her daily experiences, but it may be extremely difficult to structure teaching in a way that is consistent with the principles of behavioural instruction. In the next chapter we will explore alternative strategies for teaching language in naturalistic settings.

Chapter ten

Strategies for encouraging language development: naturalistic approaches

Introduction

One of the main problems for the behavioural approach to language teaching is that it leads to the separation of content from process, with the result that children are taught language structures and associated referential meanings within a highly restricted set of social interactions. Children do not learn to use language to serve their own communicative needs, and, for this reason, the language they do learn does not generalise to other settings and is not adequate for the induction of linguistic rules (see Harris 1984a for a more detailed disussion).

In content, interactive theories of language acquisition indicate that language development is led by the child's search for more effective ways of communicating with other people. Thus, the goal of language development is not the acquisition of rules for generating language structures. Instead, linguistic structure is a means of achieving the more immediate goal of efficient communication (Mahoney 1975). This view has a number of implications for intervention strategies.

First, a proper analysis of language disorders ought not to be confined to the child's problems or to the failure of caretakers to respond appropriately, but to the two factors together. For example, Cunningham *et al.* (1981) described patterns of interaction between mothers with normal infants (aged between 18 and 54 months) and mothers with slightly older, retarded children (aged between 28 and 96 months). They used the correspondence between the Mean Length of Utterance of mothers and their children as an indication of how intelligible the mother's language is likely to be to the child and therefore how useful it will be to a child who is trying to work out the relationship between language forms, referential meanings and the functions which language serves in communication. In this study, irrespective of whether or not the child was handicapped, the match between the MLU of the mothers and children was closely related to the child's responsiveness to interaction. Furthermore, children who spoke little, and thus provided their mothers with little information regarding their linguistic abilities, were confronted with a more directive maternal style of interaction

Figure 10.1 Developmental approaches to interactive language intervention

Physical and social context	Opportunities for language development	Increasing competence in language and communication

compared to their more talkative peers. This in turn might explain the low frequency and complexity of the spontaneous speech produced by some of these children.

Second, intervention ought to concentrate on establishing appropriate forms of social interaction between children and their caretakers, since it is only in this way that the child can learn about communicative processes and the ways in which language can be used to achieve interpersonal ends. But what constitutes 'an appropriate form of social interaction' for children with language disorders. How might such interactions be brought about between children and their caretakers?

Developmental theories of language acquisition suggest that it is helpful to think of intervention strategies on three levels:

1 the conditions or context within which language learning takes place;
2 the opportunities that are presented to the child for participating in communicative exchanges;
3 the knowledge and skills which a child demonstrates through growing competence in the communicative process.

Traditional teaching and behavioural strategies focus on describing some aspect of the child's increasing competence and then seek to improve specific skills without reference to the processes within which such skills are normally embedded. Whereas the child may achieve a degree of proficiency in using the skills in an instructional setting, lack of opportunity to practise the skill in natural communicative settings reduces the likelihood of generalisation. Naturalistic approaches describe language as part of a communicative process and the opportunities which are made available to the child for participating in communication during teaching are seen as determining what the child is able to learn about the process. If the child is provided with opportunities to learn about only some aspects of the communicative process – for example, how to respond to questions – then it ought not to be surprising that the child's skills do not extend to requests or to giving information.

A second consequence of viewing language as a process is that while form (structure), content (meaning) and use (function) provide convenient descriptive distinctions, they are not, in reality, separable; any attempt to teach relations between structure and content also implies some, possibly covert, instruction about use; conversely, an attempt to teach language use must be attached to appropriate words and phrases, which either have or will acquire some referential or interpersonal meaning. It is, therefore, desirable that teaching should occur in those contexts in which the child will experience a range of language functions and have the opportunity to practise using language to achieve a variety of interpersonal ends.

While the child's understanding of and ability to participate in linguistic exchanges with other people will be dependent upon the opportunities which have been available for language learning, the nature and variety of those opportunities will be determined by the physical setting and the perceptions of those adults who are available as conversational partners. For example, research has shown that teachers in pre-school settings provide children with different opportunities for conversational interactions compared with mothers and fathers at home (Tizard and Hughes 1984; Wood *et al.* 1980). Perceptions of the child, the child's language and the best way of helping language-disordered children will influence what the adult *tries* to achieve, while the availability of time, space, furniture and other materials will influence what the adult is *able* to achieve.

Having presented a model of language intervention in terms of relations between conditions, opportunities and competencies, it is now possible to consider how intervention strategies might be organised.

The context for naturalistic language teaching

This section is concerned with a description of activities designed to promote social interactions, and facilitate the development of language and communication. Particular emphasis is given to the creation of opportunities for the child to experience language being used in different ways and to practise using language to achieve a range of interpersonal objectives. Two kinds of activity have been explored clinically: a range of semi-structured play activities and more highly structured referential communication problems.

Play activities

A list of games together with the pragmatic language skills which they promote is presented in Figure 10.3, p. 199. Here, the aim is to engage one or more children in activities which they will find interesting and which will create opportunities for using language to achieve a range of interpersonal objectives. For this reason, it is important that the adult plays a facilitatory role but is careful not to dominate or take over control of the activity. Children may need to experience examples of language being used in different ways by others, but it is equally important that they are also able to experiment with their own use of language and discover the effects it can have on other people. Adult participation should therefore be sensitive and responsive to the attempts at verbal and non-verbal communication by the children. Above all, the adult must be aware of the way in which games may be structured to create social encounters and interpersonal problems which can be solved through verbal and non-verbal communication.

In addition to creating conditions within which communicative exchanges are likely to occur, these activities also make it more likely that children will have something to talk about – that is, something in which they are interested and involved and have organised into some kind of conceptual structure. Bloom (1973) pointed out that many of a child's first utterances are an attempt to express some idea about the world to another person. Activity in a familiar context provides the basis for the conceptual organisation which underpins these first steps into semantic coding. More recently, Brinker (1982) has attempted to chart the developing relationship between a child's actions in two play contexts and the comprehension of object names. He argues that different kinds of activity create different opportunities for the child to develop conceptual structures and that this is subsequently reflected in the child's ability to talk about these play activities.

Similarly, Nelson and her colleagues (Nelson *et al.* 1986) have argued for the importance of social routines during the early stages of language acquisition. Initially, pre-verbal communication is embedded in simple social routines such as peek-a-boo (Bruner and Sherwood 1976; Ratner and Bruner 1978) but, with time, the child begins to organise experience in relation to more complex activities such as going to a shop; visiting a café or restaurant and going to school. Nelson argues that repeated experiences in these settings gives rise to General Event Representations which provide the child with a kind of cognitive map for organising her behaviour and language when she encounters other, similar, situations. A child who is presented with a new experience which seems to fit an existing General Event Representation, will organise her activity in relation to the expectations created by that event knowledge.

The language used by the child and others forms a part of the General Event Representation which Nelson refers to as a script. Participants in routine social events take on standard roles and their language can be described in relation to a predictable script structure. Thus, the child learns language as part of a script which is inextricably linked to the social routine in which it is embedded.

The implication of this way of looking at language is that language activities designed to promote pragmatic skills may be useful only in so far as they provide children with experiences that translate into the kinds of General Event Representations and script knowledge which are applicable in other commonly occurring settings. It is for precisely this reason that formal teaching may have limited effects in other everyday situations. In the same way, pragmatic skills learned in specially constructed play activities may fail to generalise to other social interactions in naturally occurring social settings if the Event Representations afforded by the two settings are different. Should this prove to be the case, it would suggest that all language instruction ought to be conducted in situations that resemble, as far as is possible, exactly those situations in which the child needs to use language on a day-to-day basis. Ultimately, the notion of teaching language may become a question of how the language therapist provides support for the child to communicate in everyday settings so that competencies are acquired and subsequently maintained when that support is withdrawn.

Referential communication problems

Referential communication problems create a simple format in which the child must either give detailed instructions so that the adult can complete a simple task, or follow instructions given by the adult. Usually, both adult and child sit either side of a screen facing a specially chosen set of materials. A simple task might involve the child providing the adult with instructions which would permit the selection of a specific object. With a range of everyday objects this would simply necessitate naming, but if the objects used were identical except for colour or size, the child would need to modify her language accordingly. The task might be made more difficult by requiring the child to instruct the adult on how to organise materials to make a particular pattern. Various other modifications include whether the screen obscures the participants' heads and faces or merely the materials they are using, and whether the person following the instructions is able to ask questions and provide feedback.

It has been suggested that this kind of activity can be used to target specific pragmatic skills (Spekman and Roth 1982). For example, in its simplest form, the problem requires the speaker to take account of the fact that the participants do not share visual information. The speaker must therefore be able to consider the communicational needs of the listener in order to figure out which utterances are likely to be maximally informative. The speaker must also recognise that contributions which might be redundant in a situation where speaker and listener enjoyed a shared visual experience are likely to be highly relevant when this is not the case. Successful communication will thus depend upon the speaker's ability to make appropriate adjustments to his or her utterances, in the light of the perceived informational constraints experienced by the listener.

Alternatively, if the listener is able to indicate how successful the speaker's contributions are in providing information relevant to task completion, then the activity can be used to provide the speaker with opportunities for modifying or 'repairing' contributions in the light of feedback. If the language therapist takes the listener role, then feedback may be varied so that the child's communicative responsibility in the interaction is only ever slightly in advance of existing abilities (see Figure 10.3).

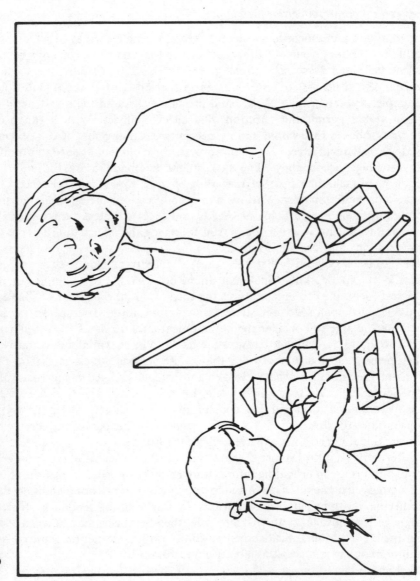

Figure 10.2 A referential communication problem

Figure 10.3 Activities for developmental language intervention

1 Activities for relating socially to others' personal needs:
Preparing a fruit salad: three children to share one knife.
Making pastry shapes of playdough models: restricted number of cutters, rolling-pins, etc.
Simple competitive team games such as skittles.

2 Activities which involve using language to direct the behaviour of self and others:
Group of children copy a pattern or collage made by the teacher–therapist.
Group of children plant seeds: one plant pot to three children.
Referential communication problems (see p. 197).

3 Giving information:
Hiding games with pictures: picture must be named before a disc is retrieved.
Communication lotto: child must describe pictures before they are claimed by those with cards.
Children take it in turns to bring a favourite object and talk to the others about it: 'show and tell'
Children act as guides for visitors.

4 Reasoning, judging and predicting:
Exploring floating and sinking with different objects in water.
Building models with simple materials.

5 Imagining and verbalising feeling of self and others:
Drama using costumes and props.
Puppet stage.
Simulated shop, café or school.

Source: Adapted from Staab (1983).

Creating opportunities for language development: social interaction and increasing competence

Within the context of different activities a variety of social and linguistic interactions may occur. This section provides a closer specification of those interactions which are consistent with the opportunities for language development. Since the child's competencies are essentially social abilities which emerge through opportunities to engage in communicative processes, they cannot easily be described in isolation, but need to be seen in relation to the child's participation in social and linguistic interactions. For this reason, this section includes both descriptions of facilitative social interactions and the social and linguistic knowledge which children acquire as a result of their involvement in such interactions.

Characteristics of adult language

Numerous research studies have shown that children with a variety of language disorders are highly responsive to the kinds of language employed by the adults around them (Chesaldine and McConkey 1979; MacDonald *et al.* 1974; Seitz 1975). As a result, it is possible to list the main features of adult language which are likely to be helpful to young language-learning children.

(1) Language which, in structural terms, is slightly more complex than the language produced by the child. This increases the likelihood that the child will understand the adult (especially if the language is used in context – see 6 below), while providing models of more complex forms. Structural complexity may be defined in a wide variety of ways, including the following:

(a) Mean Length of Utterance, expressed in either words or morphemes (see Chapter 7).
(b) Mean length of speaking turn, expressed in either morphemes or words.
(c) Grammatical complexity – particularly the use of embedded sentences and passives.
(d) Type–token ratio – that is, the frequency of different words, expressed as a proportion of all words used.

(2) Language which deals with the child's interests. For young children or those with very limited language, this is likely to mean language which refers directly to actions, objects, people and events that are present in the 'here and now'. This increases the likelihood that referential and functional meanings will be understood through context-based interpretation.

(3) Another way of achieving relevance is for the adult to make his or her contribution semantically related to that of the child's. This increases the probability that the adult's contribution will relate directly to the meanings the child is trying to express, and that the child will recognise the connection between her own communicative intentions and the language structures presented by the adult (see Chapter 5). There are a number of ways in which adult contributions may be made to relate to the meanings expressed by the child:

(a) Repetition of the child's utterance in a conventional or 'idealised form' – for example, when the child says 'buh', the adult responds with 'butter'.
(b) An expansion of the child's utterance to provide a gloss which

expresses more of the perceived meaning in the surface structure, for example, when the child says 'play bath', the adult responds with 'You want to play with your toys in the bath.'

(c) Recasting the child's utterance to illustrate an alternative grammatical structure (Nelson 1977). For example in order to demonstrate question forms, in response to the child's utterance of 'You can't get in', the adult might respond: 'No I can't get in, can I?'

(4) It is important that children receive support and encouragement for using language, and this can be achieved easily and naturally by the use of phatic responses – that is, contributions such as 'yes', 'oh', 'mmmm' and 'I see' – which indicate that the adult is listening and attending to what the child is saying (Cross 1977; Nelson 1973; Wood *et al.* 1980).

(5) In order to encourage a child who is reluctant or unable to communicate using language, it is often natural to ask questions. However, questions have a poor track record in terms of their effectiveness in stimulating conversational exchanges (Dillon 1982; Nelson 1973) and research with normal children in nursery schools suggests that a more potent way to encourage children to talk is for the adult to make meaningful personal contributions to the conversation. Thus, if a child says 'I went to the zoo yesterday,' instead of simply asking 'What did you do there?' a more effective contribution from the adult might be: 'Oh, I like zoos – all the different birds and animals.'

(6) It is important that the child is provided with models of language structures and language functions in relation to ongoing activities and the childs' interests at the time. Whenever possible, use naturally occurring conversational slots so that the adult's language fits in with other activities and the child's increasing ability to participate in verbal and non-verbal interactions.

Form and function relations

Form–function relations are concerned with the range of intentions which are understood and which the child can express through language. A complete description of such relations would include a specification at the three levels of structure, content and function described in Chapters 1, 2 and 3. Whereas formal teaching approaches usually begin with the identification of objectives in terms of form and content relations (words and phrases and their meanings), naturalistic approaches place greater emphasis on establishing the child's understanding of how linguistic forms can influence the language and behaviour of other people. Social interactions should therefore be concerned with the child's ability to use and understand the following language functions: requesting information; requesting action or directing the behaviour of others; responding to requests; making statements

ments or comments; seeking attention; greeting; protest, rejecting or disagreeing; sarcasm and humour.

Slobin has suggested a general principle that when new language forms first appear, they express existing functions and, conversely, new functions are initially tried out by the child using already established language forms (Slobin 1973). Translated into therapeutic practice, this suggests that attempts to encourage new uses for language should focus on existing words and phrases, while attempts to encourage novel forms should be introduced in the context of well-rehearsed social exchanges. For example, a child might initially express a request for an object by using the object's name; subsequently, once the request function is well established, the child might learn the new form 'give' or 'gimme'.

Presupposition

The ability to take on the listener's perspective in order to make judgements about the relevance of possible contributions to a conversation is termed 'presupposition'. It involves the ability to make judgements regarding what constitutes an informative and relevant contribution to a conversation, and what can be taken for granted or presupposed and therefore left unsaid (Bates 1976; McNamara 1972; McTear 1985; Chapter 3, this book). This includes one's ability to vary language depending upon the age or familiarity of the conversational partner and to suit the experience of the listener – for example, when retelling a story to someone who has not heard it, or talking to someone on the telephone. For the listener, it involves the ability to 'read between the lines', so that words are interpreted appropriately both in respect of the existing social and physical context, but also in terms of implicit shared understanding of past experiences.

The extent to which the adult presupposes a shared psychological context with the child will influence the complexity of the message which it is possible to convey and the likelihood of the child understanding. For example, if the sentence 'The door is open' is uttered after a child has come into a room, even a child with very little understanding of grammatical relations will probably interpret the additional meaning – 'The door should be shut' – and will close the door. On the other hand, a child who is told firmly, 'No, not now,' may not read into this the implicit message – 'But later we can do it.'

The language therapist must seek to extend the child's ability to comprehend language when presupposition is necessary for an accurate interpretation of what is meant. It may also be necessary to encourage the child to become more aware of the ability of others to presuppose meaning and to modify her language to exploit this. However, as yet our understanding of the role of presupposition in language disorder and appropriate intervention strategies is extremely limited.

Conversational skills

The ability to take an assertive role in a conversation, and hence to use language to achieve interpersonal objectives, is described in terms of conversational skills (McTear 1985; Chapter 3, this book). Social interactions should be concerned with helping the child to improve in the following areas:

increasing speech which is socially directed to another person;
turn-taking skills, including utterances which maintain a conversational topic and the ability to recognise when someone else wishes to make a contribution;
use of appropriate initiation strategies – for example, questioning;
the ability to repair a contribution when the conversational partner signals comprehension problems.

Evaluation of naturalistic approaches

Naturalistic approaches to language intervention have emerged from the burgeoning research on language development which has appeared since the early 1970s. The intervention procedures described above represent an attempt to translate our growing understanding of language acquisition among normally developing children into recommendations for helping those children whose language is delayed or otherwise impaired. The approach is based on two assumptions: first, that developmental processes rather than developmental outcomes are the most appropriate targets for intervention; and, second, that the processes described in relation to normally developing children are universal and therefore provide the best foundation for understanding the development of children with language difficulties. From this, it follows that when children do not develop normally, the best strategy is to try to support or facilitate development rather than to try to replace it with some alternative 'artificial' set of teaching procedures.

The major limitation to naturalistic methods is that, as yet, there is relatively little evidence to attest to their efficacy. Whereas behavioural methods have been introduced and systematically evaluated over a period of more than 20 years, researchers and clinicians are still at the stage of exploring the practical implications of much of the recent research on children's language. In addition, the research is still progressing and providing new insights into the processes which underlie language development. For this reason, it may be too early to seek for definitive empirical studies which can indicate the validity of this approach. For the time being, naturalistic approaches must be regarded as 'the new frontier'; there may be considerable support for the general direction in which this kind of intervention is moving, but there is also uncertainty regarding what paths to follow and the obstacles that may be encountered on the way.

To begin with, there is still considerable debate regarding the extent to which language learning is sensitive to variations in environmental support, and some studies (Heath 1983; Schieffelin 1979) have indicated that progress with spoken language may hold up quite well even under conditions in which there seems little opportunity for the elaboration of pre-verbal adult–child exchanges. Similarly, Shatz (1983) and Gleitman *et al.* (1984) have questioned whether the impact of simplified adult language addressed to young children has been exaggerated. It is, therefore, important to recognise that many of the ideas on which this approach is based are still the subject of disagreement and the focus of continuing research activity. To the extent that this research changes our ideas about the processes involved in normal language development, it will almost certainly have implications for activities concerned with helping children who experience language difficulties.

There are also problems regarding the acceptability of naturalistic approaches which stem partly from their novelty, but more importantly from the different ideologies represented in developmental theory and educational practice (J. Harris 1984a, 1986). Traditionally, teaching has been concerned with the transmission of knowledge and skills from the expert to the novice. Formal didactic instructional methods, where the teacher presents material for the pupils to learn and absorb, were initially a practical solution to the problem of one teacher having to be responsible for many students. However, the approach received considerable support with the advent of behaviourism and the appearance of derivatives such as direct instruction (Bereiter and Engelmann 1966) structured teaching and teaching to objectives. While these methods may differ in detail, they share a commitment to three principles: the specification of teaching objectives prior to the 'lesson'; teacher control over what is taught and what is learned; evaluation of outcomes in relation to the teaching objectives.

In contrast to this 'closed system' in which objectives are specified and tightly controlled, development is seen as an 'open system' (Wickens 1974) in which external environmental events are in constant interaction with the child's evolving conceptual structures. It is not, therefore, possible to make precise predictions about the occurrence of developmental outcomes for individual children. Similarly, while it might be possible to enhance opportunities for growth and developmental progress, it is not possible to construct an environment which will ensure that certain outcomes occur at particular times. Instead, naturalistic approaches seek to achieve optimal conditions for development by focusing on developmental processes. While it may be possible to make general predictions about the emergence of communicative abilities, it will only be possible to document specific outcomes retrospectively after intervention has taken place.

This contrast between traditional teaching and naturalistic approaches may give rise to a number of practical difficulties. First, it means that the language therapist must survive without a precisely stated objective to orientate his or her activities. Instead, the therapist must have sufficient confidence in and understanding of developmental processes in order to be able to evaluate the success of any lesson or activity in these terms, rather than according to whether specific outcomes were or were not achieved. This does not mean that objectives are abandoned altogether, but that they are expressed in terms of behavioural or linguistic categories which reflect a child's growing ability to participate in communicative exchanges (Seibert and Oller 1981).

Second, the language therapist must master the 'flexible response'. Instead of evaluating the child's responses in terms of a lesson objective, it is necessary to learn to evaluate each response in terms of its communicative potential at the time it occurs. Rather than knowing in advance which responses to encourage and which to ignore, it is necessary to judge how best to reply to each communicative act so that the child's understanding of linguistic communication is extended. For example, for a child with limited language, the most appropriate response to a one-word utterance might be a simple expansion and a phatic:

    Child: Train.
    Teacher: Yes, the train's coming.

On the other hand, for a more able child the teacher's best response might be: 'Yes, I wonder where it's going', or: 'Do you think it's full of people going on their holidays?'

Third, since it is not easy to predict exactly what a child learns from any single activity, evaluation of intervention is much less straightforward than with more highly structured methods. Probably the most reliable method is to assess the child's language using a profile or naturalistic recording prior to intervention and then again after a number of intervention sessions spread over several days or even weeks. The main problem with this is that, where the child's langue does improve, it may be difficult to separate the influence of the intervention procedures from other opportunities the child has for language learning, both in school and at home.

The fourth problem is that naturalistic interventions may appear so 'natural' that it is difficult to convince other people, such as the child's parents or other professionals, that anything special is happening at all. Intervention may be dismissed as 'merely playing' or 'only doing the things that everyone else does'. While it is true that this is exactly what naturalistic methods seek to achieve, it may be difficult to convince those people who have traditional views about teaching that the activities have been carefully selected and organised to maximise the child's language-learning opportunities.

Finally, naturalistic methods suffer from the surprising disadvantage that they are difficult to teach to parents and other professionals. This is partly because the methods are not amenable to formal specification in the same way that behavioural strategies can be itemised (see Chapter 9) and partly because, to be successful, the adult must learn to relinquish control and be sensitive to the child's attempts to communicate. Surprisingly, this can be far more demanding than methods which require the adult to control the direction and pace of the child's learning. In spite of these difficulties, there are many studies which have reported success in training professionals and parents in naturalistic methods (Chesaldine and McConkey 1979; McConkey and O'Connor 1980).

Chapter eleven

The implications of children's characteristics for language teaching

Introduction

This chapter considers the way in which children's backgrounds and existing abilities need to be taken into consideration when planning for language intervention. It is a cliché that all children are individuals and that good educational and clinical practice must take account of individual differences. However, there is a considerable gap between such an exhortation and an understanding of exactly how this can be achieved. This chapter focuses on those individual differences which are likely to disrupt developmental progress in general, and have direct implications for the acquisition of language. As well as providing guidance with respect to the management of these relatively extreme problems, it is hoped that it will provide practitioners with a more general sensitivity and understanding of individual differences which will assist in the design of intervention programmes for all language-disordered children.

No attempt is made to provide a general introduction to the research that has been addressed to the development of children with specific handicapping conditions or special educational needs. Rather, this chapter deals with the ways in which a variety of additional problems may lead to the modification or elaboration of those intervention strategies already described. Readers who are interested in the more general question of developmental disorders and children with special educational needs are referred to recent books by Gillam (1986), Lewis (1987), Selfe and Stow (1987), and Ramasut (1989).

Long-term hearing loss

While it is true that not all children with language difficulties experience a hearing loss, children who have impaired hearing are particularly susceptible to delayed language acquisition. The seriousness of the problem is related both to the degree of loss and the range of sound frequencies which are most affected. Hearing loss is measured in decibels (dBs). A loss of less than 40 dBs results in only moderate difficulties and affected individuals will usually still be able to hear speech. More severe impairment arises with a loss of between 40 and 55dBs, although hearing-aids may boost residual hearing so that those affected can still hear some speech sounds. Beyond a loss of 55dBs, the ability to hear speech sounds becomes severely impaired and the artificial amplification of sounds through hearing-aids is considerably less effective. However, even these profoundly deaf children with a loss of 110dBs or more have some residual hearing and show signs of making sense of what they hear when interacting with other people (Wood *et al.* 1986).

At least as important as the overall degree of hearing loss is the frequency range affected. Relatively mild hearing loss across the frequencies employed for speech production may have far-reaching effects. Moreover, since vowels, in general, are transmitted at higher intensities than consonants, a person with a 55dBs loss across all frequencies will hear more vowels than consonants. The speech which is heard will therefore be distorted and less easily intelligible. When it is possible to provide a complete audiometric assessment of a child's hearing loss, information will be provided for the level of loss in each ear across a range of frequencies. A summary statistic of the average loss across all frequencies for the least-affected ear gives a general impression of the sound intensities which the child will usually be able to detect.

Overall, about one child in 1,000 has sufficient hearing loss to be considered deaf or partially hearing and therefore in need of some form of special educational provision (Lewis 1987). However, this number varies with increasing age due to children who become adventitiously deaf. Many hearing-impaired children also experience additional problems. These include brain damage (8 per cent), cerebral palsy (7 per cent), heart disorder (6 per cent), perceptual–motor difficulties (10 per cent), emotional and behavioural problems (19 per cent) and visual deficits (18 per cent). (Statistics cited in Meadow 1978.) Similarly, the incidence of hearing impairment is much higher among groups of children who have other handicapping conditions.

Only about 10 per cent of deaf infants are diagnosed in the first year, and as many as 44 per cent are not diagnosed until after the age of 3 years (Gregory 1986). Very often, delayed language and unusual patterns of non-verbal communication are the first indicators that the child has a hearing impairment, although even this may not immediately suggest a hearing difficulty if other problems are also present.

Clearly, a child with even a moderate degree of hearing loss is likely to be at a disadvantage in terms of acquiring language, and hearing loss which is present at birth is likely to have a more pronounced impact on subsequent language functioning than loss which arises as a result of accident or injury sometime after the child has begun to speak. But exactly how might imperfect hearing influence language development? The problems go far beyond simply not being able to hear the words other people are saying.

Consider, first, the way in which infants are able to integrate visual experiences with the language of their carctakers. For normal children, adult vocalisations are able to provide a constant commentary on the child's actions and also assist in the maintenance and co-ordination of non-verbal interactions (see Chapter 5). While the child points at or grasps a toy, the adult may utter the word 'ball'; if wanting the child's attention, the adult simply speaks her name or says, 'Look at this.' Even if the child does not understand the words, intonation alone will be sufficient to attract her attention. In Chapter 5 it was suggested that this kind of experience enables children to acquire pre-verbal communicative skills, and also to infer relationships between language structures and the meanings they express.

For the hearing-impaired child, the task of translating a solitary occupation into a social activity around which communication can occur is much more difficult.

Imagine a deaf baby with little or no awareness of sound. When he looks at an object or event, he receives none of the 'mood music' that accompanies the social experiences of the hearing baby. Suppose he looks from an object of his attention to an adult who is 'sharing' the experience with him and the adult talks about what he has just been looking at. Is it obvious to the child that what they are doing is an *act of reference*? Does the infant even realise that *communication* is taking place? To discover the relationships between a word and its referent, the deaf infant has to *remember* something he has just observed and deliberately *relate* this memory to another observation. In short, the deaf child with little or no auditory awareness has to do by intellect, *in sequence*, what 'happens' to the hearing baby in parallel.

(Wood *et al.* 1986: 22)

Since the deaf infant cannot hear adult speech as a commentary on her own actions, the only way in which she can integrate the activity of the other person with her own actions is to switch visual attention back and forth between the adult and the material she is playing with. Not surprisingly, this is itself a skill which may take some time to develop. In the meantime, an adult trying to interact with the deaf infant may experience considerable frustration and sense of being ignored by a child who rarely looks up from what she is doing and seems oblivious to the adult's exclamations and verbal comments.

One frequent effect of this impaired social interaction is for adults to become controlling, to ask more questions, to give more instructions and to make clumsy and artificial attempts to get the child to look at them. Wood *et al.* argue that this is exactly the opposite of what is required for the development of language:

Whereas adults interacting with hearing babies often make what they say and do *contingent* upon their interpretation of what the child is seeing or thinking, when adults interact with deaf babies they often demand that the deaf baby attends to *them* and the baby has to work out what they mean. . . . We believe that this demand is totally unrealistic and cannot be met by infants of this age or. . . by children who are considerably older. . . . [W]e suggest that the deaf child may be frustrated not only by any lack of success in communicating his own needs and intentions, but also by the demands placed upon him when adults try to help him communicate by overcontrolling his actions and attentions.

(Wood *et al.* 1986: 23)

On the basis of their research, Wood *et al.* argue that parents and professionals concerned with helping hearing-impaired children to develop language ought, therefore, to focus initially on establishing social interactions in which child and adult share common objectives. A number of such activities were described in Chapter 10. Such interactions not only provide the conditions in which the hearing-impaired child can learn to concentrate, plan and solve problems, but also promote the kinds of communicative understanding which seem to be essential for linguistic communication (see Chapter 5).

Second, Wood *et al.* argue that group work contains too many pitfalls to be a useful context for learning about communication and that interactions in which the adult is able to support the child's activity, and respond with sensitivity to the child's attempts at communication, can occur only when the adult is able to give undivided attention to a single child.

In contrast to this interactive approach to language intervention, Kretschmer and Kretschmer (1978) have reviewed a very large number of behaviourally based intervention programmes. They conclude that these

programmes were successful to varying degrees, so that the strategy of combining developmental targets with behaviour modification techniques shows promise, particularly with children demonstrating difficulties in language learning.

(Kretschmer and Kretschmer 1978: 224)

Needless to say, the research by Wood *et al.* supports the view expressed in Chapter 5 – that behavioural approaches are not compatible with contemporary views of language acquisition. Whereas the behavioural approach systematises the process by which the adult can exert control over the child's behaviour, Wood *et al.* argue that this is precisely the opposite of what is required for effective intervention with hearing-impaired children.

Temporary hearing loss

So far we have only considered how children with permanent and relatively severe hearing loss may be disadvantaged with respect to language learning.

However, there are also large numbers of children who suffer temporary hearing impairment due to a blockage, caused by infection in the middle ear. This is referred to as 'otitis media' and is the most frequently diagnosed illness for children between birth and 3 years (Godowski *et al.* 1986) with two-thirds of pre-school children having at least one bout, and 12 per cent of all children experiencing six or more episodes by the age of 6 years (Quick and Mandell 1983). If untreated it can cause hearing loss of 26–7dBs (Downs and Blager 1982) and has been related to delayed speech and language, low intelligence-test scores and poor academic performance (Webster 1986).

Dobie and Berlin (1979) reported that children suffering from otitis media have difficulty in hearing morphological markers such as ed, ing, s, and are likely to misunderstand short words such as 'are', 'to', 'in'. They may also have problems interpreting intonation patterns, inflections and stress. They may be slower in developing word combinations and go on to be poor readers (Zinkus and Gottlieb 1980). These difficulties may cause other more obvious problems for the parent, teacher or therapist. These include inattentiveness and distractability, difficulty in understanding speech in group settings or when moving about in a room, frequently asking for questions to be repeated, confusion with multi-stage commands, difficulty in recalling verbally presented material, and inappropriate responses to questions and commands (Godowski *et al.* 1986). Considering that such relatively minor hearing loss can have such far-reaching implications, it is disturbing that the routine audiometric screening in schools generally does not lead to the identification of children with losses of 20–5dBs as being in need of follow-up and possible remedial intervention.

Apart from routine screening, evidence of otitis media is most likely to be detected by the child's parents or teachers. However, this may not immediately be interpreted as indicative of hearing loss. Webster (1986) provides the following list of warning signs of possible hearing loss.

Physical problems:

A history of ear infections or failed screening tests.
Presence of catarrh, coughs, cold and persistent breathing through mouth.
Child complains of earache, popping ears, or has visible discharge.

Problems in attending:

Child daydreams, drifts off and is more alert when close to an adult.
Watches speaker's face intently when listening to speech.
Inattentive, restless and distracting behaviour; little interest in spoken stories.
Slow to follow instructions, asks for repetition, and tends to watch for cues from other children; misunderstands instructions.

Prefers to sit close to radio or TV or asks to have volume turned up. Often slow to locate source of sounds; does not respond to own name.

Speech problems:

Softer or fuzzier speech than usual.
Speech may be limited in structure or vocabulary, with immature or confused phonology.

Learning problems:

Learns more slowly, tires more quickly; is listless and appears poorly motivated.
Asks for help more frequently.
Better at practical skills than those which involve language.
Has reading difficulties.

Behaviour problems:

Child has periods of irritability, aggression, loss of temper.

If changes in a child's behaviour suggest temporary hearing loss, then it is necessary to obtain a proper audiological assessment and appropriate medical attention to correct the problem. This is normally achieved by draining fluid which has collected in the middle ear as a result of the infection. In addition, the teacher or therapist may ameliorate the problem by following some simple practical guidelines (Godowski *et al.* 1986):

Seat the child where she is in a position to see and hear the teacher or therapist and at the front of any group.
Ensure that the child is attending before speaking.
Encourage the child to look at the speaker.
Check the child's understanding of what has been said.
Encourage the child to ask for clarification.
Where possible, provide visual aids.
Pace the rate at which speech is delivered.
Give the child plenty of time to interpret and respond to what has been said.
If necessary, provide the child with a study area which is, as far as is possible, free from distracting noise.

Visual impairment

The extent of visual impairment varies considerably. In Britain the terms 'blind' and 'partially sighted' are based upon a functional assessment of the child's ability to cope with education. Children whose sight is so limited that they need to be educated by non-visual means are termed 'blind', while those who are unable to follow the normal curriculum but can nevertheless be educated by special methods which involve sight are termed 'partially sighted'. Many of those children termed 'blind' will have some residual vision; this may be restricted to detection of light–dark variation, some sensitivity to colours or to movement. Significant loss of vision is relatively rare, with approximately four in 10,000 people in Britain being registered as either blind or partially sighted. As with children with auditory problems, there is considerable variation with respect to the age at which visual problems are detected.

For children with some useful vision, acuity can be measured by comparing their performance with that of individuals with normal vision. Typically, visual acuity improves as we approach the object being studied. Children with significant loss of vision may have to move much closer to an object to see it with anything like the clarity of normally sighted children. The Snellen Scale provides an index of relative proximity for roughly equivalent degrees of acuity. Thus, a short-sighted person might need to stand half the distance from a set of printed letters to see it with the same clarity as a person with normal vision. A child with 3/60 vision on this scale would need to stand 3 metres away from an object to see the same detail that a person with normal vision sees at 60 metres.

From a developmental point of view, the major problem for the child with very restricted vision is how to achieve a conceptual understanding of 'a world out there': space, objects, people and movement. Fraiberg (1977) vividly described the difficulties which blind children have in achieving this kind of understanding without the advantage of visual experience to link and render intelligible auditory and tactile experiences. While the sighted child seems to understand right from the beginning the interrelatedness of seeing something, being able to reach out and touch it and hear the resultant noise, the blind child is at first presented with disjointed experiences which are only gradually and rather laboriously put together as related parts of a single experience. Thus, the child's experience of her mother or teacher may be construed as discrete and unrelated sensations of sound, smell and touch that are only gradually welded into a single concept of 'mother' or 'teacher'.

The key to broadening the blind child's understanding is tactile exploration and locomotion. Ironically, since the blind child does not have access to the 'visual lures' which motivate the sighted child to approach and manipulate new objects, the very experiences which can lead to a realisation of space and objects are restricted. Even in the first months of life, the child who is unable to see her hands is less likely to bring them together in front of her face and, subsequently, less likely to use them for exploration (Fraiberg 1977).

The second problem for the blind child concerns establishing social contact with other people. Fraiberg describes a blind infant called Peter:

He was strangely uninterested in his surroundings; the unseeing eyes made the face seem blank and remote. When the mother sought contact with him through her eyes, the child's eyes did not meet hers – which feels curiously like a rebuff if you do not know that the baby is blind. The appearance of the mother's face did not cause the baby to smile. All those ways in which the eyes unite human partners were denied to this mother and baby.

(Fraiberg 1977: 60)

Urwin (1984) suggests three ways in which severe visual deficits impair the development of communication between infant and caretaker. First, the role of eye-to-eye contact in the regulation of social play is disrupted. Second, adult and child are unable to use gaze as a cue to what their partner is attending to and, third, gestures such as pointing and reaching for objects cannot have the same communicative significance for the visually impaired child. In her own study of three blind infants, Urwin found little evidence of infants referring to objects 'out there,' or of infants spontaneously offering objects to their caregivers. It is this diminished pre-verbal communication which Urwin suggests is one of the principal causes of subsequent difficulties with spoken language. For example, Urwin found that when the children did begin to use words, they needed physical contact with objects before they would name them.

Fraiberg found that it was only when mothers were taught to signal their presence through speaking to and touching the child, and to recognise the child's responses by attending to the position and motion of the child's hands instead of seeking facial cues, that reciprocal communication was established. Consider another child studied by Fraiberg:

Toni is seven months old. Her mother tells us, 'She's not really interested in her toys'. We assemble a group of Toni's crib toys, stuffed animals and dolls, and invite the mother to present them to Toni, one by one. As each of the toys is placed in her hands, Toni's face is immobile. She gives the impression of 'staring off into remote space.' Naturally, the totally blind child does not orient his face toward the toy in his hands. Since visual inspection is the sign that we read as 'interest', and averted eyes and staring are read as the sign of 'uninterest', Toni 'looks bored'.

Now we watch Toni's hands. While her face 'looks bored', her fingers scan each of the toys. One stuffed doll is dropped after brief manual scanning. A second doll is scanned, brought to the mouth, tongued, mouthed, removed, scanned again. Now we remove doll number 2 and place doll number 1 in Toni's hand. A quick scanning of fingers and she drops it again. She makes fretful sounds, eyes staring off into space. We return doll number 2 to her hands. She quiets instantly, clutches it, brings it to her mouth, and explores its contours.

In short, there is no message from the face which Toni's mother can read as 'interest' or 'preference'. But the behaviour of the hands showed clear discrimination and sustained exploration of one toy and not another.

(Fraiberg 1977: 104–5)

In the same way as the visual deficit makes it difficult for the mother to interpret the behaviour of the child, so it also poses problems for the child in learning about the 'power' or 'agency' of other people – for example, that other people have the ability to act in predictable ways in reponse to signals from the child (Lewis 1987).

In terms of language, the blind children Fraiberg studied were generally slower than normal children of the same age in respect of both vocabulary and the acquisition of grammar. She attributed this to the absence of 'pictures out there': 'the sighted child spends his days in a state of perpetual intoxication with his picture world, and the pictures lure him on into exercises in recognition, classification, naming and ultimately to the retrieval of pictures in memory.' In contrast, 'the blind child's world has large empty spaces, and learning and language must exploit near space, chance encounters and need-related experiences' (Fraiberg 1977: 242–3). This is also reflected in the fact that, whereas Fraiberg's blind children lagged behind the sighted controls in terms of naming objects 'out there', there was no delay with respect to using language to express wants and needs. Similarly, Urwin found that when the children she studied began to name objects, this only occurred when the child was able to hold or touch the object referred to. Whereas blind children may learn words associated with caregiving and familiar social routines relatively quickly (Urwin 1984), they may restrict the use of their first words to the situations in which they are first learned. In contrast, sighted infants spontaneously generalise words to other appropriate and inappropriate contexts (Lewis 1987; see also Chapter 2, this book).

Another important difference in the language of the blind children, studied by both Fraiberg and Urwin, was a considerable delay in the control of personal pronouns. For example, Fraiberg describes how Peter, at age 11 years, responded to a request from his mother at the side of a swimming pool to 'Come here and pour some water over my feet': Peter went over and carefully poured water over his own feet. For Fraiberg, this is interpreted in terms of a poorly defined self-image as a direct result of visual impairment, while Urwin sees this difficulty in terms of confusion regarding social roles following earlier problems with social interactions during the pre-verbal period.

Urwin describes a number of other ways in which the language of blind children differs from that of sighted children at a similar stage. The blind children studied by Urwin used a preponderance of 'pre-packaged' or stereotyped utterances which they often employed in a repetitive way. They were also very sophisticated at keeping 'conversations' going using their limited linguistic abilities and, as language became better established, they tended to ask a large number of questions. Urwin suggests that these characteristics may be a strategy concerned with the maintencance of social contact, although it is also possible that asking questions provides these children with an important source of information regarding their surroundings.

The most obvious implications of this research is that blind babies need considerable help in understanding the nature of the world 'out there'. On this, Fraiberg is optimistic and argues that, with sensitive support from professionals and the immediate family, blind children can acquire the same concepts and learn the same skills as sighted children, albeit via a different route. Caregivers need to be taught to 'read' the child's hands and to look for the 'stilling response' as an indication of focused attention. The child needs to be encouraged to explore with her hands; this may begin with her own body and the bodies of other people, but should then progress to toys which produce noises and can be placed just out of the child's immediate reach.

Since the child has very limited opportunities for integrating visual experiences with the language of other people, it is important that caregivers help the child integrate auditory and tactile experiences with the language she hears. This involves close attention to the child's physical actions and also monitoring of the adult's language. Urwin found that parents of the children in her study tended to talk about the child rather than about the child's surroundings. Bearing in mind the child's difficulties, it seems likely that, rather than this focus on their own needs, blind children need to hear language which can put them in touch with the world around them but which they cannot see.

Initially, it would seem to be particularly important that the blind child is encouraged to participate in simple social routines and that these routines are accompanied by a simple and repetitive commentary. Attempts by the child to make vocal contributions need to be recognised and incorporated within a 'conversation'. Gradually, as the child's understanding of the routines improves and her ability to take an active role increases, the activities need to be extended and made more complex. The focus of such routines should not be independent activity, but joint activity in which the child shares with an adult the responsibility for achieving a particular objective, and in which verbal and non-verbal communication play a dominant role (Urwin 1984).

Non-verbal children

I have chosen the term 'non-verbal' to describe those children who may appear to be socially sensitive and interested in communicating with other people, but who seem to experience considerable difficulties with either hearing and understanding or producing spoken language. This may be the case for some children with hearing impairments, particularly those who are pre-lingually deaf, and also for some children with severe learning difficulties. Other children may fail to develop spoken language for no obvious reason. When this occurs, the teacher–therapist is faced with the need to make a major decision: should language interventions continue to be focused on spoken language, even though the child appears to be making little progress? Or would it be more helpful to provide opportunities for communication using signs or symbol systems which exploit visual rather than auditory processes?

Clearly, there are arguments on either side. Possibly the child has not yet begun to use spoken language because the right combination of teaching methods has not been tried, or at least not for long enough. If the child is taught to communicate using only non-vocal means, whatever level of proficiency is achieved will facilitate communication only between those people who are proficient in the alternative system: the child may never achieve the ability to read or listen to the radio or television; moving to a new school or place of work may become problematical; and the child may find it difficult to make friends with children who are not proficient in the alternative system. Rather than expanding her social horizons, language may prove to be a barrier to the wider world of human relationships.

On the other hand, it may be preferable to settle for a system which could enable the child to communicate complex thoughts and feelings, and to exchange ideas with a small number of other people, rather than to go on with a programme of teaching that seems to be making little progress. Nor is it necessarily the case that a child who is taught to communicate using non-vocal methods will thereby have reduced opportunities for learning spoken language. Rather, the opposite may be the case, and alternative methods of communication may be introduced as a deliberate way of mediating verbal communication (Kiernan 1983). However, as Kiernan points out, if this is considered to be a realistic objective, it is not sufficient to introduce an alternative system and hope that spoken language will result 'by magic': the objectives need to be clearly stated and a programme of teaching introduced which will maximise the chances of the objectives being realised. It is also important to recognise that some children may be better suited to a programme which aims to help them to become fluent in an alternative system, while others will make better progress with a 'parallel' approach which employs the alternative system as an aid to learning spoken language.

Gestures signs and symbols

Gestural communication involves body movements to convey simple ideas or emotions. Conventional gestures include pointing as an act of reference, shoulder shrugging as an indication of indecision, and waving as a farewell gesture. Young children, and particularly those who are experiencing difficulty with spoken language, may spontaneously develop an elaborate set of idiosyncratic gestures which are understood by their immediate caretakers (Kiernan 1983). For example, a toddler may tug at her pants to indicate she wishes to go to the toilet, or touch her tongue to communicate that she is thirsty, or raise her arms to show that she wishes to be picked up (Lock 1978).

While gestures express simple ideas which are closely tied to immediate experiences, sign systems involve a much more elaborate use of hands, arms and fingers to convey complex and often highly abstract messages. While gestures are often idiosyncratic and only understood by the child and her immediate caregivers, signs are organised into formal systems of communication which are used by many different people. Individual signs can be organised into sentences on the basis of grammatical rules, much like words and sentences in spoken English. However, signs are not simply gestured words, and sign systems have a complex internal structure, the grammar of which is quite different from the grammar of any spoken language. To this extent, systems such as American Sign Language and British Sign Language may be considered to have all the structural complexities and the same potential for expressing subtle meanings as any natural spoken language (Klima and Bellugi 1979; Musselwhite and St Louis 1982).

In contrast, symbol systems employ pictures or symbols external to the body which are presented in some form of frame or on a screen. The child selects those symbols which best convey the idea she wishes to express, either by manual pointing, eye pointing or by using some mechanical or electronic device. The symbols may closely resemble the objects or events to which they refer, or they may be highly abstract. As with sign systems, it is possible to combine symbols into ordered sequences to convey more elaborate meanings. However, symbol systems are restricted in terms of the range of symbol–referent relations available and the absence of grammatical markers to modulate meanings.

For children with good intellectual abilities and normal manual dexterity, learning American or British Sign Language may be the best alternative. However, for children with physical disabilities or limited cognitive abilities, some other communication system may be more appropriate. Makaton Vocabulary is an attempt to present a subsample of BSL signs in a developmental sequence which can be easily learned by children with severe learning difficulties (Walker and Armfield 1982). Although Makaton is very widely used in special schools in Britain (Harris 1988; Jones *et al.* 1982), claims regarding its efficacy have been challenged (Kiernan 1984). The most widely used symbol system in Britain is Bliss Symbolics (Jones *et al.* 1982). This is used in place of spoken language or as a way of enhancing or augumenting the child's oral abilities. It is particularly suitable for children with poor motor control of mouth, larynx and hands (for example, some children with cerebral palsy), especially where they have the intellectual ability to learn and remember large numbers of symbol–referent relations.

One of the problems with most sign systems is that because they are quite distinct from English, the child must effectively learn a 'second language' and it is unlikely that there will be any direct carry-over from signing to speaking. Interestingly, Kiernan (1983) reported that where signs systems were being used with autistic people, signs and speech were used simultaneously, with the signs being ordered according to English syntax. Some sign or gestural systems have been specifically developed to be used alongside spoken language in the expectation that this will foster oral expression and comprehension. In the USA Signed English or Signing Exact English are frequently employed (Musselwhite and St Louis 1982), while in Britain the Paget–Gorman Sign System is more popular (Jones *et al.* 1982). These systems combine signs into sentence – such as sequences which mirror the word order of sentences in spoken English and thus facilitate signing and speaking at the same time.

Before a sign programme or symbol system is introduced, it is important to establish that it has a reasonably good chance of being successful. In a useful practical paper, Kriegsmann *et al.* (1982) identify the characteristics of weak and strong candidates for signing programmes. These are summarised in Table 11.1. In a similar vein, Russell (1984) identifies a number of questions which need to be considered before introducing augmentative symbol systems. While signs and symbol systems tend to be regarded as alternatives, it is clear that there is also a great deal of scope for combining the two in order to provide individual children with maximally effective communicative systems. However, very little research has been carried out regarding how this might be done and the likely outcomes (Kiernan 1983).

The long-term aims of an alternative communication system may range from helping the child to express basic needs, providing support for spoken language or a temporary mediating device for leading the child into verbal communication (at which point the system will be discarded), to helping the child to express complex ideas using *only* a sign/symbol system. Whenever introducing a sign or symbol system, it is important to plan so that the new system can be introduced to the child with as little disruption and with as much consistency as possible. Whatever the long-term goals, the use of signs or symbols for communication will have major implications for the childs' interactions not only in school, but also at home with her family. It is important, therefore, that these goals are realistic in terms of the child's abilities and the human resources available. At the same time, the programme will have to be designed so that the chosen aims have a good chance of being met. Most importantly, the teacher–therapist must determine what the child is to do in reponse to communications using sign or symbol, and how the new system will be incorporated into the child's daily routines with teachers, parents and other caregivers.

Non-communicating children

Whereas the term 'non-verbal' has been used to describe children who seem unable to use spoken language but who are able to communicate using signs and gestures, the term 'non-communicating' is used to describe those children who seem uninterested in communication of any kind. Such children appear to be 'remote' or 'distant' and completely indifferent to the presence of other people. Although relatively bright in other ways, they may fail to respond to simple gestures and even actively avoid situations in which other people try to communicate with them. While little is known about non-communicating children as a whole, a considerable amount of interest has surrounded a smaller, more carefully defined group of children who are termed 'autistic' (Kanner 1943).

While it is true that the crucial index of autism is 'the lack of co-ordinated social behaviour to signify social intentions', there are a number of other characteristics which are usually considered essential for this diagnosis. The condition is usually evident early on and, in the majority of cases, before the age of 30 months. The child is likely to show a strong preference for 'sameness', displaying stereotyped behaviours and an insistence on following well-established routines. These children are differentiated from psychotic children by an absence of delusions, hallucinations and other similar thought disorders, although it is quite clear that they do have serious problems in making sense of the world around them (Rutter 1985).

Autism is a broad cognitive disorder which results in impaired conceptualisation and abstractions, but it is also associated with marked language abnormalities. These linguistic difficulties stand out because they indicate deviance rather than delay, and because they are more severe, more extensive and more resistant to intervention than other language disorders (Rutter 1980). In those children who do subsequently acquire language, there are marked deviations from the pattern of progress found among normal children. These include pronominal confusion, delayed and inappropriate echoing of the speech of others, prosodic abnormalities, difficulties with speech rhythm, and problems with word meanings. However, the most obvious and disturbing feature of the autistic child's language is that it occurs in the absence of any interest in social interaction; it might therefore be termed 'language without communication'. The very marked deviance of the autistic child's language is principally associated with the way in which language is used for thinking and for social communication rather than its structural and semantic peculiarities.

Sadly, the prognosis for autistic children is very poor, with only about 50

Table 11.1 Possible candidates for signing

Needs assessment	Strong candidate	Questionable candidate
Cognitive level	Early pre-operational (above 2 years 6 months)	Late sensor-motor (s/m) Stage VI (18–24 months) (Poor) Below s/m Stage VI (Below 18-month level)
Chronological age	Generally above 2 years 6 months; decision not dependent on chronological age	(same)
Verbal comprehension	At least 1 year above production	Less than 6-month discrepancy with expressive skills (Poor) Limited meaning associated with words
Intentional communication	Varied, consistent means to express intent, needs, perceptions	Highly restricted gestural, vocal performatives (share/request/comment/inform/ask/protest)
Manual dexterity	Independent, controlled finger, hand, arm movements	Laboured, inconsistent, imprecise movements
Imitation/retention of signs	Attends well to model, self-corrects, consistent production, deferred imitation	Needs numerous presentations/prompts; cannot produce after time delay
Interest in signing	Seeks out new signs/prefers sign versus other mode	Does not focus on signer/resistive to sign training/ learning rate better in alternative system
Speech production	Unintelligible or highly restricted phonetic repertoire	Articulation patterns consistent with developmental level
Speech intervention	Minimal vocal/verbal changes after 6 months' therapy	Steady increase in vocal/verbal behaviours with therapy
Family support training	Family wants sign programme; family training available on weekly basis	Signs restricted to classroom/no family training commitment
Staff knowledge of language development	Information recent in structural/content/pragmatic (functional) areas	Limited understanding of signing as a language system
Staff support training	Staff committed to sign programme provides for regular training sessions	Responsibility for sign programme assumed by single staff person
Staff signing ability	Fluency can meet child's signing objectives	Limited knowledge of sign systems or sign production

Source: Kriegsmann *et al.* (1982).

per cent acquiring any useful spoken language. This may be interpreted as strong support for the view that pre-verbal communication plays an important role in language development, although it seems likely that, in the case of autism, the absence of pre-verbal communication is a symptom of a more profound deficit rather than the principal characteristic of the disorder. As an alternative to spoken language, a number of researchers have examined the possibilities of using sign or symbol systems with autistic individuals. In a detailed review, Kiernan (1983) is sceptical of the belief that all autistic children can benefit from an indiscriminate, total communication programme, but he argues that there is evidence that many autistic adults and children – including those in categories where the prognosis is poor – can learn to use signs to communicate their basic needs. The role of signs and symbols in language intervention has been considered above (see pp. 217–19).

In the past, because of the apparently intractable problems of autistic children, considerable attention was paid to the possibility of teaching language and communication through behavioural approaches (Lovaas *et al.* 1973). However, after more than a decade of research, the results indicate that such procedures produce only modest changes: there are problems in establishing generalisation beyond the teaching setting and very few children go on to use language spontaneously (Rutter 1980). Furthermore, the most powerful predicter of improvement is the child's existing abilities at the commencement of intervention; those with some langauge – either echolalia or single words – respond much more positively than those with no spoken language.

Rutter suggests that behavioural techniques have an important role to play – for example, in helping the child to overcome disruptive behaviour so that teaching is possible, or in learning specific linguistic skills. However, such techniques may not be effective in teaching productive language. Instead, Rutter (1980, 1985) suggests that it may be necessary to focus on the natural environment and to establish language within more natural social and conversational interactions. Because of the autistic child's resistance to most forms of social contact, it may be necessary initially to use carefully structured interactions in conjunction with reinforcement for compliance and participation from the child.

One attempt to introduce therapeutic interventions along these lines is described by Wimpory (Christie and Wimpory 1986; Wimpory 1986). Like Rutter, she argues that, in order to overcome autistic children's antipathy to communication, it is necessary to provide them with prolonged and exaggerated experiences of the kinds of social interaction which are normally made available to infants and toddlers. She describes a number of activities that are designed to establish simple communicative routines. For example, pointing is initially taught using behavioural methods. Once established, the adults respond to the communicative significance of the child's pointing, even though the child's pointing may not be intentionally communicative. Similarly, 'musical interactions' involve an adult singing action songs and encouraging the child to move rhythmically in time with the music. The adult may do most of the work in initiating actions from the child, but any spontaneous movements are interpreted as if the child were deliberately attempting to communicate.

Both of these activities represent attempts to place the child in a social setting where the adult can respond to the child's actions as if they were expressing communicative intent. Wimpory argues that the illusion of social influence and control created in these exchanges enables these children to understand how communication works and to move on to the point where they deliberately seek to communicate with other people. And, of course, such opportunities for enabling children to experience social control are not limited to contrived activities:

> Lucy is asked to clap hands but she prefers no active interaction; she avoids eye contact and even leans her head and body away from the teacher. The teacher 'compromises' with alternative games which Lucy's posture suggests to her. One game is based on Lucy's habit of sucking her thumb. The teacher . . . sucks Lucy's thumb herself and encourages Lucy to snatch it away. She thereby puts Lucy in a position where she teases and is teased . . . . In this case the teacher does not take up the powerful position of one who reprimands for thumb sucking; instead this game ultimately gives Lucy the power, for she owns the thumb.
>
> (Wimpory 1986: 4–5)

This section has referred to work carried out with children who have been diagnosed as autistic and has said very little about other children who seem to avoid social contact and do not develop any communicative skills. Given how little information is available on strategies for language intervention with non-communicating children who do not have the other symptoms of autism, it is necessary to rely upon the autistic research as a basis for language teaching. On the positive side, it seems likely that strategies that have shown promise, with such a profoundly handicapped group of children, are likely to be at least as effective with less severely affected children. Furthermore, the area which has received most attention in recent years is precisely that which is common to all non-communicating children – their inability to relate socially and to use language to express needs and intentions. Finally, the suggestions for language intervention which have been made in this section are closely in line with much of the recent research on child language acquisition described in Chapter 5 and the work on language intervention described in Chapter 10.

Children who have experienced psychological or social deprivation

Since the opportunity to hear and use language is a necessary condition for the acquisition of language, it follows that children who have very restricted language-learning experiences will be vulnerable to language delay. For example, numerous studies have shown that children who spend their early years in institutional care are likely to have speech that is delayed in respect of articulation, vocabulary, sentence length and grammar. In addition, such children often experience difficulties in using language as a means of problem-solving and for communicating ideas and concepts. While limited opportunities for language use are associated with these fairly global impairments in respect of expressive language, comprehension seems to be less affected (Cantwell and Baker 1985).

The picture presented by children who have experienced very restricted opportunities for language learning is not straightforward, since the children who are most at risk are those who have other handicapping disorders. In addition, children who have experienced linguistic deprivation are also likely to have suffered other forms of severe environmental deprivation which will affect other aspects of psychological functioning (Rutter 1981). Among the most frequent contributing factors to this form of language difficulty are inadequate child-care arrangements. The child may have very little interaction with people who are linguistically competent and therefore may be deprived of all kinds of language-learning experiences. Alternatively, the experiences that are available may be very limited in scope, so that the child gains proficiency in only a restricted number of social and cognitive uses of language (Heath 1983).

Heath (1983) describes differences in the way in which children from different backgrounds deal with requests for 'factual information' and the extent to which they are able to create a verbal narrative from their own personal experiences. While such differences are entirely acceptable at home – and, indeed, are often products of the children's home experiences of language – they are likely to be interpreted at school as evidence of more significant cognitive differences (Romaine 1984). Although such restricted experiences may indeed impair the child's ability to participate and succeed in school-based learning, it is important to remember that they arise as much from the expectations that schools have of children's language as from deficiencies in the child.

Where language differences arise solely because the opportunities for language learning at home are not consistent with the demands that are made on the child at school, problems are likely to be resolved as the child is exposed to more language and to different ways of using language. However, where environmental deprivation is associated with sensory or cognitive deficit, the outlook may be much less clear cut. To begin with, most cognitive impairments result in the child being less able to benefit from all experiences. In addition, handicapping disorders themselves may directly or indirectly affect the language-learning experiences that are made available to the child. For example, the physically handicapped child may spend a considerable amount of time in hospital for surgery, and this may severely curtail the frequency and quality of social interactions. The child with cognitive or sensory impairments may be 'unrewarding' for adults as an interactive partner, so that she is spoken to less often than children who are developing normally. Research has also shown that children with Down's Syndrome and some autistic children respond in ways that interfere with the normal pattern of verbal and non-verbal interaction between adults and young language-learning children (Lewis 1987).

Differential diagnosis of the relative contribution of environmental or experiential factors, as opposed to other impairments which have a physiological basis, is often problematical. Furthermore, such a diagnosis may add little in terms of planning an effective programme of intervention (Crystal 1984; Chapter 6, this book). Irrespective of the perceived aetiology of a language problem, intervention will be focused upon introducing environmental changes so as to improve and , hopefully, optimise the child's opportunities for subsequent language development. This may be achieved most effectively through the school or within a clinic setting, or it may involve working with the child's caregivers at home. The choice of location for intervention will, however, be more closely related to our understanding of the processes involved in language development, the pattern of linguistic strengths and weaknesses evidenced by any given child, and the problems of resource management and training, rather than to diagnosis and perceived aetiology.

In spite of the considerable amount of research and even greater amount of educational folklore regarding the relationship between social class, language delay and educational failure, the view that a working-class environment inevitable creates restricted opportunities for language development is no longer widely accepted (Stubbs 1983; Tizard and Hughes 1984). Teachers and therapists should therefore be wary of making the assumption that, because a child is part of a low-income family, her problems are a result of restricted language-learning experiences. Conversely, it is quite possible that children from middle- and high-income homes may have language problems that arise from limited learning opportunities, rather than from physiological causes. Once again, it is safer to focus on the specific pattern of abilities and disabilities shown by the child's assessment profile, rather than to seek explanations of *how* the child came to develop in a particular way.

Children with general learning difficulties

The term 'general learning difficulties' is used here to describe the large number of children who experience language problems as part of a wider cognitive deficit. These children are unable to benefit from experiences in the same way as normal children and, consequently, their developmental progress is slower than that of normal children. The causes of learning difficulties include genetic and chromosomal abnormalities, damage to the developing foetus, birth injury and post-natal environmental trauma. In many cases, there is no obvious cause and no clear physiological correlates of the learning problem.

The overall cognitive dificit may, in a sense, be responsible for the language difficulties in so far as the child has problems in attending to, interpreting and retaining all kinds of information. Here, we would expect to see a delayed pattern of development but with language abilities developing roughly in line with other aspects of psychological functioning. On the other hand, the problem with language may exist over and above the general cognitive impairment, so that, for the child with general learning difficulties, language presents a special area of concern. For children in this category, we would expect to see a pattern of developmental delay but, in addition, relatively greater delay in the area of language compared with other aspects of development.

The severity of cognitive impairment varies with two broad categories currently recognised with respect to educational provision: children with moderate learning difficulties may be integrated within an ordinary school or they may be taught in a separate school or a unit attached to a school. They will usually follow a modified form of the normal school curriculum. Children with severe learning difficulties are much more likely to be educated in a special school with a curriculum designed to match their special needs, although some of these children may stay in the ordinary school until the end of primary school. In terms of performance on intelligence tests (assuming a mean of 100 and a standard deviation of 15 points), children with moderate learning difficulties are likely to score between 55 and 70 (two to three standard deviations below the mean), while those with severe learning difficulties will usually achieve a score of below 55 (that is, more than three standard deviations below the mean).

Generally, the more severe the cognitive impairment, the more likely the child is to experience some form of language delay although, even among children with the same level of cognitive functioning, levels of linguistic ability are subject to considerable variation (Cantwell and Baker 1987). Possibly the most prevalent and marked problem among this group of children concerns articulation, with up to 95 per cent of children with severe learning difficulties affected. In terms of structure, meaning and functional characteristics, the language of children with learning difficulties tends to follow the general course of development which has been mapped out by researchers looking at normally developing children, although at a much slower pace (Snyder 1984).

However, there have been some studies which indicate moderate variations from this general pattern of slow but normal development (Harris 1983; Rondal 1976). These authors suggest that the different degrees of conceptual sophistication required for learning different aspects of language may result in children with learning difficulties being relatively more successful in some areas than in others. For example, compared to normally developing children with similar MLUs, Down's Syndrome children tend to have larger single-word vocabularies. The conceptual demands of combining words into sequences to express semantic relations may represent a challenge which, in relative terms, is much more difficult for the child with Down's Syndrome to master. As a result, they may spend much more time at the single-word stage and therefore build up larger single-word vocabularies prior to the emergence of combinatorial speech.

Children who speak English as a second language

Many children in the world learn to speak two, three or four languages quite naturally and without any disadvantage in terms of linguistic competence or general cognitive development (McLoughlin 1987). Bilingualism, therefore, is not inherently problematic. However, problems may arise for the teacher or therapist who is faced with a child who does not speak English as a first language and who seems to be experiencing serious difficulties. The most immediate question is whether this is a case of *language* disorder that is common to the child's ability in all the languages she is learning, or whether it represents a difficulty that is specific to the production and comprehension of the *English language*. Clearly, the most desirable course of action is a full language assessment with respect to the child's first language and with respect to her knowledge of English. Discrepancies between the two assessments will indicate those problems which are specific to a particular language and those which signify more general difficulties.

If the child's problems are limited to English, then it might be expected that, with the right kind of classroom support, these problems will gradually be overcome. Cummins (1984) suggests that, for immigrant children who begin learning the language of the host country before the age of 6 years, most will have achieved fluent and appropriate interpersonal language skills similar to their peers after about one and a half to two years. However, he argues that there are important differences between these interpersonal communicative language functions, which are learned relatively quickly, and the academic uses of language, which generally take much longer to learn. For this reason, face-to-face social uses of language ought not to be taken as an index of how successfully the child is dealing with the more cognitive demands of language in the classroom. In addition to taking much longer to master, proficiency with respect to academic uses of the second language is closely related to how well developed these functions are in the child's first language, and the extent to which the first language is maintained during the period in which the child is learning the second language.

If a child's difficulty seems to be restricted to the second language, the answer is not to encourage greater use of that language in the child's home, where limited proficiency may minimise opportunities for experiencing cognitive/academic language functions; rather, the child should be encouraged to develop expertise in a wide range of language functions in the first language, in the expectation that these will easily transfer to the second language as basic grammatical competence is achieved. Because of the difficulty of assessing all areas of ability in the child's first and second languages, it is important that any child who appears to have some difficulty in learning English as a second language is carefully monitored, even if it is not considered appropriate to introduce structured forms of intervention. For a more detailed discussion of bilingualism and school-based strategies for assisting second-language acquisition, the reader is referred to Cummins and Swain (1987).

If the child seems to be experiencing difficulties in both first and second languages, then the question arises as to the language most suited as a medium of intervention. While it may be regarded that a child living in an English-speaking culture should receive therapeutic intervention through the medium of English, a number of research studies have indicated that intervention will be more effective in tackling developmental problems (that is, problems which are not specific to particular languages) if it is conducted through the child's first language (Langdon 1983; Perozzi 1985). In the long term, such a strategy is likely to result in gains in English as well as in the child's first language. Where it is not possible to introduce intervention through the child's first language, then every effort should be made to support the first language – at home and in other contexts where there are native speakers – while the child is receiving more structured teaching in English.

Children with physiologically based speech disorders

Speech arises from the co-ordinated action of a number of muscle groups to expel air through the mouth and nose; the expelled air causes the vocal cords to resonate in different ways, according to the phonemes being produced. Chapter 1 described how many articulation errors occur naturally during the course of development as the child achieves voluntary control of this neuromuscular system. However, other problems arise from muscular and neuromuscular disorders or structural abnormalities of the speech mechanism. Whereas developmental problems are usually transient, problems with an organic basis are likely to be long term and potentially disruptive of the child's general language functioning. Among the most common of these problems are cleft palate, dysarthria and apraxia (Cantwell and Baker 1987).

The child with an unrepaired **cleft palate** is likely to have mispronunciation of speech sounds, delayed development of speech and even more general language delay. Particular problems occur with stop consonants, fricative consonants and affricatives. When these children speak, they frequently have a characteristic hypernasal quality which makes them sound as if they are 'talking through the nose'.

Dysarthria arises from difficulties with the control of the speech musculature. This may give rise to drooling, slow and uncoordinated oral movements and abnormal tongue protrusion during early infancy, and, subsequently, slow speech and more general language delay. Misarticulations occur most frequently in consonant clusters and slightly less often in single consonants and diphthongs. The majority of errors are distortions or omissions rather than substitutions, and individual children tend to produce consistent errors.

Apraxia is a condition in which the child has normal movements for chewing, sucking and swallowing, but abnormal movements during speech production. Articulation errors occur erratically and may include sound reversals, additions, inappropriate repetition, as well as distortions and substitutions. Errors are more frequent in consonants rather than vowels, and in sentences and polysyllabic words rather than syllables or simple words. The condition varies in intensity, with the most severely affected children limited to the imitation of single words. Problems are usually restricted to expressive language skills, with comprehension being relatively unaffected.

From the point of view of the development of language as opposed to the mechanics of speech production, these difficulties are likely to interfere with the child's ability to engage other people in meaningful dialogue. The degree of interference will depend upon how severe the child's articulation problems are. While at one extreme they may simply require the adult to attend very carefully to what the child is saying, at the other extreme they may make comprehension of even the most simple utterance problematic. This is likely to create considerable frustration for both adult and child. Furthermore, to the extent that language development arises from the child's experiences of exploring her own language in dialogue with another person, articulation disorders may place considerable constraints upon the emergence of a wide range of linguistic abilities.

The remediation of articulary disorders themselves is not a topic which this book addresses; the interested reader is referred to Eisonson (1986). Intervention for language might be directed at establishing situations in which the child could participate in activities with other people and have plenty of opportunity both to hear language and to express language which describes and comments on what is happening. Here, the context of the activity provides a framework for the child to make sense of what other people are saying and, more importantly, increases the chances that even poorly articulated utterances will be interpretable by the other participants. In cases where the child's difficulties are so extreme that, even within a 'shared' context, many utterances are uninterpretable, it may be necessary to consider the benefits of a sign or symbol system (see pp. 217–19).

Chapter twelve

Who is the best person to teach language?

Introduction

The previous three chapters have dealt in some detail with issues relating to methods of language intervention and characteristics of the child which may pose special problems for the teacher or therapist. It is now time to deal with a third crucial aspect of the therapeutic process: who should deliver the intervention?

Implicit in much of what has been said up to now is the assumption that it is the professional teacher or speech therapist who determines the structure and content of any language intervention, and that this requires a considerable amount of practical experience and theoretical knowledge. However, this does not necessarily mean that the same person will actually work in a face-to-face situation with the child. For a variety of reasons it may be expedient to utilise the services of other people to work directly with the child under the guidance of the language therapist. For example, teachers who have specific responsibility for language within a school, and speech therapists who work in schools, may find that class teachers ask them for practical advice regarding day-to-day support for children with language difficulties. Alternatively, they may feel that they could be more effective in helping children if they were able to work through other teachers, rather than directly with the child. For similar reasons, it may be seen as advantageous to involve a child's parents in a planned programme of intervention. This section considers in more detail the rationale for the involvement of relatively inexperienced people who do not have specialist qualifications in the delivery of language intervention programmes.

There are a number of specific advantages which might be derived from collaborating with parents or ordinary teachers. The language therapist with expert knowledge will often be responsible for more children than she could expect to work with regularly on an individual basis. Without the use of 'non-experts', the numbers of children who receive treatment might be relatively small. Furthermore, class teachers in primary and special schools and parents are usually with the child for a large part of the day. Naturally, both parents and teachers will have a variety of other activities which they wish to pursue and both groups may be responsible for other children; any treatment programme will have to fit in with these practical constraints. Nevertheless, it may be possible to create special slots in the day, during which time a specific child will be able to receive undivided one-to-one attention. Alternatively, it may be possible to introduce group activities that are specially designed to help the child with language difficulties to learn specific skills. In either case, providing the non-professional with guidance on remedial strategies is likely to result in a larger number of children receiving structured help than would otherwise be possible.

Second, it has been suggested that one of the drawbacks which many of the more highly structured language intervention schemes suffer from is poor generalisation from the training setting to more naturalistic contexts, such as the child's home or her usual classroom. If parents or class teachers are employed as remedial agents, then, it is argued, the problem of generalisation does not arise, since the teaching programme is introduced within the natural environment (Howlin 1984). Under closer analysis, it is apparent that this conclusion is somewhat premature. For example, if the class teacher or parent succeeds in teaching a child some aspect of language in relation to one activity, there may still be problems of generalisation to other activities and to other settings; similarly, if the child succeeds in using certain language skills with the class teacher or parent, there may still be problems of generalisation to other teachers or to other people in the family. However, to the extent that the involvement of parents and class teachers is accompanied by naturalistic strategies for intervention, it is likely that new skills would be functionally relevant and that the child will develop language to express ideas and intentions within social situations. Where this is achieved, it might be expected that the child will find it easier to transfer new skills across settings and across people to match the communicative requirements of different social encounters.

Third, in the case of parents, it is argued that motivation to achieve success is high (Howlin 1984) and that this will contribute to the successful implementation of any teaching programme and increase the chances of a positive outcome. While this may be true, it is also the case that motivation is responsive to a variety of factors which may result in positive or negative changes during the course of the programme. For example, if at the start of the programme expectations are high, but parents see little to indicate success, without appropriate counselling, confidence and motivation may be adversely affected.

Whether teachers can be regarded as being highly motivated to see an intervention strategy work is less certain. It will depend partly on the teacher's interest and understanding of the issues involved in language development, and partly on her perception of children with special educational needs. A teacher who, from choice, works with a group of such children – for example, in a special school – may respond differently from a teacher in an ordinary classroom who feels she has been landed with a particularly problematic child. Conversely, the teacher in the ordinary classroom may percieve the child as essentially 'normal' and therefore capable of improvement, while a teacher in a special school or unit may be more easily reconciled to children having long-term educational and developmental difficulties.

Perhaps the most important reason for trying to involve parents and ordinary classroom teachers concerns a rapidly growing awareness of the role of adult conversation in the development of language. In the past, when there was a greater emphasis on structured teaching and behaviour intervention strategies, it was considered appropriate to teach a child language skills in the same way that she might be taught any other practical skill – for example, learning a musical instrument. If this required specialist help, the most widely accepted model for the delivery of such treatment was temporary withdrawal of the child from the ordinary classroom for a period of intensive tuition from an expert. Subsequently, the child was returned to the classroom in possession of new skills or abilities. Unless the child's teacher was informed as to the changes which she might expect to see as a result of this intensive coaching, there was little likelihood that the child would be given planned opportunities to practise the new skills in the classroom.

The view that language is part of a social process, rather than a personal knowledge of a set of rules, raises questions about the validity of the 'intensive tuition by an expert' approach to language teaching. Instead, it has been suggested that it would be more helpful for the 'expert' to seek ways of improving the child's opportunities for language learning in the natural everyday environment. This might involve simply increasing the number of conversational opportunities made available to the child, particularly in the classroom, where children with language difficulties are easily overlooked, or trying to modify the style of interaction employed by teachers or caregivers (Howlin 1984; and Chapter 10, this book).

The fifth and final justification for the involvement of class teacher and parents is that, while the research still leaves many questions unanswered, there is a general consensus that language teaching by non-experts is an effective approach which needs further careful exploration (Howlin 1984).

Ways of involving parents and class teachers

Using teachers or the child's parents and other caregivers as therapeutic agents requires that the specialist teacher or therapist is able to train those people, who are in close daily contact with the child, to change their behaviour so that they provide better opportunities for language learning. As a result of the modified language environment provided by these people, it is assumed that the child's language will improve. This relatively simple two-stage model of intervention raises numerous issues, all of which need to be considered if the treatment is to be effective.

First, the approach assumes that at the very least the teacher or therapist will have a clear idea of what the child's problems are and how the language of those around her might be enhanced. This information is only likely to be obtained from a functionally based description derived from naturalistic observations and possibly transcribed recordings.

Second, it requires the 'language expert' to establish a relationship with the 'non-professional' which will enable strategies or skills to be taught. Depending on the complexity of the skills which the non-expert will be expected to employ, this will vary from following simple written instructions (for example, 'Make sure you ask Mike to answer at least two questions during each lesson'), to participating in a set of training workshops. If face-to-face contact is considered desirable, then a decision will need to be made about where this will take place. The child's home or her regular classroom would be appropriate from the point of view of teaching skills in a relevant context, although practical constraints may make this impossible. If training has to take place in another location, then video recordings of ordinary parent–child or teacher–child interactions are likely to be particularly helpful teaching aids.

Third, the behaviour changes required of the class teacher or parent may be straightforward and easy to explain and implement, or they may be more complex and sophisticated. For example, Chesaldine and McConkey (1979) worked with a group of parents of mentally handicapped children who were using single words but few phrases or sentences. They simply asked parents to play with their children and focus on encouraging specific two-word combinations. In contrast, Wood and Wood (1984), carried out an experimental study in which they taught teachers of deaf children to interact with their pupils using highly specific conversational styles. Clearly, simpler training objectives for the parents or class teachers are likely to be easier to implement and monitor; it is not clear how far the effort required to establish more elaborate objectives is repaid in terms of subsequent changes in children's language.

Fourth, there is likely to be considerable variation with respect to the ability, interest and time available to individual parents and class teachers. Thus, in addition to designing a programme which meets the needs of a particular child, the language therapist must be sensitive to the strengths and limitations of those people whom she seeks to involve in the therapeutic process. While such programmes may be seen as a way of increasing the adult's confidence and reducing dependence on professional help, it is also necessary to recognise that an over-ambitious programme may have the opposite effect. It may be perceived as a source of additional unwanted stress and an attempt to place too great an emphasis on the language-disordered child at the expense of the other children in the family or classroom (Clements 1985).

Finally, it should be recognised at the outset that, while involvement of other people may seem to offer a time-saving way of treating children, the approach actually involves an attempt to modify the language and behaviour of two people instead of one. If the treatment is to be properly evaluated, pre- and post-intervention assessment should consider changes in the child's performance *and* the extent to which the adult is able to maintain the modified forms of interaction prescribed by the teacher or therapist. Only when the language therapist is in possession of this information will it be possible to determine the extent to which the adult's language is implicated in the changes observed in the child's language and, if the programme does not work, the extent to which this is a reflection of poor performance by the parent or class teacher. It is also worth noting that most studies have found that it is extremely difficult to persuade parents or teachers to maintain regular and detailed records of children's language and behaviour.

In summary, while there are a number of good reasons for seeking the involvement of parents or class teachers, this will usually involve a commitment from both parties to a long-term process which will require frequent monitoring, and the gradual development of an effective approach to intervention.

Working with language programmes

The term 'language programme' is often used to describe any explicit plan of action designed to improve a child's language ability; this would include relatively simple *ad hoc* strategies introduced by teachers, as well as more elaborate and carefully prepared approaches introduced by trained language therapists. In this section, I want to consider programmes and packages which are commercially produced for use by a wide range of professionals, including teachers, speech therapists and psychologists. Programmes may be used directly by the professional, or as a way of helping other professionals and parents to work more effectively in improving children's language abilities. In addition to considering the advantages and disadvantages of commercially produced programmes in general, this section will consider some of the ways in which such programmes might be used and the criteria which should be employed when selecting a programme.

In a review Harris (1984c) described four types of commercially available programmes. These programmes were classified according to the amount of work involved in their development and hence their level of sophistication:

Speculative programmes are those which have not been subjected to any empirical evaluation but are presented as preliminary research reports during the development stage of a project.

Programmes based upon practical experience are usually books written by teachers, speech therapists or psychologists. They use a blend of research evidence, clinical experience and anecdote as a basis for establishing guidelines for language intervention.

Language kits are complete packages containing instruction manuals, teaching materials and assessment sheets.

Video courses are highly structured teaching programmes which attempt to train parents or teachers to use specific skills considered useful for working with language-impaired chidren.

In each of the four categories there are examples of programmes which employ highly structured behavioural strategies, as well as those that seek to generate more effective interactions within naturalistic environments. Furthermore, while the degree of development work involved in producing the different programmes varies considerably, there is an almost uniform disregard for systematic evaluation of the effectiveness of the programme. Out of 23 programmes reviewed by Harris (1984c), six were classified as providing limited 'evidence regarding effectiveness' and only two as having 'strong' empirical support for their claims. This suggests that practitioners need to be extremely wary of published language intervention materials and should not assume that because a programme has been accepted for publication it has been rigorously evaluated.

There are two main reasons for using a published language programme: the first is that the programme may claim to deal effectively with an area of language intervention about which the practitioner has little first-hand experience or, for other reasons, does not feel confident in tackling without help. The second reason is that the programme may provide a set of guidelines which the language therapist can pass on for use to a classroom teacher or parent who has requested help. For example, the language therapist may have insufficient time to provide detailed guidance for a teacher who is 'desperate' for some practical advice. Alternatively, if it is possible to find a programme which clearly describes an appropriate sequence of activities, this may be used as a form of back-up for more direct work with the teacher or parent. Whatever the reason for turning to a language programme, it is important to be aware of their limitations and to bear in mind the following criteria during selection (Harris 1984c):

Target groups. What kinds of children do the programme designers consider most likely to benefit from the approach described? Consider what modification might be necessary if the programme is to be used with a different group.

Range of language objectives. What levels of language ability does the programme address and what assumptions does it make about existing abilities?

Theoretical framework. What theoretical framework (if any) does the programme draw upon? To what extent are the instructions for intervention consistent with that framework?

Language features. To what extent does the programme emphasise structural, semantic and functional aspects of language?

Production and comprehension skills. How much emphasis is given to encouraging production as opposed to comprehension skills?

Procedures. Are the procedures for encouraging language clearly described?

Provision for assessment. Does the programme include or refer to assessment instruments which can be used to measure success in achieving the specified objectives?

Individuals or groups. Has the programme been designed for work with individual children or with groups?

Evidence for effectiveness. What evidence is presented regarding effectiveness? Does this include comparison of experimental and control groups? To what extent have problems of generalisation been dealt with?

Flexibility. To what extent is it possible to incorporate suggestions in the programme with other activities? How much disruption of existing routines would the programme create if introduced into a child's home or a classroom?

Expert knowledge. Does implementation of the intervention procedures require specialist knowledge?

Presentation. Is the programme clearly presented in an easily accessible format? Could the programme be used without the provision of expert support?

Consideration of these practical issues may help the language therapist to select the most useful programme for a particular situation. In spite of some of the claims which are made, it is probably advisable to see most of these programmes as valuable additions to the resources which a language therapist can bring to bear on a problem, rather than a panacea which provides all the answers. When a programme is employed, it is necessary to monitor progress and evaluate outcomes just as carefully as when any other intervention strategy is introduced (see Chapter 6).

It is also important to bear in mind that the professional manner in which many programmes are presented may actually conceal from the unwary user major theoretical and practical limitations. When used by untrained and inexperienced teachers or parents, the professional appearance of the programme packaging may sustain the adult in a series of, at best, unproductive or, at worst, positively detrimental 'teaching activities'. A related problem is that the rapid growth in research on children's language during the last 25 years has meant that language programmes very quickly become dated, both in relation to their theoretical base and any empirical data they employ (Harris 1984c; Kiernan 1984). All commercially produced programmes should therefore be treated with caution until the language therapist has first-hand experience of the way in which they can be used and their efficacy in a variety of different situations. A summary evaluation of various language programmes is provided in Table 12.1.

Table 12.1 Evaluation of language-teaching programmes: summary table

	Target groups	Range of language curriculum	Theoretical framework	Language features specified	Production (P)/comprehension skills (C)	Procedures	Provision for assessment	Relevance to individuals (I), and groups (G)	Evidence for efficacy	Flexibility	Previous knowledge req'd by adult	Presentation
Speculative programmes												
Guess et al. (1974)	Mute; ESN(S); CA 5–15	O-GC(5)	Behav'al	Structure; concepts; functions	P+C	Operant	X	–	–	–	Beh. mod.	Art book
Bricker and Bricker (1970, 1974)	ESN(S); CA 5–15	O-GC (3+)	Behav'al	Structure	P+C	Operant	X	–	–	–	Beh. mod.	Art book
Stremel (1972)	ESN(S)	SW-GC(3)	Behav'al	Structure	P	Operant	X	–	•	–	Beh. mod.	Art journal
Miller and Yoder (1972, 1974)	ESN(S)	SW-GC (2,3,4)	Devlpt'al	Semantic	P+C	Elicitation in context+RF	X	–	–	•	Lang. dev.	Art books
MacDonald et al (1974)	ESN(S); (DS)	SW-GC(2)	Devlpt'al/ behav'al	Semantic	P	Elicitation in context+RF	✓	–	•	–	Lang. dev.	Art journal
Rees (1978)	ESN(S)	O-GC(5+)	Devlpt'al/ behav'al	Structure and concepts	P+C	Operant	✓	–	•	•	Beh. mod.	Book
Programmes based on practical experience												
Kent (1974)	ESN(S); multiply handi-capped	O-GC(2)	Behav'al	Structure and concepts	P+C	Operant	✓	–	–	–	Beh. mod.	Book
Kirk and Kirk (1972)	ESN(S); Sp. delay; CP; blind; DS	Mediating processes	Psycho-linguistic	Processes	P+C	Elicitation drills	✓	–	–	–	Psycho-linguistic	Book
Ainley et al. (1980)	ESN(M); ESN(S)	Linguistic concepts	None	Structure and concepts	P+C	Elicitation drills	X	–	•	–	None	Book
Crystal (1979, 1982) Crystal et al. (1976)	Lang. delay and dys-function	SW-GC(5+)	Linguistic/ devlpt'al	Grammar	P	Elicitation drills	✓	–	–	•	Grammar	Books
Lee et al. (1975)	Lang. delay	SW-GC(5+)	Devlpt'al	Grammar	P+C	Structured dialogue	✓	I+G	•	•	Grammar	Book

Study												
Leeming et al. (1979)	ESN(S)	SW-GC(3+)	Devlpt'al	Semantic; function; vocab	P+C	Elicitation drills and RF; structured dialogue	✓	—	—	*	None	Book
Gillham (1979, 1983)	ESN(S)	SW-GC(2+)	Devlpt'al	Vocab; semantic	P+C	Modelling in context; reading	✓	—	—	*	None	Books (illustrated)
Cooper et al. (1978)	Lang. delay dysfunction; MA1½–4½	Cog'+social-; pre-req's lang for thought	Devlpt'al	Function	P+C	Structured play	✓	—	*	*	Lang. dev.	Book
Jeffree and McConkey (1976)	Lang. delay	O-GC(3+)	Devlpt'al	Semantic; function	P+C	Structured play; Elicitation + RF	✓	—	—	**	None	Books (illustrated)
Hastings and Hayes (1981)	Lang. delay	O-GC(3+)	Devlpt'al	Semantic; function	P+C	Modelling in context; play	X	—	—	**	None	Books (illustrated)
Commercially produced 'kits'												
Thomas et al. (1978)	ESN(S)	Vocab. SW-GC(5+)	None	Structure; concepts; vocab.	P+C	Elicitation drills	X	—	—	*	None	Picture cards and booklet
Hermans (1982)	ESN(S)	GC(2–5+)	Devlpt'al	Structure	P+C	Elicitation drills	X	—	—	*	None	Picture cards and booklet
Burnett and Fletcher-Wood (1983)	Lang. delay; CA 3–5	SW-GC(5+)	None	Structure; concepts	P+C	Elicitation drills; modelling in context	✓	I+G	—	—	None	Activity cards, assess. sheets
Clements et al. (1983)	ESN(S)	O-GC(5+)	Behav'al; devlpt'al	Structure; semantic	P+C	Operant	✓	—	—	—	None	Activity cards; assess. sheets; manual
Knowles and Masidlover (1982)	ESN(S)	O-GC(5+)	Devlpt'al	Structure; semantic; function	P+C	Modelling in context; play; prompted role reversal	✓	I+G	—	*	Lang. dev.	Resid. course; 3 manuals; assess. material

Table 12.1 Evaluation of language-teaching programmes: summary table

	Target groups	Range of language curriculum	Theoretical framework	Language features specified	Production (P)/ comprehension skills (C)	Procedures	Provision for assessment	Relevance to individuals (I), and groups (G)	Evidence for efficacy	Flexibility	Previous knowledge req'd by adult	Presentation
Video courses												
Robson (1982)	ESN(S)	GC(2–5+)	Behav'al; devlpt'al	Structure; semantic	P	Operant; structured dialogue	✓	I+G	**	*	None	Video mini-course
McConkey and O'Connor (1981)	ESN(S)	SW–GC(2+)	Devlpt'al	Structure; semantic; function	P	Modelling in context; play	✓	I	**	**	None	Video mini-course

Notes: RF = Reinforcement
SW = Single words
GC = Grammatical constructions; the figures in brackets indicate the approximate MLU (in words) of these constructions.
CA = Chronological age
MA = Mental age
Sp. delay = Speech delay
CP = Cerebal Palsy
DS = Down's Syndrome
ESN = Educationally subnormal

Evidence for Efficacy has been rated on a simple star system:
– = no evidence
* = limited evidence
** = strong evidence

Flexibility has been rated on a simple star system:
– = very few opportunities for modification or elaboration
* = moderate opportunities for modification or elaboration
** = extensive opportunities for modification or elaboration

Source: Harris (1984c)

References

Ainley, J., Attridge, B., Catchpole, C. and Clarke, R. (1980) *Early Language Programme*, Basingstoke: Globe Education.

Anthony, A., Boyle, D., Ingram, T. and McIsaac, W. (1971) *The Edinburgh Articulation Test*, Edinburgh and London: E. and S. Livingstone.

Austin, J. L. (1962) *How to do Things with Words*, Oxford: Clarendon Press.

Bates, E. (1976) *Language and Context: The Acquisition of Pragmatics*, New York: Academic Press.

Bellugi, U. (1971) 'Simplification in children's language', in R. Huxley and E. Ingram (eds) *Language Acquisition: Models and Methods*, New York: Academic Press.

Bellugi, U. and Brown, R. (eds) (1964) 'The acquisition of language', *Monographs of the Society for Research in Child Development* 29.

Bereiter, C. and Engelmann, S. (1966) *Teaching Disadvantaged Children in the Pre-school*, Englewood Cliffs, New Jersey: Prentice-Hall.

Berko, J. (1958) 'The child's learning of English morphology', *Word* 14: 150–77.

Berry, P. and Mittler, P. (1984) *The Language Imitation Test*, London: NFER-Nelson.

Binet, A. and Simon, T. (1905) 'Methodes nouvelles pour le diagnostic du niveau intellectuel des anormaux', *L'année psychologique* 11: 191–244.

Bishop, D. V. M. (1982) *Test for Reception of Grammar*, Medical Research Council. Available from the Department of Psychology, University of Manchester.

Bishop, D. V. M. (1983) 'Comprehension of English syntax by profoundly deaf children', *Journal of Child Psychology and Psychiatry* 24 (3): 415–34.

Blackham, G. J. and Silberman, A. (1975) *Modification of Child and Adolescent Behaviour*, 2nd edn, Belmont, California: Wadsworth Publishing Co.

Blackman, D. E. (1984) 'Functional analysis of verbal bahaviour: a foundation for behavioural approaches to language remediation', in D. J. Muller (ed.) *Remediating Children's Language: Behavioural and Natur-*

alistic Approaches, London: Croom Helm.

Blank, M. (1973) *Teaching Language in the Pre-school: A Dialogue Approach*, Columbus, Ohio: Charles E. Merrill.

Blank, M. and Franklin, E. (1980) 'Dialogue with preschoolers: a cognitively-based system of assessment', *Applied Psycholinguistics* 1: 127–50.

Blank, M., Gessner, M. and Esposito, A. (1979) 'Language without communication: a case study', *Journal of Child Language* 6: 329–52.

Blank, M., Rose, S. A. and Berlin, L. J. (1978) *The Language of Learning*, New York: Grune Stratton.

Bloom, L. (1970) *Language Development: Form and Function in Emerging Grammar*, Cambridge, Massachusetts: MIT Press.

Bloom, L. (1971) 'Why not pivot grammar', *Journal of Speech and Hearing Disorders* 36 (1): 40–50.

Bloom, L. (1973) *One Word at a Time*, The Hague: Mouton.

Bloom, L., Hood, L. and Lightbrown, P. (1974) 'Imitation in language development: if, when, why', *Cognitive Psychology* 6: 380–420.

Bloom, L. and Lahey, M. (1978) *Language Development and Language Disorders*, New York: Wiley.

Bowerman, M. (1973a) *Early Syntactic Development: A Cross Linguistic Study with Special Reference to Finnish*, Cambridge: Cambridge University Press.

Bowerman, M. (1973b) 'Structural relationships in children's utterances: syntactic or semantic', in T. E. Moore (ed.) *Cognitive Development and the Acquisition of Language*, New York: Academic Press.

Bowerman, M. (1976) 'Semantic factors in the acquisition of roles for word use and sentence construction', in D. Morehead and A. Morehead (eds) *Directions in Normal and Deficient Child Language*, Baltimore, Maryland: University Park Press.

Braine, M. D. (1963) 'The ontogony of English phrase structure: the first phrase', *Language* 39: 1–14.

Braine, M. D. (1976) 'Children's first word combinations', *Monographs for Society of Research in Child Development* 41: 104.

Bremner, J. G. (1988) *Infancy*, Oxford: Blackwell.

Bricker, D. D. and Bricker, W. A. (1973) *Infant, Toddler and Preschool Research and Intervention Project Report: Year III*, Institute on Mental Retardation and Intellectual Development, Nashville, Tennessee: George Peabody College for Teachers.

Bricker, W. A. and Bricker, D. D. (1970) 'A program of language training for the severely language handicapped child', *Exceptional Children* 37: 101–13.

Bricker, W. A. and Bricker, D. D. (1974) 'An early language training strategy', in R. E. Schiefelbusch and L. L. Lloyd (eds) *Language Perspectives: Acquisition, Retardation and Intervention*, Baltimore,

Maryland: University Park Press.

Brinker, R. P. (1982) 'Contextual contours and the development of language', in M. Beveridge (ed.) *Children Thinking Through Language*, London: Edward Arnold.

Brown, R. (1958) 'How shall a thing be called?', *Psychological Review* 65: 18–21.

Brown, R. (1973) *A First Language*, London: Allen & Unwin.

Brown, R. and Hanlon, C. (1970) 'Derivational complexity and order of acquisition', in J. R. Hayes (ed.) *Cognition and the Development of Language*, New York: Wiley.

Bruner, J. S. (1975) 'The ontogenesis of speech acts', *Journal of Child Language* 2: 1–19.

Bruner, J. S. (1983) *Child's Talk: Learning to Use Language*, Oxford: Oxford University Press.

Bruner, J. S. and Sherwood, V. (1976) 'Early rule structure: the case of peekaboo', in J. S. Bruner, A. Jolly and K. Sylva (eds) *Play: Its Role in Evolution and Development*, Harmondsworth: Penguin.

Burnett, P. and Fletcher-Wood, V. (1983) *Let's Play Language*, Wisbech: Learning Development Aids.

Cantwell, D. P. and Baker, L. (1985) 'Speech and language: development and disorders', in M. Rutter and L. Hersov (eds) *Child and Adolescent Psychiatry: Modern Approaches*, 2nd edn, Oxford: Blackwell.

Cantwell, D. P. and Baker, L. (1987) *Developmental Speech and Language Disorders*, New York: Guilford Press.

Carney, E. (1979) 'Inappropriate abstraction in speech-assessment procedures', *British Journal of Disorders of Communication* 14: 123–35.

Carrow, E. (1973) *Test of Auditory Comprehension of Language*, London: NFER-Nelson.

Carrow-Woodfolk, E. (1985) *Test for Auditory Comprehension of Language*, rev. edn, London: NFER-Nelson.

Cavallaro, C. C. (1983) 'Language interventions in natural settings', *Teaching Exceptional Children* 16 (1): 65–70.

Cavallaro, C. C. and Poulson, C. L. (1985) 'Teaching language to handicapped children in natural settings', *Education and Treatment of Children* 8 (1): 1–24.

Chapman, R. (1981) 'Computing Mean Length of Utterance in Morphemes', in J.F. Miller (ed.) *Assessing Language Production in Children*, Baltimore, Maryland: University Park Press.

Chappell, G. E. (1977) 'A cognitive-linguistic intervention program: basic concept formation level', *Language Speech and Hearing Services in Schools* 8: 15–22.

Chesaldine, S. and McConkey, R. (1979) 'Parental speech to young Down's Syndrome children: an intervention study', *American Journal of Mental Deficiency* 83: 612–20.

References

Chomsky, C. (1969) *The Acquisition of Syntax in Children from 5 to 10*, Research Monograph 57, Cambridge, Massachusetts: MIT Press.

Chomsky, N. (1959) 'Review of *Verbal Behaviour* by B. F. Skinner', *Language* 35: 26–58.

Chomsky, N. (1965) *Aspects of Theory of Syntax*, Cambridge, Massachussetts: MIT Press.

Chomsky, N. and Halle, M. (1968) *The Sound Pattern of English*, New York: Harper & Row.

Christie, P. and Wimpory, D. (1986) 'Recent research into the development of communicative competence and its implications for the teaching of autistic children', *Communication* 20 (1): 4–7.

Clark, E. V. (1983) 'Meanings and concepts', in J. H. Flavell and E. M. Markman (eds) *Handbook of Child Psychology*, 4th edn, New York: Wiley.

Clark, R. (1977) 'What's the use of imitation?', *Journal of Child Language* 4 (3): 341–58.

Clarke-Stewart, K. A. (1973) 'Interactions between mothers and their young children: characteristics and consequences', *Monographs of the Society for Research in Child Development* 38.

Clements, J. (1985) 'Update – training parents of mentally handicapped children', *Association of Child Psychology and Psychiatry Newsletter* 7 (4): 2–9.

Clements, J., Evans, C., Jones, C. and Upton, G. (1983) *Early Language Training Programme for the Mentally Handicapped Child*, Cardiff: Drake Educational Associates.

Cole, K. N. and Dole, P. S. (1986) 'Direct language instruction and interactive language instruction with language delayed pre-school children: a comparison study', *Journal of Speech and Hearing Research* 29: 206–17.

Conant, S., Budoff, M., Hecht, B. and Morse, R. (1984) 'Language intervention: a pragmatic approach', *Journal of Autism and Developmental Disorders* 45: 456–62.

Condon, W. S. and Sander, L. (1974) 'Synchrony demonstrated between movements of the infant and adult speech', *Child Development* 45: 456–62.

Connell, P. J. (1982) 'On teaching language rules', *Language Speech and Hearing Services in Schools* 13: 231–40.

Connell, P. J. (1986) 'Teaching subjecthood to language disordered children', *Journal of Speech and Hearing Disorders* 29: 481–92.

Connell, P. J. (1987) 'An effect of modelling and imitation teaching procedures in children with and without specific language impairment', *Journal of Speech and Hearing Research* 30: 105–13.

Connell, P. J., Spradlin, J. E. and McReynolds, L. V. (1977) 'Some suggested criteria for the evaluation of language programs', *Journal of*

Speech and Hearing Disorders 42: 563-7.

Connolly, J. H. (1979) 'Some remarks on the teaching of LARSP', in D. Crystal (ed.) *Working with LARSP*, London: Edward Arnold.

Conrad, R. (1979) *The Deaf School Child: Language and Cognitive Function*, London: Harper & Row.

Cooper, J., Moodley, M. and Reynell, J. (1974) 'Intervention programmes for preschool children with delayed language development: a preliminary report', *British Journal of Disorders of Communication* 9: 81-91.

Cooper, J., Moodley, M. and Reynell, J. (1978) *Helping Language Development: A Developmental Programme for Children with Early Language Handicaps*, London: Edward Arnold.

Cooper, J., Moodley, M. and Reynell, J. (1979) 'The developmental language programme: results from a five-year study', *British Journal of Disorders of Communication* 14: 57-69.

Corrigan, R. (1978) 'Language development as related to stage 6 object permanence development', *Journal of Child Language* 5: 173-89.

Costello, J. M. (1977) 'Programmed instruction', *Journal of Speech and Hearing Disorders* 42: 3-28.

Courtright, J. A. and Courtright, I. C. (1976) 'Imitative modelling as a theoretical base for instructing language disordered chidren', *Journal of Speech and Hearing Disorders* 19: 635-63.

Cromer, R. F. (1974) 'The development of language and cognition: the cognition hypotheses', in B. M. Foss (ed.) *New Perspectives in Child Development*, Harmondsworth: Penguin.

Cromer, R. F. (1981) 'Reconceptualising language acquisition and cognitive development', in R. Schiefelbusch and D. Bricker (eds.) *Early Language: Acquisition and Intervention*, Baltimore, Maryland: University Park Press.

Cronbach, L. J. (1984) *Essentials of Psychological Testing*, 4th edn, New York: Harper & Row.

Cross, T. G. (1977) 'Mothers' speech adjustments: the contribution of selected child listener variables', in C. E. Snow and C. A. Ferguson (eds) *Talking to Chidren: Language Input and Acquisition*, Cambridge: Cambridge University Press.

Crystal, D. (1979) *Working with LARSP*, London: Edward Arnold.

Crystal, D. (1981) *Clinical Linguistics*, Vienna: Springer-Verlag.

Crystal, D. (1982) *Profiling Linguistic Disability*, London: Edward Arnold.

Crystal, D. (1984) *Linguistic Encounters with Language Handicap*, Oxford: Blackwell.

Crystal, D., Fletcher, P. and Garman, M. (1976) *The Grammatical Analysis of Language Disability*, London: Edward Arnold.

Cummins, J. (1984) 'Minority students and learning difficulties: issues in assessment and placement', in Y. Lebrun and M. Paradis (eds) *Early Bilingualism and Child Development*, Amsterdam: Swets Publishing Service. Reprinted in J. Cummins and M. Swain (eds) (1986) *Bilingualism in Education*, London: Longman.

Cummins, J. and Swain, M. (eds) (1986) *Bilingualism in Education*, London: Longman.

Cunningham, C.C. and Sloper, P. (1984) 'The relationship between maternal ratings of first word vocabulary and Reynell Language scores', *British Journal of Educational Psychology* 54 (2): 160–7.

Cunningham, C. E., Reuler, E., Blackwell, J. and Deck, J. (1981) 'Behavioural and linguistic developments in the interactions of normal and retarded children with their mothers', *Child Development* 52: 62–70.

Curtiss, S. (1977) *Genie: A Psycholinguistic Study of a Modern-day 'Wild Child'*, New York: Academic Press.

DePaulo, B. M., Bellam, A. and Bonvillian, J. D. (1978) 'The effect on language development of the special characteristics of speech addressed to children', *Journal of Psycholinguistic Research* 7: 189–211.

Dillon, J. T. (1982) 'The effect of questions in education and other enterprises', *Journal of Curriculum Studies* 14 (2): 127–52.

Dobie, R. A. and Berlin, C. I. (1979) 'Influence of otitis media in learning and development', *Annals of Otology, Rhinology and Laryngology* 88 (supp. 60): 26–58.

Dore, J. (1973) 'The development of speech acts', unpublished PhD thesis, New York: City University.

Dore, J. (1974) 'A pragmatic description of early language development', *Journal of Psycholinguistic Research* 4: 343–50.

Dore, J. (1977) 'Children's illocutionary acts', in R. O. Freedle (ed.) *Discourse, Production and Comprehension*, Norwood, New Jersey: Ablex Publishing Corporation.

Downs, M. and Blager, F. B. (1982) 'The otitis prone child', *Journal of Developmental and Behavioural Paediatrics* 3 (2): 106–13.

Dunn, L. M., Whetton, C. and Pintilie, D. (1982) *The British Picture Vocabulary Scale*, London: NFER-Nelson.

Edwards, P. (1973) 'Sensory motor intelligence and semantic relations in early child grammar', *Cognition* 2 (4): 395–434.

Eimas, P., Siqueland, E. R., Jusczyk, P. and Vigorito, J. (1971) 'Speech perception in infants', *Science* 171: 303–6.

Eisonson, J. (1986) *Language and Speech Disorders in Children*, New York: Pergamon.

Fenn, G. (1973) 'Language development in severely subnormal children', *Cambridge Journal of Education* 3: 35–41.

Fenn, G. (1979) *Word Order Comprehension Test*, London: NFER-Nelson.

Ferguson, C. A. and Farwell, C. B. (1975) 'Words and sounds in early language acquisition', *Language* 51: 419–39.

Fillmore, C. J. (1968) 'The case for case', in E. Bach and R. T. Harms (eds) *Universals in Linguistic Theory*, London: Holt, Rinehart & Winston.

Folger, J. P. and Chapman, R. S. (1977) 'A pragmatic analysis of spontaneous imitations', *Journal of Child Language* 5: 25–38.

Forehand, R. and Peed, F. (1979) 'Training parents to modify the non-compliant behaviour of their children', in A. J. Finch and P. C. Kendall (eds) *Clinical Treatment and Research in Child Psychopathology*, New York: Spectrum.

Fraiberg, S. (1977) *Insights from the Blind*, London: Souvenir Press.

Francis, H. (1980) 'Language development and education', *Educational Analysis* 2: 25–35.

Fraser, C., Bellugi, U. and Brown, R. (1973) 'Control of grammar in imitation, comprehension and production', in C. A. Ferguson and D. I. Slobin (eds) *Studies of Child Language Development*, New York: Holt, Rinehart & Winston.

Garcia, E. E. and DeHaven, E. D. (1974) 'Use of operant techniques in the establishment and generalisation of language: a review and analysis', *American Journal of Mental Deficiency* 79 (2): 169–78.

Geller, E. F. and Wollner, S. G. (1976) 'A preliminary investigation of communicative competence of three linguistically impaired children'. Paper presented at the New York State Speech and Hearing Association, Grossingers.

Gillham, W. (1979) *The First Words Language Programme*, London: Allen & Unwin.

Gillham, W. (1983) *Two Words Together: A First Sentences Language Programme*, London: Allen & Unwin.

Gillham, W. E. C. (ed.) (1986) *Handicapping Conditions in Chidren*, London: NFER-Croom Helm.

Gleitman, L. R., Newport, E. L. and Gleitman, H. (1984) 'The current status of the "Motherese" hypothesis', *Journal of Child Language* 11: 43–79.

Gleitman, L. R. and Wanner, E. (1982) 'Language acquisition: the state of the art', in E. Wanner and L. R. Gleitman (eds) *Language Acquisition: The State of the Art*, Cambridge: Cambridge University Press.

Godowski, B. S., Sanger, D. D. and Decker, T. N. (1986) 'Otitis media: effect on a child's learning', *Academic Therapy* 21 (3): 283–91.

Goldman, R. and Fristoe, M. (1969) *The Goldman–Fristoe Test of Articulation*, Circle Pines, Minnesota: American Guidance Service Inc.

Gordon, D. and Lakoff, G. (1975) 'Conversational postulates', in P. Cole and J. L. Morgan (eds) *Syntax and Semantics* (vol. 3) *Speech Acts*, New York: Academic Press.

Greenfield, P. M. and Smith, J. H. (1976) *The Structure of Communication in Early Language Development*, New York: Academic Press.

Gregory, S. (1986) 'Advising parents of young deaf children: implications and assumptions', in J. Harris (ed.) *Child Psychology in Action*, London: Croom Helm.

Grice, H. P. (1975) 'Logic and conversation', in P. Cole and J. L. Morgan (eds) *Syntax and Semantics* (vol. 3) *Speech Acts*, New York: Academic

Press.

Grunwell, P. (1981) 'The development of phonology: a descriptive profile', *First Language* 3: 161–91.

Grunwell, P. (1982) *Clinical Phonology*, London: Croom Helm.

Guess, D., Sailor, W. and Baer, D. M. (1974) 'To teach language to retarded children', in R. E. Schiefelbusch and L. L. Lloyd (eds) *Language Perspectives: Acquisition, Retardation and Intervention*, Baltimore, Maryland: University Park Press.

Gunzberg, H. C. (1973) *Primary Progress Assessment Chart of Social Development*, London and Birmingham: NSHMC/SEFA Publications.

Halliday, M.A.K. (1973) *Explorations in the Functions of Language*, London: Edward Arnold.

Halliday, M.A.K. (1975) *Learning How to Mean – Explorations in the Development of Language*, London: Edward Arnold.

Hammill, D. D. and Larsen S. C. (1974) 'The effectiveness of psycholinguistic training', *Exceptional Children* 41: 5–14.

Hare, B., Hammill, D. D. and Bartel, W. (1973) 'Construct validity of selected ITPA subtests', *Exceptional Children* 40: 13–20.

Harris, J. (1984a) 'Teaching children to develop language: the impossible dream', in D. J. Muller (ed.) *Remediating Children's Language: Behavioural and Naturalistic Approaches*, London: Croom Helm.

Harris, J. (1984b) 'Encouraging linguistic interactions between severely mentally handicapped children and teachers in special schools', *Special Education: Forward Trends* 11 (2): 17–24.

Harris, J. (1984c) 'Early language intervention programmes: an update', *Association of Child Psychology and Psychiatry Newsletter* 6 (2): 2–20.

Harris, J. (1986) 'The contribution of developmental psychology to the education of mentally handicapped children', in J. Harris (ed.) *Child Psychology in Action*, London: Croom Helm.

Harris, J. (1988) *Language Development in Schools for Children with Severe Learning Difficulties*, London: Croom Helm.

Harris, J. C. (1983) 'What does Mean Length of Utterance mean? Evidence from a comparative study of normal and Down's Syndrome children', *British Journal of Disorders of Communication* 18 (3): 153–69.

Harris, M. (1986) 'The acquisition of number markers', in K. Durkin (ed.) *Language Development in the School Years*, London: Croom Helm.

Harris, P. J. (1986) 'Presenting psychological knowledge to mothers of young children', in J. Harris (ed.) *Child Psychology in Action*, London: Croom Helm.

Hastings, P. and Hayes, B. (1981) *Encouraging Language Development*, London: Croom Helm.

Hawkins, P. (1984) *Introducing Phonology*, London: Hutchinson.

Heath, S. B. (1983) *Ways with Words*, Cambridge: Cambridge University Press.

Hermans, C. J. P. (1982) *Syntax: Language Teaching Programme*, Wisbech: Learning Development Aids.

Howe, C. J. (1975) 'The meanings of two-word utterances in the speech of young children', *Journal of Child Language* 3: 29–47.

Howlin, P. (1984) 'Parents as therapists: a critical review', in D. J. Muller (ed.) *Remediating Children's Language: Behavioural and Naturalistic Approaches*, London: Croom Helm.

Hughes, D. L. (1985) *Language Treatment and Generalisation: A Clinician's Handbook*, London: Taylor & Francis.

Hughes, M., Carmichael, H., Pinkerton, G. and Tizard, B. (1979) 'Recording children's conversations at home and at nursery school: a technique and some methodological considerations', *Journal of Child Psychology and Psychiatry* 20 (3): 225–32.

Hymes, D. (1971) 'Competence and performance in linguistic theory', in R. Huxley and E. Ingram (eds) *Language Acquisition: Models and Methods*, London: Academic Press.

Ingram, D. (1974) 'Phonological rules in young children', *Journal of Child Language* 1: 49–64.

Ingram, D. (1976) *Phonological Disability in Children*, London: Edward Arnold.

Ingram, D. (1979) 'Phonological patterns in the speech of young children', in P. Fletcher and M. Garman (eds) *Language Acquisition*, Cambridge: Cambridge University Press.

Ivimey, G. P. (1975) 'The development of English morphology: an acquisition model', *Language and Speech* 18: 120–44.

Jeffree, D. and McConkey, R. (1976) *Let Me Speak*, London: Souvenir Press.

Jeffree, D., Wheldall, K. and Mittler, P. (1973) 'Facilitating two-word utterances in two Down's Syndrome boys', *American Journal of Mental Deficiency* 78 (2): 117–22.

Jones, L. M., Reid, B. D. and Kiernan, C. C. (1982) 'Signs and symbols: the 1980 survey', in M. Peter and R. Barnes (eds) *Signs, Symbols and Schools: An Introduction to the Use of Non-vocal Communication Systems and Sign Language in Schools*, Stratford: National Council of Special Education.

Kahn, J. V. (1975) 'Relationship of Piaget's sensori-motor period of language acquisition in profoundly retarded children', *American Journal of Mental Deficiency* 79: 640–3.

Kanner, L. (1943) 'Autistic disturbances of affective contact', *Nervous Child* 2: 217–50.

Karmiloff-Smith, A. (1979) *A Functional Approach to Child Language*, Cambridge: Cambridge University Press.

Keenan, E. O. (1974) 'Conversational competence in children', *Journal of Child Language* 1: 163–83.

Kent, L. R. (1974) *Language Acquisition Program for the Retarded or Multiply Handicapped*, Champaign, Illinois: Research Press.

Kiernan, C. (1981) *Analysis of Programmes of Teaching*, Basingstoke: Macmillan Globe Educational.

Kiernan, C. (1983) 'The use of non-vocal communication techniques with autistic individuals', *Journal of Child Psychology and Psychiatry* 24 (3): 339–76.

Kiernan, C. (1984) 'Language remediation programmes: a review', in D. J. Muller (ed.) *Remediating Children's Language: Behavioural and Naturalistic Approaches*, London: Croom Helm.

Kirk, S. A. and Kirk, W. D. (1972) *Psychological Learning Disabilities: Diagnosis and Remediation*, Urbana, Illinois: University of Illinois Press.

Kirk, S. A., McCarthy, J. J. and Kirk W. D. (1968) *Illinois Test of Psycholinguistic Abilities*, Illinois: University of Illinois.

Klima, E. S. and Bellugi, U. (1979) *The Signs of Language*, Cambridge, Massachusetts: Harvard University Press.

Knowles, W. and Masidlover, M. (1982) 'Derbyshire language scheme', unpublished – limited availability through Derbyshire County Council.

Kretschmer, R. R. and Kretschmer, L. W. (eds) (1978) *Language Development and Intervention with the Hearing Impaired*, Baltimore, Maryland: University Park Press.

Kriegsmann, E., Gallagher, J. C. and Meyers, A. (1982) 'Sign programs with non-verbal hearing children', *Exceptional Children* 48 (5): 436–45.

Labov, W. and Labov, T. (1978) 'Learning the syntax of questions', in R. Campbell and P. T. Smith (eds) *Recent Advances in the Psychology of Language*, New York: Plenum.

Langdon, H. W. (1983) 'Assessment and intervention strategies for the bilingual language disordered student', *Exceptional Children* 50 (1): 37–46.

Lawton, D. (1983) *Curriculum Studies and Educational Planning*, London: Hodder & Stoughton.

Lee, L. L. (1966) 'Developmental sentence types: a method for comparing normal and deficient syntactic development', *Journal of Speech and Hearing Disorders* 31 (4): 311–30.

Lee, L. L. (1969) *Northwestern Syntax Screening Test*, Evanston, Illinois: Northwestern University Press.

Lee, L. L. (1974) *Developmental Sentence Analysis*, Evanston, Illinois: Northwestern University Press.

Lee, L. L., Koenigsknecht, R. A. and Mulhern, S. (1975) *Interactive Language Development Teaching*, Evanston, Illinois: Northwestern University Press.

Leeming, K., Swann, W., Coupe, J. and Mittler, P. (1979) *Teaching Language and Communication to the Mentally Handicapped*, Schools

Council Curriculum Bulletin, No. 8, London: Evans/Methuen.

Lenneberg, E. H. (1967) *Biological Foundations of Language*, New York: Wiley.

Leonard, L. B. (1975) 'Modelling as a clinical procedure in language training', *Language Speech and Hearing Services in Schools* 6: 72–85.

Lewis, V. (1987) *Development and Handicap*, Oxford: Blackwell.

Lieven, E. (1978) 'Conversations between mothers and young children: individual differences and their possible implications for the study of language learning', in N. Waterson and C. E. Snow (eds) *The Development of Communication*, Chichester: Wiley.

Lock, A. (1978) 'The emergence of language: on being picked up', in A. J. Lock (ed.) *Action, Gesture and Symbol: The Emergence of Language*, London: Academic Press.

Lock, A. (1980a) *The Guided Reinvention of Language*, London: Academic Press.

Lock, A. (1980b) 'Language development, past, present and future', *Bulletin of the British Psychological Society* 33: 5–8.

Longhurst, T. M. (1977) 'Language acquisition and assessment', in *Normal and Handicapped Pre-school Children: A Review of the Literature*, formal report vol. 2, Topeka, Kansas: Kansas Neurological Institute.

Lovaas, O. I., Koegel, R., Simmons, J. Q. and Long, J. S. (1973) 'Some generalisation and follow-up measures on autistic children in behaviour therapy', *Journal of Applied Behaviour Analysis* 6: 131–66.

McCauley, R. J. and Swisher, L. (1984) 'Psychometric review of language and articulation tests for pre-school children', *Journal of Speech and Hearing Disorders* 40: 34–42.

McConkey, R. and O'Connor, M. (1980) 'Implementation of classroom research findings on the early language development of mentally handicapped children', *First Language* 1: 67–77.

McConkey, R. and O'Connor, M. (1981) 'Putting two words together', unpublished video-course, limited availability through St Michael's House, Stillorgan, Dublin.

MacCorquodale, K. (1969) 'B. F. Skinner's *Verbal Behaviour*: a retrospective appreciation', *Journal of the Experimental Analysis of Behaviour* 12: 831–41.

MacDonald, J. D. and Blott, J. P. (1974) 'Environmental language intervention: the rationale for a diagnostic and training strategy through rules, context and generalisation', *Journal of Speech and Hearing Disorders* 39 (3): 244–56.

MacDonald, J. D., Blott, J. R. Gordon, K., Spiegal, B. and Hartmann, M. (1974) 'An experimental parent assisted treatment program for pre-school language-delayed children', *Journal of Speech and Hearing Disorders* 39 (4): 395–415.

McGee, G. G. Krantz, P. J. and McClannahan, L. E. (1985) 'The facilitative effects of incidental teaching on preposition use by autistic children', *Journal of Applied Behaviour Analysis* 18 (1): 17–31.

McLean, J. E. and Snyder, L. S. (1978) *A Transactional Approach to Early Language Training*, Columbus, Ohio: Charles E. Merrill.

McLoughlin, B. (1987) *Theories of Second Language Learning*, London: Edward Arnold.

McNamara, J. (1972) 'Cognitive basis of language learning in infants', *Psychological Review* 79: 1–14.

McNeill, D. (1970) *The Acquisition of Language: The Study of Developmental Psycholinguistics*, New York: Harper & Row.

McTear, M. F. (1985) *Children's Conversation*, Oxford: Blackwell.

Mahoney, G. J. (1975) 'Eclological approach to delayed language acquisition', *American Journal of Mental Deficiency* 80 (2): 139–48.

Maratsos, M. P. (1983) 'Some current issues in the study of the acquisition of grammar', in J. H. Flavell and E. M. Markman (eds) *Handbook of Child Psychology*, 4th edn, New York: Wiley.

Maratsos, M. P. and Chalkley, M. P. (1980) 'The internal language of children's syntax: the ontogenesis and representation of syntactic categories', in K. E. Nelson (ed.) *Children's Language*, vol. 2, New York: Garden Press.

Martin, G. and Pear, J. (1988) *Behaviour Modification: What It Is and How to Do It*, 3rd edn, Engelwood Cliffs, New Jersey: Prentice-Hall.

Mead, G. H. (1934) *Mind, Self and Society*, Chicago: University of Chicago Press.

Meadow, K. P. (1978) 'The "natural history" of a research project: an illustration of methodological issues in research with deaf children', in L. S. Liben (ed.) *Deaf Children: Developmental Perspectives*, New York: Academic Press.

Meltzoff, A. H. and Moore, M. K. (1977) 'Imitation of facial and manual gestures by human neonates', *Science* 198: 75–8.

Meltzoff, A. H. and Moore, M. K. (1983) 'Newborn infants imitate facial gestures', *Child Development* 54: 702–9.

Menyuk, P. (1964) 'Comparison of grammar of children with functionally deviant and normal speech', *Journal of Speech and Hearing Research* 7: 109–21.

Menyuk, P. and Menn, L. (1979) 'Early strategies for the perception and production of words and sounds', in P. Fletcher and M. Garman (eds) *Language Acquisition*, London: Cambridge University Press.

Miller, J. F. (1981a) *Assessing Language Production in Children*, London: Edward Arnold.

Miller, J. F. (1981b) 'Eliciting procedures for language', in J. F. Miller (ed.) *Assessing Language Production in Children*, London: Edward Arnold.

Miller, J. F. and Yoder, D. E. (1972) 'A syntax teaching program', in J.E. McLean, D. E. Yoder, and R. L. Schiefelbusch (eds) *Language Interven-*

tion and the Retarded: Developing Strategies, Baltimore, Maryland: University Park Press.

Miller, J. F. and Yoder, D. E. (1974) 'An ontogenetic language teaching strategy for teaching retarded children', in R. L. Schiefelbusch and L. L. Lloyd (eds) *Language Perspectives: Acquisition, Retardation and Intervention*, Baltimore, Maryland: University Park Press.

Miller, W. and Ervin, S. (1964) 'The development of grammar in child language', in U. Bellugi and R. Brown (eds) 'The acquisition of language', *Monographs of the Society for Research in Child Development* 29 (92).

Morris, C. W. (1938) 'Foundations of the theory of signs', in O. Neurath, R. Carnap, and C. Morris (eds) *International Encyclopaedia of Unified Science*, Chicago: University of Chicago Press. Reprinted in C. W. Morris 1971.

Morris, C. W. (1971) *Writings on the General Theory of Signs*, The Hague: Mouton.

Morse, P. A. (1972) 'The discrimination of speech and non-speech stimuli in early infancy', *Journal of Experimental Child Psychology* 14: 477–92.

Morse. P. A. (1974) 'Infant speech perception: a preliminary model and a review of the literature', in R. L. Schiefelbusch and L. L. Lloyd (eds) *Language Perspectives: Acquisition, Retardation and Intervention*, Baltimore, Maryland: University Park Press.

Morse, P. A. (1979) 'The infancy of infant speech perception: the first decade of research', *Brain Behaviour and Evolution* 16: 351–73.

Mowrer, D. E. (1984) 'Behavioural approaches to treating language disorders', in D. J. Muller (ed.) *Remediating Children's Language: Behavioural and Naturalistic Approaches*, London: Croom Helm.

Musselwhite, C. R. and St Louis, K. W. (1982) *Communication Programming for the Severely Handicapped*, San Diego, California: College Hill Press.

Nelson, K. (1973) *Structure and Strategy in Learning to Talk*, Monographs of the Society for Research in Child Development 30 (1–2).

Nelson, K. in collaboration with Gruendel, J. *et al.* (1986) *Event Knowledge: Structure and Function in Development*, Hillside, New Jersey: LEA.

Nelson, K. E. (1977) 'Facilitating children's syntax acquisition', *Developmental Psychology* 13 (2): 101–7.

Newcomer, P., Hare, B., Hammill, D. D. and McGettigan, J. (1974) 'Construct validity of the ITPA sub-tests', *Exceptional Children* 40: 509–10.

Newson, J. (1979) 'Intentional behaviour in the young infant', in D. Shaffer and J. Dunn (eds) *The First Year of Life: Psychological and Medical Implications of Early Experiences*, Chichester: Wiley.

Ninio, A. and Bruner, J. (1978) 'The achievement and antecedents of labelling', *Journal of Child Language* 5: 1–15.

Ochs, E. (1983) 'Conversational competence in children', in E. Ochs and B. Schieffelin (eds) 1983.

Ochs, E. and Schieffelin, B. B. (eds) (1979) *Developmental Pragmatics*, New York: Academic Press.

Ochs, E. and Schieffelin, B. B. (eds) (1983) *Acquiring Conversational Competence*, London: Routledge & Kegan Paul.

Osgood, C. E. (1957a) 'Motivational dynamics of language behaviour', in M. R. Jones (ed.) *Nebraska Symposium on Motivation*, Lincoln, Nebraska: University of Nebraska Press.

Osgood, C. E. (1957b) 'A behaviouristic analysis of perception and language as cognitive phenomena', in H. E. Gruber, K. R. Hammond and R. Jesser (eds) *Contemporary Approaches to Cognition*, Cambridge, Massachusetts: Harvard University Press.

Perozzi, J. A. (1985) 'A pilot study of language facilitation for bilingual language handicapped children: intervention implications', *Journal of Speech and Hearing Disorders* 50: 403-6.

Peter, M. and Barnes, R. (eds) (1982) *Signs, Symbols and Schools*, Stratford: National Council of Special Education.

Piaget, J. (1970) 'Piaget's theory', in P. H. Mussen (ed.) *Carmichael's Manual of Child Psychology*, 3rd edn, New York: Wiley.

Piaget, J. and Inhelder, B. (1969) *The Psychology of the Child*, London: Routledge & Kegan Paul.

Quick, C. and Mandell, C. (1983) 'Otitis media and learning disabilities: more than a relationship', paper presented at the annual international Convention of the Council for Exceptional Children, Detroit, 4–8 April 1983.

Ramasut, A. (1989) *Whole School Aproaches to the Education of Children with Special Educational Needs*, Brighton: Falmer Press.

Ratner, N. and Bruner, J. (1978) 'Games, social exchange and the acquisition of language', *Journal of Child Language* 5: 391–401.

Rees, N. S. (1978) 'Pragmatics of language: applications to normal and disordered language development', in R. L. Schiefelbusch (ed.) *Bases of Language Intervention*, Baltimore, Maryland: University Park Press.

Reynell, J. and Huntley, M. (1985) *The Reynell Development Language Scales*, 2nd edn, London: NFER.

Richards, M. P. M. (ed.) (1974) *The Integration of the Child into a Social World*, Cambridge: Cambridge University Press.

Robson, C. (1982) *Language Development Through Structural Teaching*, Cardiff: Drake Educational Associates.

Romaine, S. (1984) *The Language of Children and Adolescents*, Oxford: Blackwell.

Rondal, J. (1976) 'Maternal speech to normal and Down's Syndrome children matched by Mean Length of Utterances', unpublished research report, Minnesota: University of Minnesota.

Ruder, K. F. (1978 'Planning and programming for language intervention', in R. L. Schiefelbusch (ed.) *Bases of Language Intervention*, Baltimore, Maryland: University Park Press.

Russell, M. (1984) 'Assessment and intervention issues with the non-speaking child', *Exceptional Children* 51 (1): 64–71.

Rutter, M. (1980) 'Language training with autistic children: how does it work and what does it achieve?', in L. A. Hersov and A. R. Nicol (eds) *Language and Language Disorders in Childhood*, London: Pergamon.

Rutter, M. (1981) *Maternal Deprivation Reassessed*, 2nd edn, Harmondsworth: Penguin.

Rutter, M. (1985) 'Infantile autism and other pervasive developmental disorders', in M. Rutter and L. Hersov (eds) *Child and Adolescent Psychiatry: Modern Approaches*, 2nd edn, Oxford: Blackwell.

Schaffer, H. R. (1977) *Studies in Mother–Infant Interaction*, London: Academic Press.

Schiefelbusch, R. L. (1984) 'Speech, language and communication disorders of the mentally handicapped', *Folia Phoniat* 36: 8–23.

Schieffelin, B. B. (1979) 'Getting it together: an ethnographic approach to the study of the development of communication competence', in E. Ochs and O. B. Schieffelin (eds) *Developmental Pragmatics*, New York: Academic Press.

Schlesinger, I. M. (1971) 'Production of utterances and language acquisition', in D. I. Slobin (ed.) *The Ontogenesis of Grammar: A Theoretical Symposium*, New York and London: Academic Press.

Schlesinger, I. M. (1974) 'Relational concepts underlying language', in R. L. Schiefelbusch and L. L. Lloyd (eds) *Language Perspectives: Acquisition, Retardation and Intervention*, Baltimore, Maryland: University Park Press.

Searle, J. R. (1969) *Speech Acts: An Essay on the Philosophy of Language*, Cambridge: Cambridge University Press.

Searle, J. R. (1975) 'Indirect speech acts', in P. Cole and J. L. Morgan (eds) *Syntax and Semantics* (vol. 3) *Speech Acts*, New York: Academic Press.

Seibert, J. M. and Oller, D. K. (1981) 'Linguistic pragmatics and language intervention strategies', *Journal of Autism and Developmental Disorders* 11: 75–88.

Seitz, S. (1975) 'Language intervention – changing the language environment of the retarded child', in R. Koch and F. de la Cruz (eds) *Down's Syndrome (Mongolism) Research Prevention and Management*, New York: Bruner Mazel.

Selfe, L. and Stow, L. (1987) *Children with Handicaps*, London: Hodder & Stoughton.

Shatz, M. (1983) 'Communication', in J. H. Flavell and E. M. Markman (eds) *Handbook of Child Psychology*, 4th edn, vol. 3, New York: Wiley.

Sinclair, H. (1970) 'The transition from sensory motor behaviour to symbolic activity', *Interchange* 1 (3): 119–26.

Skinner, B. F. (1957) *Verbal Behaviour*, New York: Appleton-Century-Crofts.

Slobin, D. I. (1973) 'Cognitive prerequisites for the development of grammar', in C. E. Ferguson and D. I. Slobin (eds) *Studies of Child Language Development*, New York: Holt, Rinehart & Winston.

Slobin, D. I. and Welsh, C. A. (1973) 'Elicited imitation as a research tool in developmental psycholinguistics', in C. A. Ferguson and D. I. Slobin (eds) *Studies of Child Language Development*, New York: Holt, Rinehart & Winston.

Smith, N. V. (1973) *The Acquisition of Phonology: A Case Study*, Cambridge: Cambridge University Press.

Snow, C. E. (1977) 'Mothers' speech research: from input to interaction', in C. E. Snow and C. A. Ferguson (eds) *Talking to Children: Language Input and Acquisition*, Cambridge: Cambridge University Press.

Snyder, L., Lovett, T. C. and Smith, J. O. (1975) 'Language training for the severely retarded: five years of behaviour analysis research', *Exceptional Children* 42: 7–16.

Snyder, L. (1984) 'Communicative competence in children with delayed language development', in R. L. Schiefelbusch (ed.) *The Acquisition of Communicative Competence*, Baltimore, Maryland: University Park Press.

Sparrow, S. S., Balla, D. A and Cicchetti, D. V. (1984) *Vineland Adaptive Behaviour: Scales Interview Edition, Survey Form*, Circle Pines, Minnesota: American Guidance Service.

Spekman, N. J. and Roth, F. P. (1982) 'An intervention framework for learning disabled students with communication disorders', *Learning Disability Quarterly* 5: 429–37.

Spekman, N. J. and Roth, F. P. (1984) 'Intervention strategies for learning disabled children with oral communication disorders', *Learning Disability Quarterly* 7 (1): 7–18.

Staab, C. F. (1983) 'Language functions elicited by meaningful activities: a new dimension in language programs', *Language, Speech and Hearing Services in Schools* 14: 164–70.

Stampe, D. (1969) 'The acquisition of phonetic representation', in *Papers from Fifth Regional Meeting*, Chicago: Chicago Linguistic Society.

Stampe, D. (1979) 'A dissertation in natural phonology', unpublished doctoral dissertation, Chicago: University of Chicago.

Stremel, K. (1972) 'Language training: a program for retarded children', *Mental Retardation* 10: 47–9.

Stubbs, M. (1983) *Language Schools and Classrooms*, 2nd edn, London: Methuen.

Taenzer, S. F., Cermak, C. and Hanlon, R. C. (1981) 'Outside the therapy room: a naturalistic approach to language intervention', *Topics in*

Language Learning and Hearing Disabilities, 1 (2): 41–6.

Terman, L. M. (1916) *The Measurement of Intelligence*, Boston: Houghton Mifflin.

Thomas, B., Gaskin, S. and Herriot, P. (1978) *Jim's People*, 2nd edn, St Albans: Hart-Davis Educational.

Tizard, B. and Hughes, M. (1984) *Young Children Learning*, London: Fontana.

Tough, J. (1976) *Listening to Children Talking*, London: Ward Lock Educational.

Tough, J. (1977) *The Development of Meaning*, London: Allen & Unwin.

Urwin, C. (1984) 'Communication in infancy and the emergence of language in blind children', in R. L. Schiefelbusch and J. Pickar (eds) *The Acquisition of Communicative Competence*, Baltimore, Maryland: University Park Press.

Vygotsky, L. S. (1962) *Thought and Language*, Cambridge, Massachusetts: MIT Press.

Vygotsky, L. S. (1978) *Mind in Society*, Cambridge, Massachusetts: Harvard University Press.

Walker, M. and Armfield, A. (1982) 'What is the Makaton Vocabulary?' in M. Peters and R. Barnes (eds) *Signs, Symbols and Schools*, Stratford: National Council for Special Education.

Warren, S. F. and Kaiser, A. P. (1986) 'Incidental language teaching: a critical review', *Journal of Speech and Hearing Disorders* 51: 291–9.

Webster, A. (1986) 'Update: the implications of conductive hearing loss in childhood', *Association of Child Psychology and Psychiatry Newsletter* 8 (3): 4–14.

Weener, P., Barrit, L. and Semmel, M. I. (1967) 'A critical evaluation of the ITPA', *Exceptional Children* 33: 373–80.

Wells, G. (1974) 'Learning to code experience through language', *Journal of Child Language* 1: 243–69.

Wells, G. (1979) 'Influences of the home on languge development', paper given to the SERC and SCRE Seminar on Language in the Home, Cardiff, January 1979.

Wells, G. (1981) *Learning through Interaction: The Study of Language Development*, Cambridge: Cambridge University Press.

Wells, G. and Harrison, G. (1979) 'Transcription analysis and writing up', in *Project Manual 2: Language Development Course E3G2 Cognitive Development*, Milton Keynes: Open University Press.

Wickens, D. (1974) 'Piagetian theory as a model for open systems of education', in M. Schwebel and J. Raph (eds) *Piaget in the Classroom*, London: Routledge & Kegan Paul.

Willbrand, M. L. (1977) 'Psycholinguistic theory and therapy for initiating two word utterances', *British Journal of Disorders of Communication* 12: 37–46.

Wimpory, D. (1986) 'Developing sociability in pre-verbal autistic children', paper presented at the British Psychological Society, Developmental Section, Annual Conference, University of Exeter, September 1986.

Wood, D. J. (1988) *How Children Think and Learn*, Oxford: Blackwell.

Wood, D. J., McMahon, L. and Cranstoun, Y. (1980) *Working with Under Fives*, London: Grant McIntyre.

Wood, D. J., Wood, H. A., Griffiths, A. and Howorth, J. (1986) *Teaching and Talking with Deaf Children*, Chichester: Wiley.

Wood, H. A. and Wood, D. J. (1984) 'An experimental evaluation of the effects of five styles of teacher conversation on the language of hearing impaired children', *Journal of Child Psychology and Psychiatry* 25 (1): 45–62.

Yule, W. and Berger, W. M. (1975) 'Communication, language and behaviour modification', in C. C. Kiernon and F. P. Woodford (eds) *Behaviour Modification with the Severely Retarded*, Amsterdam: Elsevier.

Zigler, E. and Balla, D. (eds) (1982) *Mental Retardation; The Development–Difference Controversy*, Hillsdale, New Jersey: Lawrence Erlbaum Associates.

Zinkus, P. W. and Gottlieb, M. I. (1980) 'Patterns of perceptual and academic deficits related to early chronic otitis media', *Pediatrics* 66: 246–53.

Name index

Subject index